A LIFE STRIPPED BARE

Hi January &
        Darren

Thanks for the other day,
its always great to
catch up'

As I finished this book
id thought you would
get a lot of use from
it!

        Shawn xox ☺

Also by Leo Hickman

A Good Life: The Guide to Ethical Living

A LIFE STRIPPED BARE

my year
trying to
live ethically

LEO HICKMAN

TRANSWORLD PUBLISHERS
61–63 Uxbridge Road, London W5 5SA
a division of The Random House Group Ltd

RANDOM HOUSE AUSTRALIA (PTY) LTD
20 Alfred Street, Milsons Point, Sydney,
New South Wales 2061, Australia

RANDOM HOUSE NEW ZEALAND LTD
18 Poland Road, Glenfield, Auckland 10, New Zealand

RANDOM HOUSE SOUTH AFRICA (PTY) LTD
Isle of Houghton, Corner of Boundary Road & Carse O'Gowrie,
Houghton 2198, South Africa

First published 2005 by Eden Project Books
a division of Transworld Publishers
in association with Guardian Books
an imprint of Guardian Newspapers Ltd

This paperback edition published 2006

Typeset in 11.5/15pt Minion by
Falcon Oast Graphic Art Ltd.

Printed and bound in Great Britain by
Cox & Wyman Ltd, Reading, Berkshire.

3 5 7 9 10 8 6 4

Papers used by Transworld Publishers are natural, recyclable products
made from wood grown in sustainable forests. The manufacturing
processes conform to the environmental regulations of the country of origin.

eden project books   **theguardian**

Acknowledgements

Special thanks to my ethical auditors – Hannah Berry, Mike Childs and Renée Elliott – for turning my family's life upside-down.

Thanks also to my ethical editors – Lisa Darnell at Guardian Books, and Susanna Wadeson and Kate Samano at Eden Project Books – for turning my words the right way up.

Finally, thanks to all the people who took time to write to me with their own experiences of ethical living. I hung on every word.

Foreword

IT WAS ONCE DESCRIBED TO ME as the Mangetout Moment: the rush of guilt that tells you that what you're doing – buying, say, a small pack of mangetout that's been air-freighted out of season from a field in Kenya to the supermarket shelf before you – is somehow a negative force on the world. But it quickly passes when you realize that, hell, you've got half an hour to shop, get home, have a shower and start rustling up something impressive before the in-laws arrive for dinner. Concerns about 'food miles', the exploitations of cheap labour and excessive plastic packaging can wait till tomorrow.

But tomorrow never comes. Not in my household, anyway. The good intentions and empathy with the world's problems are there, but if acting on them means interrupting or changing my habits then it's likely to play second fiddle to doing the laundry, commuting to work, paying the bills, changing nappies, going shopping, having a beer and all the other things that consume my days. In recent years the guilt has started to nag at me increasingly, but I can't seem to transform that caring instinct somewhere inside me into any kind of meaningful action.

We are all struck at some point in our lives – for me when

I had my first child – by the urge to answer some of life's Big Questions: Who am I? What am I doing with my life? Is this it? Am I a good person? And what is it, I have wondered, that blocks me from getting up out of my chair and doing something that might actually prove to be a positive force – however insignificant – on the world?

The irony of our Western lifestyle, of course, is not that we are blissfully ignorant of the negative impact it has on ourselves, our neighbours and the environment, but that we choose to journey on regardless, blinded by a convenient fog of inertia and apathy. I can't get through a day, it seems, without reading stories about mercury-filled salmon, deodorants being linked to cancer, increasing levels of social exclusion and inequality, or landfill sites reaching full capacity. I gasp at the saddening and maddening facts about our wasteful and self-obsessed lives: that globally, US$33 billion is spent on make-up and perfume annually, whereas just US$29 billion a year would be required to eliminate hunger and provide clean water to all; or that the US has more private vehicles on the road than people licensed to drive them; or that half the world's population survive on the equivalent of two dollars a day – less than I spend on a coffee on the way into work.

But I prefer to turn to Ceefax for the football results or take my daughter out for a walk round the park rather than dwell too long on all that nasty, negative stuff. Besides, what can I do about it all, anyway? That's why we vote, isn't it?

It was against this backdrop that I was set a challenge by the *Guardian*, where I work as a journalist. Could I – someone living a typically comfortable and routine life in a city suburb – take a step back from my daily habits and consumer choices, and try to understand their true impact? Could I, over the course of a few months, start to lead a more 'ethical' life, in which I reduced, to use a popular idiom, my 'footprint on the earth', as well as being a more positive force both to myself and those around me? Could I join the small but growing proportion of society striving to live more thoughtfully and less wastefully; those who, according to the Ethical Consumerism Report 2004, pushed sales of organic food well over the billion-pound mark, up from £390 million in 1999, and which in 2003 spent £24.7 billion on a wide range of ethical purchases, from free-range eggs to A-rated energy-efficient appliances?

This wasn't to be an exercise in dropping out and taking up life as a hermit on a croft in the Scottish Highlands. Nor was it to be an attempt to replicate Tom and Barbara's stab at Good Life self-sufficiency in the suburbs. I wouldn't have a manifesto as such pinned to my fridge for constant reference; the idea was simply to see where the journey would lead me. There was certainly no anticipation of a day when I would, like a Weight Watchers champion, proudly crack open the organic champagne and declare, 'I've done it. My life is completely guilt-free.'

But I spotted a problem immediately. I was going to need some help – someone to kick my weak-willed, unethical butt whenever I wavered and started to show signs of giving up. However, I wasn't interested in having some Zenned-out, love-bead-wearing hippy who eats only tofu burgers and is in touch with their *chi* telling me what to do. I'm cynical enough at the best of times. If I was to connect with this experiment, I wanted serious professionals who could explain with reason – and preferably some hard science – why I needed to make changes to my life.

Upon reflection, I felt that I needed help in three key areas: the food I eat, the environmental damage I'm responsible for, and understanding more about the power that big corporations and government hold over us all.

Three people answered my call: Renée Elliott, council member of the Soil Association and founder of the Planet Organic shops in London; Mike Childs, campaigns director at Friends of the Earth; and Hannah Berry, writer and researcher at *Ethical Consumer* magazine. Between them, I hoped they would provide the spur I required.

However, a second – and probably more fearsome – hurdle I faced was my family. If I wasn't to give up after the first weekend, I was going to have to bring my wife Jane and our baby daughter Esme along too. Jane, it has to be said, needed some convincing, especially after I explained how the challenge would commence, with the three 'ethical auditors' visiting us and asking us a series of probing, personal questions about our lifestyle. The thought, she said, of anyone rummaging through our kitchen cupboards or asking us what loo paper we use was abhorrent. I agreed, but managed to sign her up with the promise that the experiment might lead me to take more of an interest in how the house got cleaned.

Next, we had to define what we meant by a more ethical lifestyle. The intention wasn't to create a diet-like set of rules that we would fret about if we broke. ('If you enter that McDonald's, you won't just be letting me down, you'll be letting yourself down.') Rather, it was to be about living out a daily battle where we fought to establish priorities and tackle dilemmas: if you have to choose, is fair-trade coffee better than organic? Are disposable nappies OK to use at night if washable ones leak? Should I always give loose change to someone holding a collection box in their hand? In terms of pollution, is it better to get the bus or the train to work? Should I let my child watch television adverts?

I also knew early on that I wanted to hear from as many other people as possible about their thoughts and experiences of going through a similar life experiment – if only to act as further motivation. So I placed a plea on the *Guardian*'s website for help and set about writing a web diary for others to follow my family's progress, a diary that was later to transmute into a year-long series of articles for the *Guardian*. But I soon got requests for further information about my personal circumstances, because people wanted to offer me ever more detailed and tailored advice. So, in one particularly self-exposing early website posting, I attempted to answer as many of the queries as possible:

> Some of you have asked for more details about my life in order to help issue further tips and recommendations. So, with as much honesty as I can muster, and in no intended order of importance or apparent impact on the planet or those around me, here goes . . .
>
> I eat meat
> I don't smoke
> I don't own a car
> I live in a Victorian three-bedroom terraced house in south London with my partner Jane and our young daughter, Esme

I heat my house using a gas combination boiler

I commute to work by train (a twenty-minute journey)

I don't exercise regularly

I am signed up to the green tariff with the electricity supplier

I work in an open-plan office sitting in front of a computer all day

I shower once a day

I watch TV – quite a bit

I favour fly/drive holidays

I donate a small amount each month to charity through my payslip, thus avoiding the taxman

I vote when asked to

I shop at Sainsbury's once a fortnight, getting a taxi home afterwards

I top-up shop at local convenience stores every few days

I drink about three units of alcohol a week

I am not politically active

I don't eat ready meals, but try to prepare meals from scratch

I know my immediate neighbours, but do not know anyone else on my street

I don't do any voluntary work

I bank with a high-street bank

I wasn't too sure what people would take away from this list – probably that I was a middle-class white-collar worker living out a somewhat predictable and safe life in the suburbs.

Whatever people thought, many said they recognized a lot of their own lives in my checklist. In fact, I was staggered by the scale of the response. I received well over six hundred letters and emails from people across the world, all with their own stories about how they too often felt a similar feeling of inertia and guilt about not being able to lead a more ethical life. Some felt they had made a successful switch in their lives, whereas others felt that their efforts had been a miserable, even worthless, failure. Either way, all their words were welcome and, whether inspiring, dispiriting or even downright insulting, they proved in combination to be my greatest catalyst for change. This is the story of my struggle to make that change. The story, if you like, of how I turned my own Mangetout Moment into a Mangetout Momentum.

1

IN THE US, PRISONERS ON DEATH ROW famously get to choose their final meal before facing their executioner. You might think that imminent events would conspire to put them off their food, but many decide to take the opportunity to truly pig out. Why not? When there's no point fretting about cholesterol levels and love handles any more, where's the harm in loading up on as much salt, fat, sugar, red meat, and excessive carbs as you can push through your lips?

The night before the ethical auditors arrive, I ask Jane whether we should be having our own 'last supper' before our lives are turned upside-down. I propose that we mark the moment with a feast of things we fear will be stripped from our kitchen. For inspiration, we look up on the internet what the most recently executed death-rowers ordered up for their last supper. A little distasteful, I know, but we're feeling vulnerable. After scrolling around the most recent requests it's apparent that those facing execution largely dream of one thing only – fast food, and piles of it. Take John Hooker, who was executed on 25 March 2003 in Oklahoma. He evidently knew precisely what he wanted – he'd had many years to think about it, after all – and was quite particular when making his request:

Three chicken breasts and three chicken wings from KFC
Broccoli spears with cheese sauce
A baked potato with sour cream and chives
Two bacon cheeseburgers
Two slices of cherry cheesecake
Two 7-Ups

In fact, of the sixty-five people executed in the US in 2003, thirteen of them requested burgers, twelve fried chicken and nineteen French fries. If there's anything to be learned from these last-meal requests, it's that people turn to comfort food in times of high anxiety. No shock there, but the evidence seems to suggest that the higher the anxiety, the higher the pile of food.

Interpret our own stress levels as you will, but our anxiety about the pending ethical audit leads us to break from our normal weekday run of meals such as chilli con carne, salads-in-a-bag, lasagne, spag bol, baked potatoes, lamb chops, sausage and mash and such like, and instead phone for a take-away curry – poppadoms, Peshwari naan, lamb pasanda, samosas, shish kebab, chicken tikka masala, onion bhaji, pilau rice, the works. Everything is consumed with gleeful vigour except the on-the-house onion and lettuce salad – we always leave that untouched.

As we await the arrival of the auditors, we panic about what we should give them for lunch. After all, what does an ethical auditor eat for lunch? Will they be vegetarians, vegans or that thing where you only eat windfall fruit? Does everything have to be organic? Or fair trade? And what will they want to drink?

There's always that flurry before guests arrive when you go around plumping up cushions, checking the bath for tide marks, digging out a hand towel and 'guest soap' to posh up the bathroom, sniffing to see whether a squirt of air-freshener is in order, putting away the laundry hanging on the clothes horse and other such acts of paranoia mixed with house pride. Jane generally minds much more about these things than I do. But on this occasion I'm flitting around too.

'Do you think we should hide some of these remotes?' I ask. 'We don't want them thinking we just sit in front of the telly all day, when we don't.'

'No, just leave everything where it is. We've got to let them see precisely how we live.'

'What about all those packs of nappies in Esme's bedroom?'
'Leave them.'

I can see that Jane is anxious too, but she is determined that we act as if we've got nothing to be ashamed of. But just as we are starting to slip into another debate about what to give them for lunch, there's a knock on the door.

Hannah Berry is the first to arrive. She works for *Ethical Consumer*, a bimonthly magazine that aims to inform readers about the 'social and environmental impacts of products, and the ethical records of the companies that make them'. Hannah seems a little nervous, too, as she steps into our sitting room and takes a seat. Her hooded top, short hair and jeans bring to mind communes, cats and lentil bakes.

I ask her whether she wants tea or coffee, realizing that I am beginning the process of revealing the details of our lives for critical analysis.

'Coffee, please,' says Hannah.

'I can make some real coffee instead of instant, if you prefer.' For some reason I imagine that Hannah will score us positively for having fresh coffee. I sense a scowl from Jane.

As I walk to the kitchen to put on the kettle, I speculate about what labels Hannah has no doubt already drawn up for us, just from knowing our names, our address, our jobs and so on: middle-class, professional urbanites who probably shop at Sainsbury's, own an estate car, go on several minibreaks a year and drink Pinot Grigio and eat cashew nuts while watching property shows or arts documentaries.

As the kettle boils, Mike Childs arrives. He is the UK campaigns director of Friends of the Earth, the international network of environmental groups, and has travelled by train to London for the day from his home in Yorkshire. Dressed in jeans, T-shirt and a green loose shirt, he has the relaxed, devil-may-care look of an environmental campaigner. I introduce him to Hannah and offer him a drink, then Jane and I retire to the kitchen to resume our panic about what to serve up for lunch. We rifle through our cupboards and fridge, looking for something that will ooze class and sophistication as well as earning ethical brownie points, but we just keep pulling out tins of baked beans, packs of pasta and jars of mango chutney (a guilty reminder of last night's curry). Jane berates me for not planning this meal ahead. I pop my head round the sitting-room door and ask if there's anything in particular they'd like for lunch, but they kindly and politely (but not in the least helpfully) try to put us at ease by asking us just to serve something that we would typically eat. So we settle on a salad niçoise: some lettuce, a few eggs, green beans, a tin of tuna and olives. At least it's healthy, we think.

I can hear a black cab pull up outside our house. Surely ethical auditors don't travel by taxi? Shouldn't they stick to walking, cycling and public transport? I peer out of the window and see a smartly dressed woman with shoulder-length blond hair stepping out of the cab. She looks a bit glam to be an ethical auditor to me, but she is walking towards our front door.

'Hello, you must be Leo,' says Renée Elliott, council member of the Soil Association and founder of the London chain of Planet Organic shops. Her breezy confidence, clothes and manner combine to present the image of a ball-breaking businesswoman, and her east-coast American accent cements this perception. I would have struggled to think of someone more diametrically opposed to the slightly shy and apprehensive Hannah sitting on the sofa in the next room. If anyone is going to be brutally honest about the way Jane and I live, I sense that Renée will be more than willing to oblige.

As everyone is now here, I declare an official start to proceedings.

'Many thanks for coming. First of all, Jane and I are obviously a bit nervous about what horrors you are going to uncover, so please be easy on us. At first, at least. I'm not really sure how we should proceed with this, but I guess it would make sense if we go through the house room by room, and you take notes and ask us about what we buy, how we live our lives, that kind of thing. Then we can all have lunch. Where shall we start?'

'Oh, the kitchen, definitely,' says Renée immediately. 'You can tell so much by looking at someone's kitchen.'

The other two nod in agreement, so we walk through to the back of our Victorian terraced house.

There's not too much to say about our kitchen. Twelve foot square, it's a little drab, not having been decorated since we moved in six months previously. It was fitted by the previous owners with what we suspect are Ikea kitchen units, wooden work surfaces and a tiled floor. We have all the standard fitted appliances – big fridge-freezer, electric double oven, gas hob, washer-dryer and dishwasher. The room isn't big enough for a family-sized kitchen table, so we tend to eat off our laps most nights in front of the telly. On the rare occasion when we have people over for a meal, we bring out a small antique table with an extendable leaf and eat in the sitting room. We are planning to get builders in to knock through the wall between the kitchen and our downstairs bathroom and, by moving the bathroom upstairs, enlarge the kitchen to a much bigger and more family-friendly room with French doors opening out on to our small back garden – so Esme will not always have to sit in her highchair in splendid isolation.

We relay our structural plans to the auditors as they step into the kitchen, each armed with a clipboard and pen. At this point Esme awakes from her morning nap and joins the tour in Jane's arms.

'Do you mind if we look in your fridge?' asks Renée bluntly.

'Er, feel free,' I mumble.

As she scrutinizes the contents, I feel as if she is reading my diary. Are we a margarine or butter family? Do we eat ready meals? How long has that tin of tuna with cling film over it been languishing at the back? Didn't you know that cooked and uncooked meat should be kept apart?

Soon the auditors are holding up packs of mangetout and tutting about where they were grown. And noting that our milk is organic, whereas our eggs are free-range but not organic.

Each item that they pull out of the fridge seems to be throwing up more and more problems: food miles, pesticide residues, additives ... One key issue is whether Jane and I should become vegetarians. Hannah, who has been a vegetarian since the age of nine, explains in the kind of toe-curling detail that would deter even the most ardent fan of bangers and burgers what goes on down on our farms and in our abattoirs. However, Renée – also a vegetarian – is keen to stress that it is a personal choice and one that we should come to alone. I turn to Mike and ask him if he eats meat. 'Only if it's from an animal reared on the hills and dales near where I live,' he says. I look out of the window and see a London-reared pigeon land in our garden.

All this talk leaves me feeling even more nervous about lunch. What are they going to make of the tuna and eggs? Should we quickly rustle up something else with the remaining ingredients? A lettuce and green bean salad? That's hardly a meal. How about pasta instead? I'm just trying to work out what we could use for a sauce when Renée opens one of our kitchen units.

She squeals with pleasure. 'I love ferreting around in other people's food cupboards.' She seems to be enjoying this a little too much.

Mike and Hannah seem less excitable as they watch while Renée starts to empty our store cupboards on to the kitchen worktop. Perhaps it's the out-of-date ginger nuts or the split bag of self-raising flour among the growing pile that are curtailing their enthusiasm?

After a few minutes of vigorous rifling, muted gasps and knowing looks, before us lies what looks to me like a harvest festival display but to the others more probably the reduced-to-clear aisle end at the supermarket. There are dozens of items, ranging from cans of baked beans and chopped tomatoes to packets of pasta (we count seven varieties, even though I swear we only ever alternate between spaghetti, fusilli and penne), pots of spices and cartons of juice. There's also bread, rice, bottles of wine, beer, various condiments, packets of nuts and dried fruit, and an assortment of tea and coffee. I realize how much stuff goes untouched for months at a time, stranded at the back of the cupboard.

A pattern is emerging: the auditors violate every nook and cranny, before listing the many ways in which what they find is harming us, others or the environment. Everything is fair game: wine, tins of tuna, eggs, frozen pastry, fresh fruit, packs of rice, biscuits, even the salt and pepper grinders.

I don't know about Jane, but I'm already in need of a stiff drink and we haven't even got out of the kitchen yet. I look at the cooking brandy now sitting on the worktop, which is no doubt feeling, like us, a little exposed and abused. But it's not even lunchtime yet so I put the kettle back on for another coffee. A mistake, as it happens.

'I suppose this might be a good time to talk about your use of kitchen appliances,' says Renée, watching me spark up our gas hob to boil the water in our whistle kettle. Surely they can't criticize this – it doesn't even have to be plugged in. Mike and Renée begin to discuss whether it's more energy efficient to boil water on a gas hob or to use an electric kettle.

After some debate about how much flame should be on show beneath the kettle, Hannah interjects, 'The inherent inefficiency of conventional electricity production makes gas preferable in terms of carbon emissions. Unless your supplier draws completely on renewable energy sources, in which case I'd recommend a UK-made steel, concealed-element kettle like those made by Russell Hobbs. Steel is longer lasting, won't potentially leach chemicals into the water and you can boil as little as you want.'

I begin to get the hang of how this all works – the auditors weigh up the energy and resources required to produce an item, how best to use it in terms of energy efficiency, and then gauge its tendency to cause further pollution. In other words, they perform what they call a 'life-cycle analysis' on everything in our home.

Next come our washing machine and dishwasher, then pots, pans and kitchen gadgets. They quickly unearth a crème brûlée torch, sandwich toaster and juicer, all of which show no sign of use. I catch Hannah rolling her eyes as she opens a drawer to find a tangle of skewers, chopsticks, mashers, corkscrews, carving forks, egg poachers and whatever else we've bought during those delusional moments when, inspired by Nigella, Delia or Jamie, we've popped to the nearest kitchen shop for the latest must-have toy.

'You only ever need one set of pots and pans,' says Hannah. 'So when you need to replace them, go for something hard-wearing, like cast-iron pans with a flat base, snugly fitting lid and welded handle. And it's best to buy either second-hand or locally made crockery – bear in mind that anything made from bone china – real bone – may not appeal to vegetarian dinner guests.'

I start to feel like a child, and scrabble for any scraps of recognition that not everything about our lives leads to climate change, global poverty, the destruction of the world's eco-system or a combination of all three. 'We don't have a microwave,' I point out. 'Surely that's a good thing?'

Yes, that's true, they say – up to a point. While their safety is still being debated by some and they require lots of energy and resources to make and ship, microwaves do actually save energy if you use them for heating and warming food instead of conventional ovens.

'But I wouldn't say go out and buy one,' adds Hannah.

I hand everyone a refill of coffee, but this only seems to steer the conversation back to how much energy we use in our home. We talk about the energy rating of our fridge-freezer, our gas combi-boiler, washing-machine cycles, even the merits of having the small oven clock on at all times.

Renée soon drifts away to carry on rummaging through our cupboards. She lets out a little shriek. Oh God, has she found one of the mice that seem to have signed a new tenancy agreement on the space behind the kitchen sink? But no, she lifts up a bottle of bleach she's found under the sink.

'Look,' she says. 'There's also Cif cream, limescale remover, Bold laundry liquid, Sainsbury's dishwasher tablets and Milton sterilizing tablets for "complete protection from germs". Here's proof that as a nation we're obsessed with completely eradicating germs from our lives.'

Now all three of them are looking through our cleaning products.

'Why keep so many poisons in a room where you prepare food, Leo?' asks Hannah, holding up a can of oven cleaner. The auditors are all in agreement – this cupboard is highly toxic and its contents are in need of an urgent ethical overhaul.

Bleach is a particularly evil substance to be releasing into our sewers, states Mike. 'You evidently use a bleach product to clean the floors and the loo. Bleach contains some very effective toxic chemicals, which is why it kills germs. It's powerful stuff and should be used sparingly.'

Jane has clearly had enough. She is sitting on the step leading from the hall down to the kitchen, silently holding Esme tight to her chest, no doubt wondering what on earth we have let ourselves in for. To give her a breather from the onslaught, I propose that I show them around the garden while Jane tosses the salad, even though she looks as if she would prefer to toss a caber. In the auditors' direction.

As soon as we step outside, I sense that once again they're not too impressed with what they see, even though this late spring day is filling the south-facing space with sunshine. The garden is almost entirely covered in the wooden decking fitted by the previous owners and the only tree – a cherry – is lifeless and bare. At fifteen foot square it's more of a patio than a garden – there are a couple of garden-centre plants in pots, a sack of charcoal for the barbecue and a big bag of peat-based compost.

Renée, however, is keen to suggest that it should be seen as a blank canvas. 'Although the garden is a bit lifeless,' she says, 'it's wonderful to have a patch of outdoor space, particularly with a baby in the family.'

Mike agrees. 'You are really lucky to have access to outside space in London and you should make the most of it. Even with just a small space, it's possible to create an attractive environment, and even to grow a few vegetables.'

My defence for our barren garden is that we've only recently moved in and, with a new baby in the house, haven't yet found the time to liven it up with some plants. The auditors see this in a positive light, saying that we can now make every effort to plant out an exclusively organic garden and to attract as much wildlife as possible. This rejuvenates me a little and I'm buoyed further by the enthusiasm they all show for the many ways we can transform the garden. We return to the kitchen, and I tell Jane that this time next year we could be eating home-grown produce.

'Lunch is ready when you are,' she says.

I pour a jug of tap water and lead everyone into the sitting room.

As they all sit down I bring in our large walnut salad bowl which we bought in Morocco a few years back on holiday. I had assumed before the auditors arrived that this would lead to a positive score for being 'authentic', but their lack of a reaction suggests to me that either they're too transfixed by the prospect of what's in it, or too hungry to care. Given the dressing-down we've already had, I think we get off lightly. It occurs to me that the bowl may not be from a sustainable timber source – I am already being brainwashed by the auditors.

As the bowl is lowered into position in the centre of the table, I anxiously wait for their reaction. I look round cautiously to see everyone peering inside the bowl. Has a tuna salad ever come under such extreme scrutiny? I may as well be awaiting the verdict of a Michelin reviewer, such is the tension in the air.

'Who wants some salad then?' I ask.

'Are these the non-organic eggs from your fridge?' asks Renée. Jane and I had previously congratulated ourselves on our perfectly soft-boiled eggs.

'Yes, sorry, I'm afraid they are.' Why am I apologizing? Of course they're the eggs from my fridge. What does she think? That they're from a free-range chicken coop in our garden, the one they all missed behind the bag of compost?

'Is that tuna in there, Leo?' says vegetarian Hannah.

'Don't you eat fish?' asks Jane.

'No, I don't eat any meat or fish. Well, I do eat fish on the rare occasion,' responds Hannah, possibly out of politeness.

'I'll just give everyone some and they can leave what they don't like,' I say, a little curtly perhaps, piling salad on to the first plate, which is passed round the table to Mike. At first I think this is because nobody wants it. Then I start to wonder if there's some kind of feminist anti-ladies-first thing going on.

Mike thanks me and then begins to look more closely at the ingredients.

'Where are these beans from? Have they been air-freighted in from abroad or grown locally?' asks Mike.

'I don't know, actually,' says Jane. 'We bought them in Sainsbury's. I can get the packaging if you like.'

'I'll go,' I say. 'I've got to get the bread out of the oven anyway.'

'Have you been baking bread?' asks Renée, clearly impressed.

'Er, no. It's one of those pre-bake ciabatta thingies. Sorry.'

Renée's face visibly deflates.

I dash to the kitchen to search for the packaging of the beans and to collect the bread, then I hand the packet to Mike.

'Kenya,' he says. No one needs to say another word.

As everyone tentatively starts to eat, the conversation turns to food miles, wasteful packaging and food eaten out of season. At times I'm not sure whether what they are saying is meant to be a series of jibes directed at the food we've just served up, or intended to be educative. Either way, my usually voluminous appetite feels like it's been left in the garden. There's nothing quite like watching your guests pick apart the constituent parts of the meal you've prepared to put you off your food.

'Let's talk about something else other than food,' pleads Jane. 'There must be lots of other questions you've got for us.'

It is a welcome relief to move on to new topics such as our holiday habits, how we travel to work, where we bank, how we dress Esme, where we buy our own clothes, whether we know our neighbours and use local shops, how much rubbish we put out each week, whether we have ever considered doing voluntary or charity work, and so on.

Half an hour later, the plates are mostly clear. But I still feel as if I've just forced a herd of sheep into a pen full of wolves. I don't ask if they want any dessert.

After sharing a meal with guests, most people either stay at the table to continue chatting over tea or coffee, or move to more comfortable seating. We all get up and go to the bathroom together.

We had talked over lunch about our bathroom habits, among other things – how long we spend in the shower or bath, what toothpaste, cosmetics and toiletries we use. And so the auditors now express a desire to check out the bathroom to get an 'accurate picture' of what we typically get up to in there. I think they're just after a good old pry.

Like our kitchen, the downstairs bathroom (which contains just a bath and a hand basin; the loo is upstairs) is a little drab, not yet having been decorated since we moved in. But it's not the tiling they're interested in – although they all do momentarily study our bath's shower attachment to assess water efficiency – it's the bathroom cabinet they're after.

I spot a potential flare-up immediately as Renée reaches for Jane's beloved range of Clarins products. 'Please don't criticize those,' I plead silently. She starts to reel off the list of ingredients, passing comment on most of them. Cosmetics seem to be a keen interest of Renée's – she's mentioning terms I haven't heard since GCSE chemistry, and explaining what potential harm they could be having on our bodies. Renée carefully inspects the entirety of the cabinet.

'Do you know what this soap does to your skin every time you use it?' she asks. 'And just look what's in this moisturizer.'

Esme saves the day by interrupting proceedings with a perfectly timed 'special delivery'. I wonder later if this is induced by the strength of Jane's grip as judgement is passed on her beauty regime. Anyway, it serves to move us all to Esme's bedroom, where we keep all her nappy-changing para-phernalia on what new parents seem rather loftily to call a 'changing station'.

But the analysis doesn't abate: there's nappy cream to discuss; nappy brands to assess; toys to examine. Being lectured on how to bring up your child is hard enough to take with humour and grace when the advice comes from family members, but taking it from strangers is a new one on us. Even though we know the auditors only have our and Esme's best interests at heart, it is hard not to feel that we have somehow been marked down as bad parents.

Hannah seems particularly concerned by the potential sources of toxins in the room. 'The nursery was obviously freshly painted in preparation for Esme's arrival and a new carpet has been laid,' she says. 'But artificial-fibre carpets of this sort are not generally recommended for small children, as they can contain traces of dangerous compounds such as brominated flame retardants.'

This is a concern for Mike and Renée, too. We must try at all costs to avoid products made from synthetic materials, stresses Mike. 'Babies and toddlers are particularly vulnerable to the effects of chemicals in the environment, and yet toiletries for babies often contain chemicals known to disrupt our hormone system, or to build up in our body fat. It's better to use water than these wipes to keep your baby clean. Avoid perfumed creams and lotions, too, as these often contain dodgy chemicals, and take care with plastic bottles, feeding cups and bowls, which have been found to leach chemicals when the surface gets scratched.' I interrupt to say that we do use water and cotton wool, but the items he's found seem to condemn us.

Like most parents, we thought we had done everything we possibly could to give our baby the best start in life – read all the books, attended antenatal classes, made a cosy nursery, breastfed and so on. So to hear that the environment we have lovingly created for Esme contains toxins, and furthermore that the manner in which we are raising her is bad for her environment, leaves us feeling somewhat dejected.

I'm not sure how much more we can take of this so I beckon everyone down to the sitting room to wrap things up.

'Have you seen all you need to?' I ask.

'We could go on for hours, I suspect,' says Renée. 'But I think we have a pretty good idea now of how you live.'

It's agreed that they can ask further questions at any time in the future and that they should contact us if they have any more thoughts or guidance. There's one final burst of inter-rogation about our gadget habit – Mike can't help but comment on his way out on how big the TV is – then they make their way to the front door. I don't think they realize quite what an impact their visit is going to have on my family's life.

*   *   *

How do you respond to that? Make a nice soothing cup of tea? We don't have any fair-trade teabags. Have a long, hot, relaxing bath? Baths are water and energy inefficient and expose you to the many synthetic ingredients found in toiletries. Plonk yourself in front of the telly and watch something truly escapist? That will expose you to corrupting advertising and use up electricity needlessly. Go for some retail therapy? I don't even need to answer that.

After we shut the front door, Jane and I look at each other, shell-shocked.

'Well?' I say.

Jane carries Esme into the sitting room and sinks into the sofa without a word. I know from experience that that expression means she needs to be left alone, for both our sakes. I start to clear the table and take the plates through to the kitchen.

Everything is still arrayed on the worktops. Each item – the tins, the packets, the boxes, the bottles, the crockery, even the empty plastic salad bag – seems to be nagging at me, all of them saying 'guilty'.

The whole experience has been like viewing a house with an estate agent – but in reverse. Instead of hearing the merits of each room talked up, we have been taken on a tour of our own home – and to a certain extent our own lives – and the vast majority of what was found has been criticized, even condemned. Is it possible to live in the way the auditors propose? Where everything you do, buy and eat is analysed in such depth? Can nothing be spontaneous any more, or done without thinking of the long-term consequences? Surely the auditors have days off now and again? Don't they ever treat themselves to a Starbucks cappuccino? Out-of-season strawberries? A hire car? And do they beat themselves up about it if they do? Should this kind of life be viewed as one long diet, but instead of restricting the chocolate éclairs, crisps and full-fat milk, you cut back on greenhouse emissions, toxins and selfish habits?

Or maybe I'm looking at it the wrong way. Maybe it's not always about suffering for your cause. To be fair, the auditors did all make the point that both Jane and I need to feel happy about what we are doing, otherwise we'll soon lose the will for living ethically – just like those who stray quickly from their diets, or stop going to the gym they so enthusiastically signed up to a few months before.

'They're simply not being realistic,' says Jane, walking into the kitchen to help me clear up. 'No one can live like that.'

'I don't think they were saying that from this second forth we have to adopt every single thing they said.' I try my best to win her over. 'I suppose their message was that, basically, everything we do or buy has a knock-on effect of some sort – and often it's a negative one. We should try to reduce our impact whenever we can, for the good of ourselves, Esme and the wider environment. Be responsible for our actions. I don't think we have to beat ourselves up each time we stray from the path of righteousness. It's not a religion.'

'Well, they seemed to feel it was, the way they preached on.' Jane sounds weary.

'Why don't we try just a handful of things first? Just to get us going,' I suggest. 'We'll take it one step at a time and see how we get on.'

'Whatever we do, I don't want to feel forced into it if it isn't working out,' says Jane. 'And if they think I'm giving up my Clarins then they can think again.'

2

WHERE TO START? So much of what the auditors had to say
to us seemed to hinge on our shopping habits – the
rubbish we produce, the type of food we eat, the chemicals we
expose ourselves to every day through household products, the
journeys we make. And considering that Jane and I buy most
of our everyday items from the Sainsbury's a couple of miles
from our home, it seems that if we are to implement the proposed changes we will need a drastic review of this particular
fixture in our lives.

We've done a lot of talking since the auditors left, but now
that we're standing outside Sainsbury's it seems all too real. I
feel a little nervous about how we are going to come through
this. Shopping trips aren't the best of times for Jane and me.
Some might call it determined debating, but I would call what
we end up doing as soon as we reach the first aisle simply
bickering. The fact that we now have to enter this shop and
question each of our purchases doesn't bode well for the
harmony of our relationship come the check-out. The safest
and most sensible tack is just to relinquish full control to Jane:
shut up, push the trolley and smile my way through the next

hour or so of drudgery. After all, Jane has always insisted that she actually enjoys shopping, whereas I can think of dozens of things I'd rather be doing. Perhaps that's why I'm so keen to see this fortnightly trip, if not abandoned, then at least drastically curtailed.

When we enter I quickly adopt my familiar position. I fall behind Jane with the trolley and let her advance alone to the fruit and veg aisle. Then, starting with the lettuces, tomatoes and mushrooms, she criss-crosses from side to side, selecting and bagging as she goes. I keep the trolley close at hand so that she can drop the items in and move on, while I avoid the traffic snarl-ups that build up near the weighing and bagging points. If I'm honest, I tend to disconnect myself from the whole process. Only this time I soon notice a problem – the auditors' advice keeps running through my head.

Mike seems to be particularly interested in our fruit – a Brazilian mango, a punnet of strawberries grown in Kent, a bunch of white grapes, a packet of salad tomatoes and an 'exotic fruit selection' containing fruit from South Africa, Colombia and Thailand.

'You evidently enjoy cooking and use lots of fresh fruit and veg, which is a good start,' he says. 'But you buy them at the supermarket, which means they are often imported or have travelled up and down the country before making it on to the shelves. It is common for green beans to be imported from Zimbabwe and Kenya, asparagus to be flown in from Peru and apples imported from New Zealand and the US, which means they've been packed for transportation, creating extra waste, and will have contributed to climate change en route.'

He picks up some Turkish dried apricots. 'Food that is transported around the world clocks up "food miles", which generate significant amounts of carbon dioxide, one of the gases that cause climate change. Even when produce is grown in the UK, the big supermarkets transport it around the country to be processed and packaged before it reaches the customer. Smaller regional supermarkets are more likely to source food, process it and sell it within the same region.'

Hannah is keen to highlight the self-defeating practice of importing organic produce from abroad. 'The environmental benefits of growing organic fruit and veg can be cancelled out when they've come halfway across the world. Currently, 70 per cent of organic food sold in UK supermarkets comes from overseas – even at the height of the British apple season, more than half the apples on sale in most major supermarkets are imported, with some travelling twenty thousand kilometres before they arrive on our shelves.'

I glance at Jane to see her reaction as she watches the auditors pore over the contents of our fridge. I feel a little violated, to be honest, and I can sense that she is squirming too.

But Renée seems to disagree with the other two. 'The issue of food miles is not as cut and dried as people think,' she says. 'Food transported long distances by ship uses much less fuel than everyone driving to the supermarket in their cars. Don't misunderstand me – one of the organic mantras is to buy local. If you buy British, you are supporting the farmers in your own country and buying what is in season. Fantastic. But I also take a more global view. You see, we ban chemicals like DDT in the West, but companies keep manufacturing them and sell them to developing nations. We then buy and eat the produce they grow with those same chemicals. So if you believe in organic, I think you must support organic agriculture in developing nations as well; otherwise it just doesn't make sense. Surely it's not just about making sure that our own little patch of land is not being ruined?'

Hannah is staring at the floor and chewing her lip, unconvinced by this argument. She stresses that buying local, organic produce should always be our overriding goal. 'The best way is through a box-delivery scheme. This encourages quality, healthy eating with freshly picked seasonal fruit and vegetables, reduces packaging, ensures fair prices for the farmers and supports organic and low-input agriculture, thus enriching biodiversity and wildlife. Next best is local produce bought from a market, or, even better, direct from the farmer, but always express a preference for organic. If you can't get organic, you might find it helpful to know that aubergines, peppers, cabbages, frozen peas, garlic, leeks, marrow, radishes, swedes, sweetcorn and turnips tend to have the lowest pesticide residues.'

What about when I fancy something a bit more exotic, such as lemongrass, limes and bananas?

'You should opt for Europe-grown when in season,' says Hannah. 'It's more likely to have travelled by ship than by air. And avoid food from oppressive regimes, such as Zimbabwe.

Look out for produce that's labelled as fair trade and organic. Currently, this largely means bananas, pineapples, mangoes and oranges. Where you have to choose between them, fair trade over organic is probably best. As well as providing workers with a fair wage, acceptable living conditions and freedom to join trade unions, part of the fair-trade premium is used to encourage and support the implementation of more environmentally friendly methods of production. Farmers are encouraged to convert to organic methods wherever possible. Conversely, there are no criteria for wages and working conditions in organic production.'

Is organic produce really what it's cracked up to be? I ask the auditors. Isn't it just a marketing wheeze to appeal to middle-class sensibilities?

'Take pesticides,' says Mike. 'Supermarkets demand certain cosmetic standards for their produce, which encourages farmers to use more pesticides. Apples are naturally quite often blemished – and a perfect skin can mean the fruit has been doused in potentially toxic chemicals. The Pesticide Safety Directorate tests pesticide levels in fruit and veg, but their safety levels only apply to one pesticide at a time. But fruit and veg can contain traces of several pesticides together and very little is known about the combined effect these have on health. So far only the Co-op and Marks and Spencer are making a real effort to get risky pesticides out of their food and even they have a long way to go before their produce is pesticide-free.'

Jane and I look to Renée for her view. After all, selling organic produce is her living, so if anyone should be able to convince us of its benefits, she should.

'Are organic fruit and vegetables better for you?' she asks rhetorically. 'There is evidence to show that the levels of some vitamins and minerals, such as vitamin C, magnesium, iron and phosphorus, are higher in organic crops, but more research is still needed. But remember that conventional farming relies on artificial additives to give plants their nutrients, while organic food is produced using nutrients from natural sources.

'The government says that the residues of poisons such as pesticides, herbicides and fungicides – and they *are* poisons, designed to kill bugs, weeds and diseases – left on our foods are safe. Quite frankly, I'm not convinced and many environmentalists dispute their claim. Many food crops are sprayed with more than one chemical – Cox's apples can be sprayed up to sixteen times with thirty-six different pesticides. But no one knows how these chemicals interact with each other and what the effects could be on our health. If someone handed you a lettuce that had been sprayed with chemicals, and one that hadn't, which would you choose? It's not rocket science. And it's not as if all of those chemicals wash off – some are designed to be consumed internally by the plants. And I'm not keen on peeling fruit and veg, as the government has previously recommended, because a lot of the goodness is just under the skin, as well as in the fibre of the skin. For me, buying organic just makes sense.'

Jane says that she has always been tempted by the idea of buying organic produce, but just can't swallow the prospect of paying such a premium.

'A question many people ask me,' responds Renée, 'is what organic produce to get if they can't buy exclusively organic. I always say, especially in regard to children, to buy what you or your kids eat the most of. If Esme eats apples constantly, then buy organic apples. If you live on rice, then buy brown for all the added nutrients, and make sure it's organic. Organic isn't expensive if you are buying carrots, onions, potatoes, beans or grains.'

I hold up a lettuce that Jane has just dropped in the trolley. 'Look, it's grown in Spain. Isn't there a locally produced one?'

We look around, but can't find a lettuce grown in the UK anywhere. We can't get a bag of salad either, as they don't say where the leaves are grown.

'Shall we just go without lettuce?'

It's one of the staples we buy on every trip to the supermarket. In fact, our shopping list hardly ever varies – we rarely stray from the stock ingredients that make up our favourite meals. At some point in the week we will invariably have a baked potato with butter, taramasalata and grated cheese on top and some salad on the side. It's a simple, easy meal for the end of a busy day at work. The thought of not having our back-up lettuce leaves us a little uneasy, but we bravely decide to press on without it.

As I follow Jane, with Esme fast asleep in the baby sling on my chest, I look at all the produce laid out so invitingly on the shelves. The range has always seemed so amazing – melons, parsnips, pears, kiwis, chillies, yams, apples. And then there are all the varieties. Take the apples, for example: Gala, Braeburn, Golden Delicious, Bramleys, Granny Smiths and Cox's.

But now all I can think about are the dozens of countries that the fruit and veg must have been grown in; the thousands of miles it must have travelled to get here; the people who must have picked and harvested it. And then I start to dwell on how much we throw away each week because it gets forgotten about at the back of the fridge. Only this morning we cleared out an old, softening cucumber and some mushy grapes to make space for what we are about to buy.

This plentiful array always has the same effect on us – we whizz round loading up our trolley, only to get home and realize that we've got far more than we're likely to eat. Sure enough, within a few days we're beginning to pick blackened bananas out of the fruit bowl.

I can't say we're that adventurous either, despite the wide choice. Winter or summer, we always bring back the same things: bananas, oranges, apples, a melon, a punnet of strawberries, baking potatoes, tomatoes, onions, parsnips, avocados, new potatoes, carrots, peppers, chillis, a bag or two of salad, some mangetout or beans, an aubergine, mushrooms, broccoli, some leeks. These will be cooked up into the same kinds of meals on weekdays: lasagne, chilli con carne, spag bol, curries, stir-fries and various meat-and-two-veg combos. We like cooking but most nights we just go into cruise control and knock up something quick and familiar, that can preferably be eaten as leftovers the next day. Only at weekends will we pull down a recipe book and go for something a bit more adventurous.

So today I suggest that we try to buy less fruit, as this is what we seem to waste the most. Jane agrees, adding that we could restrict what we buy by only choosing fruit that's in season. The trouble is that we can't really tell what is in season and what isn't. We know the basics – strawberries in summer, apples in autumn and so on – but there's no indication here of what's seasonal, as everything is available all year round. It's no surprise that we don't know what month things grow in – we don't need to.

I look down to see what's in the trolley so far. There's a bag of potatoes, broccoli, mushrooms, onions and spinach. These are the only things we could find that were grown in the UK, and are therefore presumably in season. It doesn't seem enough to last us a couple of days, let alone a fortnight. We've also struggled to find organic vegetables, even though we had decided to give them a go, because so many of them have been grown abroad and, in some cases, have clearly been air-freighted. For example, the mangetout we want have come all the way from Zambia, in a plastic tray wrapped in cling film – and they cost about £1.50 for just 150 grams. We also see fruit and veg from Thailand, Mexico, Spain, Egypt, the US, even Burkina Faso. It seems madness. In fact, we spend so long playing 'Spot the Country' that it's no wonder our trolley is so sparse.

Ready meals are not something we normally go for. We might very occasionally buy the odd pizza, packet of fresh pasta with a pot of sauce, or 'country kitchen' soup when we really can't be bothered to cook anything. But these will be bought on the way home from work rather than on the fortnightly shop. So we head straight for the fresh meat, fish, eggs, milk, cheese and butter. This is where we normally spend the most time – and money.

The auditors had rifled through our freezer drawers and fridge, pulling out any meat or dairy products they could find. Before them lay packs of mince, sausages, cartons of milk, spreadable butter, tins of tuna, Cheddar cheese and eggs.

'I feel so strongly about meat and dairy,' says Renée, clutching a frozen packet of Irish stewing beef. 'Not because I'm a vegetarian trying to convert the rest of the world, but because there are so many health and environmental issues that need to be considered.'

She's now holding up a packet of Sainsbury's Taste the Difference sausages – one of our favourites. 'Look,' she says, pointing at the label. 'These contain sodium metabisulphite, or E223. The book *E is for Additives* says that E223 is an antimicrobial preservative, antioxidant and bleaching agent that can cause food aversion and allergic skin reactions. But what is really interesting is that treating foods with sulphite reduces their thiamine (vitamin B1) content, so foods which contain a significant amount of thiamine, such as meat, should not be treated. And look at this yoghurt. It's full of sugar and additives you just don't need.'

But Renée says that additives should not be our primary concern when choosing meat and dairy products – the way the animal is reared and the effect this process has on the environment are a much bigger worry.

'The majority of beef, pork and poultry farmers – most of whom are struggling to make a living – try to rear as many animals as they can on as little land as possible and feed the animals with the cheapest feed. When animals are crowded together, disease can spread rapidly and farmers become reliant on vaccines and antibiotics.'

Mike surprises me by saying that much of the meat we eat is raised on genetically modified soya and grains. To illustrate this point, Hannah picks up our pack of Lurpak spreadable butter and says that it is a product of Arla, Europe's largest dairy, which currently does not guarantee its cows are fed non-GM crops.

'GM feed is one major issue to be aware of,' adds Mike, 'but meat production has another side effect. The pressure to produce soya for the meat industry is intense and is leading to the destruction of large areas of the Amazonian rainforest. Satellite images from the National Institute for Space Research show that more than 25,000 square kilometres of Amazonian rainforest have been destroyed since last year, much of it related to soya production for the meat industry.' This figure sticks with me and I later find it's an area about the same size as the Scottish Highlands.

Hannah says it is crucial that meat-eaters appreciate this point. 'According to a US science think-tank, eating meat is the second most environmentally harmful consumer activity, after buying and using cars. Water pollution is one of the most serious consequences. Silage, for example, is 200 times more polluting than raw sewage. And it takes 21,000 litres of water to produce a kilo of beef, as opposed to 210 litres for a kilo of wheat – and demand for grazing land is the major cause of deforestation worldwide.'

Renée now brings up animal welfare. 'Intensively reared chickens typically live in a space no greater than an A4 sheet of paper, with 40,000 birds housed in the same unit with no natural light or ventilation, thereby creating an ideal breeding ground for disease. And intensively reared pigs are often kept indoors all of their lives, in units that house thousands of animals on concrete floors with no bedding. Reliance on drugs is high in both sectors.'

Hannah adds, 'If you believe it's acceptable to farm and eat animals so long as they are treated with care and respect whilst briefly alive, you'll need to be able to distinguish meaningful welfare claims from half-hearted or misleading ones. Certified organic meat from small producers ensures the highest welfare standards. Organic methods ban growth promoters and the pre-emptive use of drugs, as well as specifying much more space and freedom for animals than other welfare systems. This also applies to eggs and dairy products. However, the dairy industry probably entails greater animal suffering than the beef industry. Calves are removed from their mothers, leading to high levels of mastitis and lameness for the cows kept in a constant cycle of pregnancy and lactation. In egg production, surplus male chicks are often gassed or minced alive. Under so-called 'free-range' systems, hens continue to be pumped full of antibiotics, endure beak trimming and may never see the light of day.'

What about eating less meat and more fish, I ask. Would
that be better?

'Over-fishing is wiping out many fish stocks and
destroying marine environments,' says Mike. 'If you want to
eat fish you should try species caught on hand lines like sea
bream, Dover sole and mackerel, all of which are
recommended by the Marine Conservation Society. Avoid
Atlantic cod, salmon, seabass, haddock and tuna. Even
organic salmon farming causes problems because of the way
in which the fish are kept and the discharge from their oil-
rich high-energy diet.'

Hannah seems to agree that eating fish instead of meat is
rarely an ethical alternative. 'Contrary to myth, fish have fully
developed nervous systems, long-term memories and
complex social relationships. Up to 70 per cent of marine
fisheries are now fully or over-exploited and many modern
fishing methods wreck the aquatic environment or create vast
amounts of "bycatch", while fish farms can be hugely
polluting and risk damaging wild populations through the
escape of unnaturally large, often genetically modified fish.
It takes four tonnes of caught fish – often the food source for
beleaguered wild species – to produce fish feed for a tonne of
farmed salmon.'

So should we just become vegetarians, or even
vegans?

'I don't think it's about becoming a vegetarian,' says
Renée. 'It's about understanding what happens in the
conventional meat, chicken and dairy industries and then
making an informed, intelligent decision about what you eat

and why. If you're concerned about the cost, buy organic but eat less meat.'

Mike adds that if we do choose to eat meat there are some golden rules to follow. 'Look for organic free-range meat that has been reared in the UK rather than transported halfway around the world. Lamb from hill-grazed sheep is a good option, as well-managed sheep farming helps maintain the biodiversity of our dales and hillsides, as well as supporting struggling rural economies. Look for Welsh or Yorkshire lamb. You should also source dairy products from local suppliers to reduce transport-related emissions. Much of the butter, cheese and yoghurt we consume is imported from all over the world. Some Cheddar comes from as far away as Australia. Yet dairy farmers in the UK have been struggling to get a fair price. By cutting back on the amount of meat, fish and dairy products you buy and choosing what you eat carefully, you will substantially reduce your environmental impact.'

Hannah is the only one who overtly encourages us to be vegetarians. 'You need to decide whether exploitation of non-humans can fit with a concept of ethical living,' she says. 'Vegetarianism is a powerful form of boycott because it directly reduces demand for meat. However, just eating less meat and fish, and choosing carefully sourced products, will have a direct positive effect, too. The 138 million "meat reducers" in Europe are responsible for substantial environmental, human-health and animal-welfare benefits.'

We are still mentally scarred from serving lunch to the auditors. After they left, we resolved that once we had eaten up all the food we had in the house, we would start implementing their advice bit by bit. Out of all the areas of our life they looked into, what we ate was probably going to need the biggest overhaul.

Jane approaches the eggs. We don't usually buy many – maybe half a dozen, for a cooked breakfast at the weekend. Eggs, though, are the one thing where, over recent years, we have started to buy free-range. It's those repeated images of chickens crammed into tiny cages that put us off battery eggs. But as we now stand looking at the variety of eggs available, I pick up some organic ones to see the price. They cost £1.50 for half a dozen large eggs, whereas their free-range brethren are just under a pound.

I place them in the trolley, thinking that we need to at least taste the organic ones before deciding whether we should start buying them. But as we move down the aisle towards the milk and butter, we soon realize that we need to make this decision for just about everything we buy today. By the time we reach the cheese, I am wondering whether we should limit ourselves to organic produce.

Jane doesn't think we can afford to, pointing out that the organic produce seems to be a third, even half, more expensive. Convinced by what the auditors said about reducing the amount of pesticides we are exposed to, she thinks we should certainly buy exclusively organic food for Esme when she starts weaning. But she's not sure that we can follow that through all the time when it comes to us.

'It seems to come down to how much we care about two things,' I say. 'Reducing our intake of pesticide residues, and animal welfare. I don't think we can ignore either of them, really. But I'm not sure whether we should spend more money on our food, eat less, or try to cherry-pick certain organic things.'

I pick up some organic Cheddar cheese and put it in the trolley, but decide to walk past our staple Parmesan as I can't find any that's organic. Jane, meanwhile, has already reached the fridge containing sausages and bacon.

'Look at the price of these.' She holds up a pack of Duchy Original sausages. 'And they're not even organic. It says they're free-range and "naturally reared and naturally fed". What do you think that means exactly?'

I shrug, but we decide to try them, as well as the organic smoked back bacon I spot on a shelf nearby. But as I reach out for it I notice the 'price per kilo' total on the label – £17.99. On the shelf next to it I notice some 'low price' back bacon for just £3.23 a kilo.

I am shocked. 'Maybe we should just be vegetarians, as Hannah suggested. It would certainly be a lot cheaper.'

Since the auditors left, we have both refused to confront the thorny issue of vegetarianism – I suspect because we know what upheaval making such a change would involve. Standing amid the body parts of hundreds of animals, now seems like an opportune moment.

'I couldn't do it,' says Jane. 'How could you go without bacon, or sausages, or steak, ever again? I just love meat too much. I don't mind being a "meat reducer", as Hannah said, but not a vegetarian.'

I agree, but wonder whether we should try going without

meat for a while, just to see whether we'd be able to cope.

Jane takes the bacon from me and puts it firmly in the trolley. 'Maybe, but this isn't the time. We'd need to really plan ahead, read up on vegetarian recipes and make a proper shopping list, otherwise it would be baked potatoes every night, I suspect.'

Again, we leave the aisle with the trolley much emptier than usual. As we turn into the first row of tinned goods, I wonder if this shopping trip was really worth the effort.

'An ethical store cupboard should be a relatively empty cupboard,' says Mike, 'with just the essential ingredients to add to your diet of fresh, locally sourced organic food. Nuts, dried lentils, pasta, flour and rice all come in handy, as well as seasoning and spices. But given that it is often not practical to go and buy fresh ingredients every day, tins of tomatoes and ready-soaked beans, for example, have a role to play. You should be careful not to overstock your cupboard, though. Dried goods like pulses do have a shelf-life, as do tins. There is no point in stocking up on useful ingredients that you are not going to eat.'

I think he's referring to the cannellini beans that we never quite get round to soaking.

After looking through all our store-cupboard goods, Renée says that we're doing well to buy certain everyday items such as pasta and rice in bulk, so reducing packaging. She's also pleased that she hasn't found too much tinned stuff: 'I'm not crazy about tins. Not from an ethical standpoint, but because they have so little nutritional value. Frozen is better, in general.'

Jane and I receive a hat-trick of back slaps when Hannah comments that she hasn't spotted too much processed food, either, although she chides us for having lots of perishable items in small packets, such as dried apricots, mixed nuts, tomato purée and jars of mustard, which tend to get half used then forgotten about.

But it's the sight of my homemade muesli that, somewhat surprisingly, raises Hannah's hackles. I thought that this would have gone down well, given muesli's reputation for being the lifeblood of eco-warriors, but when I announce that I make it by mixing Quaker oats with some supermarket own-brand bran flakes and raisins, Hannah winces.

'Quaker is owned – as is Tropicana, who make your cartons of orange juice – by PepsiCo, who are a significant financial supporter of the Bush administration,' she explains. 'Along with General Mills, who also make your tins of Green Giant sweetcorn, and Nestlé USA, it is part of Grocery Manufacturers of America, a powerful food, beverage and consumer brand association that has opposed proposed restrictions on marketing in schools and has lobbied for GM technology. And it's hard to know for sure, but your own-brand bran flakes might be supplied by Cereal Partners, another Nestlé/General Mills collaboration.'

Hannah is now on a roll and starts holding up item after item, pointing out which multinational is behind each brand and why we should be concerned.

'Your Twinings Earl Grey tea comes courtesy of Wittington Investments, owner of the UK's third-largest animal-feed manufacturer, ABN, which is one of the biggest users of GM crops in the country.'

I've never even heard of Wittington Investments. Hannah says that most consumers, like me, have never heard of the largely faceless holding companies that now own many familiar names. More importantly, most consumers are blind to these companies' other activities and investments, many of which may not necessarily chime with their ethical standards. Hannah then somewhat deflates my pride at having some organic produce in our cupboards.

'You should learn to recognize which brands are just the organic face of the same old multinationals,' says Hannah. 'Seeds of Change, for example, is owned by Mars. And Meridian, which makes your organic sesame oil, is owned by Hazelwood, one of Europe's leading manufacturers of convenience foods, which in turn is owned by Greencore, which by its own admission is Ireland's largest sugar manufacturer. It also claims to be at "the forefront of developing the next generation of pizza, quiche, readymeals and novelty cakes".'

But Renée's view couldn't be more different. 'A question I get asked a lot is whether organic retailers, such as myself, should sell products from the so-called "big bad" companies who now have a range of organic foods. I say a resounding "yes". Firstly, I think you're on dangerous ground when you start judging the ethics of companies you don't have an intimate knowledge of. Secondly, if you buy organic products from a company you have reservations about and sales of those products do well, the big boys will put more money into organic agriculture because they will follow the market and the profits.'

Mike, meanwhile, is rummaging through our tins. He holds up a can of kidney beans, which we use to make chilli con carne. 'Some food cans are lined with a chemical called Bisphenol A, which is a suspected hormone disrupter,' he says. 'Some research has shown it to advance puberty in mice. So as a precaution, you might want to cut down on canned food. But you should think about where food comes from, too. A lot of typical store-cupboard ingredients are produced in the developing world and imported to the UK. When local alternatives are not available – tea, coffee and rice, for example – buying fair-trade products will ensure that the growers get a fair price. Also, you should be aware that some ingredients are under pressure from the promotion of GM varieties, such as GM maize and soya. Fortunately, most supermarkets are resolutely opposed to stocking GM products, although vigilance will be needed to ensure that they live up to their promises.'

Hannah is looking at the label on some cans of lager. I can sense more coming about the omnipresence of the multinationals in our cupboards. 'These Stella Artois are made by Interbrew, the world's second-largest brewing conglomerate. Your cans of Guinness are made by Diageo, which also produces Smirnoff, Baileys and Johnnie Walker among its many brands.'

Hannah moves on to the bottles of wine. 'Thankfully, your wine from Australia and Chile uses real corks. The proliferation of plastic corks is causing profound problems for Europe's cork dehesas, which are sustainably managed habitats rich in wildlife.' She goes on to tell me that vineyards account for 10 per cent of farmed land in parts of Europe, but are responsible for over 75 per cent of the pesticides and herbicides used in those areas.

'Your wine does seem to have clocked up a fair few "alcohol miles" en route,' observes Mike. 'Wines from Australia, New Zealand and South Africa have grown in popularity in recent years, which is bad news for the climate as they will be contributing to climate change in transit. If English wine is not to your taste, stick to European wines, and support small vineyards where you can. And when it comes to drinking beer, support local brewers rather than buying imports. The Campaign for Real Ale has plenty of advice about where to get quality beer from micro-breweries.'

The first tinned foods we usually reach for are tomatoes and baked beans, followed by tuna in spring water and mackerel fillets. We buy these every fortnight, but we'll also less regularly pick up tins of kidney beans, sweetcorn, olives and soup. Then our trolley glides its way towards the pasta and rice, of which we always have plentiful supplies. Wine and beers are next, although again it's not every week that we buy these, and we finish off with some sliced granary bread and any condiments we need to top up, such as mustard and peppercorns. We speed past the frozen foods on the way to the check-out, pausing briefly for frozen peas. We hardly ever buy any other frozen foods. Well, maybe the odd tub of ice cream in the summer.

As we reach the check-out and start to unload, we stare at

our meagre purchases. We have a tradition of trying to guess the total – sad, I know – usually anything between £130 and £150. I look at what's in the trolley and guess that we've probably only spent £50 for what should be our fortnightly supply of food for two (one of whom is a breastfeeding mother, the other 'a pig').

We have largely failed at what we set out to do: act on the auditors' advice and change our food-buying habits. Instead, we've been indecisive about what to buy, and have ended up simply not choosing to buy much as a solution.

I reach into my wallet to find my Nectar card. We're not even going to earn a decent amount of points. This rankles me a little as we always save up our points for our big Christmas shopping trip, managing to knock about £50 off the bill. But then I remember Hannah telling me that loyalty cards should be ripped up, as they are little more than data-collecting devices for the supermarkets. Their rewards are largely meaningless, she said, given how much we spend on food, but worse, they benefit the supermarkets by providing them with useful information about our shopping habits, which they can then use to manipulate us into buying more. But somehow I can't seem to resign myself to losing the £50 Christmas discount. The bill just tops £70, which pleases me until I look at how little we've bought. I sign the debit-card slip, glance at my points total on the receipt, and join Jane in packing the shopping.

The final straw is that we've forgotten to bring any plastic bags from home to re-use. I look at the pile of carrier bags that the cashier has kindly shaken open for us. 'This trip has been a disaster, hasn't it?' I mutter. Jane doesn't even look up.

It's just been too much to remember. We've had to think about so much: food miles, excess packaging, what's in season, animal welfare, vegetarianism, pesticide residues, wasteful plastic bags, GM food, avoiding multinationals. And by doing so we've even forgotten to buy ourselves our little treat for the way home. I think sorrowfully of the jam doughnut or pork pie that we often scoff guiltily in the cab – we don't have a car – on the way home. Maybe the mistake was trying to persist with our routine shopping trip. Maybe we should try to cut back on supermarket shopping, as the auditors suggested.

The only saving grace, I ponder, is that Esme has slept her way through the entire trip.

3

I<small>T'S THE PILE OF PLASTIC BAGS</small> we're left with that cements in my mind that our shopping trip has been a failure. Maybe it's because I've still got the auditors' mantra about waste running through my head. We were told to think carefully about the impact of our lives on the environment: how wasteful we are, how the way we live can cause others suffering and harm. We must be a positive force for our daughter, ourselves, our local community, the world, they said.

As I write down 'Change our lives for the good' next to 'Pay lecky bill' and 'Pick up photos from chemist' on our to-do list, I recall the auditors' views on our wastefulness. To truly understand the scale of the problem, they suggested I should follow our rubbish from our garden gate to its final resting place, wherever that may be. If we all knew what happens to our waste, we might wake up a little and make more effort to reduce what we send to the landfill.

As Hannah pulls the lid off our flip-top bin in the kitchen to inspect the contents, she notices that it is lined with a white purpose-bought bin-liner. 'Why don't you use these instead?' she says, glancing at the large bundle of plastic shopping bags scrunched down the side of the dishwasher.

'Household waste is a growing problem for the UK,' explains Mike. 'We produce some 25 million tonnes of the stuff every year, most of which ends up in landfill. That's an average of 386kg of waste for every adult and child in your borough of Lambeth.'

'And it's increasing by 3 per cent a year,' adds Hannah. 'About half could be recycled, but so far only 12 per cent is. It's appalling, as landfill sites generate significant quantities of carbon dioxide and methane, as well as toxic leachate that can contaminate groundwater. Incineration isn't much better, either. Though it generates fewer greenhouse gases, there are health concerns around its dioxin-containing emissions, while the residue, which is often toxic and is around a quarter of the original mass, still has to be landfilled.'

Wealthy countries convert the world's resources into waste – a one-way flow in which the lifespan of products has become very brief. I'm told that we need to reverse this trend, and that little things can make a difference.

But I already recycle, I protest. Every week, we diligently set aside waste paper, glass and cans in our 'green box' for the council's Friday morning pick-up. What else can I do?

'We need to minimize our waste,' says Mike. 'We can do this by the famous Three Rs – reducing, re-using and recycling. Buying less stuff that can only be used once before it goes in the bin, buying things that can be re-used, and recycling things we have really finished with. The average bin contains 35 per cent kitchen and garden waste which could be composted, 25 per cent paper which can be re-used and then recycled, 9 per cent glass and 9 per cent metals, which can all be easily recycled.'

But people are showing how it can be done, say the auditors. Daventry council in Northamptonshire has apparently achieved a 44 per cent recycling rate at a cost of just £56 a year per resident. And in Peterborough wheelie bins are being barcoded so that people who throw out less rubbish can be monitored and qualify to receive council tax reductions. Where there's a will, there's a way, they all stress.

'To reduce the amount of garbage you create,' says Renée, 'try not to buy what you don't need, buy products with less packaging, buy in bulk, and if, for example, you must use the drycleaner, ask them to put several items in one plastic covering. If you can't think of a use for something you don't want, take it to a charity shop. Save good packaging to re-use, like paper, boxes, bags and bubble wrap. And get things mended that would otherwise be thrown out. This may mean buying something of a higher quality in the first instance, instead of something cheap and poorly made that won't last. Not always possible, but do it when you can.'

Hannah points out that rubbish isn't just created when we throw things away – huge amounts are generated during manufacture. 'Every year each UK citizen disposes of about half a tonne of rubbish, which will have created a further two and a half tonnes at the manufacturing stage and ten tonnes when the raw materials were extracted.'

OK, I say, I'm shocked at what we're doing – who isn't? – but ask for some practical solutions.

'You're lucky that you have a doorstep recycling service, so there's no excuse for not recycling all your paper, cans and glass,' says Mike. 'New legislation that Friends of the Earth campaigned for means that every home will benefit from this service by 2010 at the latest, meaning that everyone can increase the amount they recycle. But since your doorstep box scheme doesn't collect plastic or card, these still form a substantial chunk of your rubbish that goes to landfill. So try to cut back on buying cardboard and plastic packaging. For example, buy loose vegetables rather than pre-packed ones, and glass bottles rather than plastic ones wherever possible. You also need to tackle your plastic-bag mountain. Re-use them when you go shopping, or as bin-liners. Better still, use a long-lasting canvas bag or a basket for shopping, and say no to shop assistants who offer plastic bags you don't need. Other boroughs in London do provide facilities for recycling plastic, so make sure you ask your council why it isn't doing so too.'

Hannah throws in some other ideas. 'The website www.recyclemore.co.uk helps you track down nearby plastic-recycling facilities, but it might be easier to avoid plastic packaging as much as possible. I notice that your fridge contains fruit and meat in cellophane-covered trays. Plastic can take about 450 years to degrade in landfill sites. Tetrapaks are a problem too. Why not write to your MP and press for legislation – in Germany people are encouraged to leave excess packaging in the store, and there's a 10p tax on plastic bags in Ireland.'

The ideas keep coming. I'm beginning to feel a little overwhelmed. 'You should also lobby retailers to stock recycled products,' continues Hannah. 'We must stimulate a market for waste and a need for re-processing plants to be built. The website www.recycledproducts.org.uk is a useful guide to seeing what recycled goods are available. You could write to retailers and manufacturers and tell them that producing bags from recycled plastic rather than virgin polythene reduces energy consumption by two-thirds, produces a third of the sulphur dioxide and half the nitrous oxide, and uses an eighth of the water. Likewise, making new aluminium cans from recycled ones cuts the energy by 75 per cent, and there'd be twelve million fewer full dustbins every year if all the aluminium cans in the UK were recycled. And newspaper production is polluting too – it's energy and water intensive, and relies on more and more monoculture tree plantations. If not recycled, newspapers would make up a third of all household waste.'

Mike thinks that much of the solution lies at government level, but that as voters and citizens we must pressurize our politicians as much as possible. 'If the government encouraged manufacturers to make more long-lasting products, and taxed natural resources more highly, it would help enormously. Cheap natural resources fuel our consumer-led economy, making it easy for us to buy more and more things we don't need.'

'Use charity shops, textile banks, the Furniture Recycling Network and schemes that donate appliances to low-income households,' adds Hannah. 'And get a battery recharger, so you don't add to the 20,000 tonnes of poisonous batteries landfilled every year. Make sure you buy the new rechargeable batteries which don't contain mercury or cadmium.'

In fact, I had already been on the phone to Lambeth council about my rubbish several months before the auditors swept through our home. Soon after we'd moved house and after a long weekend unpacking dozens of boxes, a huge pile of flattened cardboard was stacked against our wheelie bin. But when the council's normal recycling round didn't take them away, I rang to find out what had happened.

'We don't recycle cardboard in Lambeth,' I'm informed. 'Or plastic either. They're too expensive to transport and store as they're so bulky. Just paper, glass and cans.'

This perplexed me. I'd expected to receive the same recycling service as we had in Kensington and Chelsea in west London. There we'd lived in a small second-floor flat and each week put all our recyclables into one bag – plastic, cardboard, bottles, cans, the lot – and left it in the plastic dustbin provided outside marked for recycling.

I was always a bit suspicious about this system, having seen the binmen throw the bag into the back of their dustcart along with all the other rubbish. Even though it went into a separate side compactor, I suspected that it probably all went the same way in the end.

But in our new house there's a different system. There are two different rounds each week – one to collect waste from the wheelie bin, and one to collect the recyclable contents of our green box, which is sorted kerbside by the binmen. But since plastics and cardboard aren't collected, we have to put them in the wheelie bin, destined for the landfill.

We keep our green box next to the bin in the corner of the kitchen. This seems the most convenient place for it though I've noticed that many people on our street leave theirs outside all the time. Their boxes always seem to be emptier than ours. Is this because we are producing more rubbish than them, or because having the green box in the kitchen encourages us to use it more?

The auditors have got me thinking about what happens to our rubbish. I know it must end up in a landfill somewhere, but I haven't a clue where. I can't remember having seen a landfill site before. I've been to the municipal dump every now and again, but I've never come across one of those huge land-fills you see on the telly sometimes, the ones with a mass of seagulls flying overhead and huge dumper trucks driving over the rubbish. So I contact Luke Henry of Lambeth council's waste-management team to ask for permission to accompany my rubbish to its final resting place. He agrees – but warns me that it won't be a comfortable journey.

It's eight forty-five on a bright Monday morning and I'm stand-ing outside my house watching our wheelie bin being emptied of its rotting load. A mechanical arm lowers the bin on to the road and the dustcart lumbers forward towards the next cluster of bins. The driver beckons me to join him, so I leap up into the cab and settle down behind him next to Luke, who is already inside. It's going to be a long, hot and smelly day.

It takes four hours to complete the shift. In this time we

collect twelve tonnes of waste from the twenty residential streets that surround my house. As we drive down these Victorian terraced streets, the driver tells me about some of his bugbears.

'The worst thing is people who don't tie up their bags,' he says. 'They just throw them into their bins untied and when we come to collect them the rubbish spills out and we're the ones left to clean up. Just a small thing like that – it doesn't take a second – makes a huge difference to us. Doesn't cross their minds, though.' He shakes his head in disgust, and goes on to say that his crew seems to be collecting more and more rubbish each year.

'I was doing this job when wheelie bins first started in the early 1990s. Before then we had to pick up those old metal rubbish bins. Murder, they were. They'd break your back. Wheelie bins are much easier, but it seems that people now throw more and more into them. Give them a bigger bin and they'll fill it.'

Once the dustcart is full, it's a forty-minute drive to the vast transfer station at Smugglers Way on the bank of the Thames in Battersea. It is here that I learn the ultimate fate of my rubbish: it is loaded on to barges, then floated downriver on a two-day journey to a landfill site. The contents of my green box, meanwhile, are destined for a separate sorting site in Norwood, about three miles south of my house.

The transfer station is huge. About thirty dustcarts are queuing to enter the vast hangar-like building. I can't help but notice that there is a smart-looking modern block of flats backing on to the site.

'Seems like an odd place to build flats,' I remark.

'The rumour is that the estate agent didn't exactly inform prospective buyers from the outset about what goes on at Smugglers Way,' says the driver. 'I wouldn't be best pleased if I'd paid a small fortune for a flat only to find out that the large warehouse next door is actually where London says goodbye to its rubbish.'

'I think I'd have been curious to find out what it was,' says one of the dustmen now sitting in the cab with us. 'Can't exactly miss it, can you?'

Luke explains that Smugglers Way is one of four transfer stations for London and that it serves the boroughs of Wandsworth, Lambeth, Hammersmith and Fulham, and Kensington and Chelsea – hence the number of dustcarts queuing to enter the site.

As we wait our turn, I ask the crew about the waste business. London faces a huge problem disposing of its effluence, says Luke. Due to space restrictions, most of the city's waste is dumped in huge holes in the ground across half a dozen sites in neighbouring counties. Such sites within greater London have long since been filled and closed. In other words, London is now dumping its waste on its neighbours. All the rubbish collected at Smugglers Way is sent down the Thames to a hundred-acre landfill site at Mucking in Essex. But the Mucking site is due to close in 2007, so pressure is already building on local politicians, councils and private contractors, who need to find an alternative.

When the landfills are full, what are we going to do with our rubbish? Incinerate it? Dump it at sea? Pay another area in the UK to landfill it for us?

Why, I ask, can't more be recycled? There are two big problems, says Luke. First, people need to be encouraged to sort their rubbish much more at home. This is by far the most cost-effective and efficient place for it to be done. Second, there needs to be a market for recyclable goods. At present, there is very little profit in recycling: brown glass currently sells at £70 a tonne, green glass (60 per cent of all glass) at £30 a tonne, paper goes for £25 a tonne and steel (baked-bean cans and the like) gets £10 a tonne. The exception is aluminium, which can go for as much as £600 a tonne, but generally it is hard to eke a profit from recycling. Add to this the fact that it costs councils just £66 a tonne to dump their rubbish at Smugglers Way and it is clear how the economics are currently stacked towards landfilling rubbish rather than recycling it.

I watch a huge truck filled with broken green glass lurch its way to the exit. 'Where's that going?' I ask Luke.

'Probably to the United Glass plant in Harlow, where glass is crushed to make what they call "cullet", which is then used to make new glass. That's where much of our glass is taken to be recycled nowadays.'

'How long would it take the citizens of Lambeth to use enough glass to fill that truck?' I speculate.

'Oh, bearing in mind all the glass cleared up from our streets, about two to three days. That truck weighs about forty tonnes.'

I watch the truck head off down the road, emitting a large, lingering puff of diesel fumes as it goes.

We are finally waved into the transfer station, and the driver reverses the dustcart towards one of dozens of what appear to be large plastic doors. I jump out of the cab with Luke and we watch the vehicle reverse until the door is pushed open to reveal a dark hole. The back of the dustcart starts to rise slowly and all the crushed rubbish inside begins to fall out, slowly at first, but then with gathering force until about a minute later a watching crew member gives the thumbs up for the driver to move away. Somewhere amid the tonnes of rubbish that have just dropped into the containers below, ready to be loaded on to the waiting barges, is a week's worth of my family's waste – two large black bin-liners filled with plate scrapings, dirty nappies, vegetable peelings, milk cartons, plastic bottles, cardboard, cotton buds: all the things that we have discarded without a thought about where they will end up.

Two days later, as I wait for the huge barge with my rubbish on board to dock at Mucking landfill in Essex, I know that what I'm about to see is going to shock me even further. I'm already unsettled by the huge wall of rubbish behind me.

Mucking has been taking some of London's waste since the late nineteenth century. It is owned by Cory Environmental, one of the country's largest waste-management companies, and Ian Edwards, the site's operations manager, is beside me watching one of three large cranes glide across to meet the barge as it snuggles up to the dock.

'We have fifty-eight barges that dock here,' says Ian, 'thirty of which come from Smugglers. That's six hundred truck journeys a day through London that are saved by bringing rubbish down the river. In fact, we create the most river traffic on the Thames, which shows how little the river is used nowadays.' I sense that he is proud of his operation here in the heart of what the government has quaintly labelled the Thames Gateway for future mass-housing developments. Gateway to hell, more like, given the sweet, putrid stench that fills my nostrils.

Ian explains that 15 per cent of London's rubbish is dumped at Mucking – about the same amount as is incinerated. The locals don't like it, of course – the only things that do are the nine different types of seagull that are found on the site, some of which have come from as far away as Russia.

I ask him why the site is closing in 2007. 'Europe,' he says curtly. The Landfill Directive from Brussels demands that landfilling is ultimately to cease across Europe, and our government backed this up with the publication of its *Waste Strategy 2000 England and Wales*. Its targets include recycling or composting 25 per cent of household waste by 2005, and 33 per cent by 2015.

The rest of Europe are generally ahead of us in that they incinerate more and at a more local level. And they recycle more, too. This is certainly something to aim for, but the current targets are just not realistic, Ian laments.

'Some cities in the US, such as Seattle, have achieved 40 to 45 per cent recycling rates, but have never been able to push on from that. I think the long-term targets of the government strategy unit are unachievable.'

Ian says that although we are making great strides to meet these recycling levels, sometimes he wonders whether the UK is the only country sticking strictly to the rules. He chuckles to himself. 'My wife loves me – when we're on holiday I always try to visit the local rubbish dumps. I went to a site in Crete recently. They were tipping there all day, then this guy just poured on some paraffin and set light to the whole thing. I would be put in jail if I did that here.'

As the cranes begin to lift the containers of rubbish off the barge and on to huge yellow transporter trucks, we climb into Ian's Land Rover and drive up on to the landfill. Seagulls circle around us. I ask Ian how deep the rubbish is buried here.

'Oh, about twenty to thirty metres down.' I'm shocked. That's about the height of a fifteen-storey building. I think of all the history buried beneath us. What will archaeologists make of this when they dig it up in centuries to come? That we drove a lot of cars, probably, given the huge number of tyres I can see lying about on the surface.

'The tyres are real buggers,' Ian says. 'You can bury them as deep as you like but over time they keep floating to the surface.' I find this more than a trifle disconcerting: is this surface safe to be driving over?

Ian then explains how the site is managed. The transporters bring the containers up off the barges on to the landfill, where they dump their contents into 'cells' – areas about the size of a football pitch that are completely sealed over with earth once filled. Buried pipes are then used to pump away the methane that builds up. This is collected at a generator on site and used to produce about twenty-three megawatts of electricity. 'Enough to power a small town,' says Ian proudly. 'In fact, 25 per cent of our profits actually come from methane extraction.'

Mindful of what Hannah has told me about leachate, I ask if the site is guaranteed not to leach poisonous liquid into the groundwater, or the neighbouring fields and gardens.

'Once closed in 2007, this site will be totally sealed over with two foot of engineered clay. It will take at least eighty years for any liquid to escape from here and by that time it will be totally inert. You could drink it, it will be so clean.'

As if to prove his point, Ian explains that after 2007 there will be a farm for rare animals on the site, as well as forest walks, picnic areas and a cycle track. Whereas no buildings are allowed to be constructed on the site, farming is permitted. 'We've even had Aberdeen Angus herds grazing on some of our reclaimed land before,' he says.

This thought unsettles me. Can pasture or crops really not be affected by thirty metres of landfill below? Ian invites me to get out of the Land Rover.

'This is one small step for a man, one giant heap for mankind,' I joke to Ian through his open window, but he can't hear me over the noise of the transporters working around us. Somewhat like Neil Armstrong, I'm a little unsure whether the surface will take my weight (even though it has happily supported a Land Rover), or whether I will sink into a putrefying hellhole.

The ground is reassuringly firm and I wander across to a mound of recently dumped rubbish to take a closer look. As I go, I step gingerly on all sorts of things we might throw out at home ourselves – shampoo bottles, cereal packets, toys, blackening chicken bones, magazines. What strikes me is how much of it could be recycled. I even find a copy of the *Guardian* dated just a week earlier, showing perfectly how quickly rubbish is swept from our homes and dumped out of sight.

'How can we get more people to recycle?' I ask Ian, once back in the Land Rover.

'I've always felt that most people see second-hand or recycled goods as second class. One thing I would do is not tell people when they are buying something that is made with recycled materials. Maybe it's best that they just don't know. That way they won't think it's inferior.'

I notice that the smell doesn't seem to be as bad as when I first reached the site. Ian explains that you soon get used to it, and that deodorizing agents are constantly being sprayed into the air.

'You should be here on a hot day, though,' he says. 'Then the neighbours really do start complaining.' I look over to a housing estate a few hundred metres from where we are parked. I can't imagine what it must be like trying to live and raise children in the shadow of this mountain of waste.

As we drive back to Ian's office on the fringes of the site, he tells me what I guess must be his party-piece anecdote about Mucking.

'We get all sorts of people ringing us up saying that they've lost something and please can they come down and look for it – wedding rings, money, photos, everything. When I tell them that the site is over a hundred acres that usually puts them off. But one day I had this tearful secretary from some City firm saying that she needed to come down and look for her firm's computers! Apparently, they had been thrown out by accident by some removal men. The trouble was they contained some really important data on their hard-drives and had to be found otherwise it might cost the firm millions. The reason why she was in such a state was that it had happened when her boss was away and she had been in charge of the computers being moved.

'Anyway, she came down here and we helped her look for them. What people don't know is that we have to keep really detailed maps and records of where we tip rubbish in case the police need to come looking for a dead body, or something like that – which has happened before, by the way. Well, we ended up finding the missing hard-drives, and what's more, her boss never even found out.'

'Go and get showered,' orders Jane as I step through the door. 'You stink.'

Is this how Ian is treated when he gets home from work each day, I wonder? I don't think I smell too bad, but Jane's reaction suggests otherwise. It's only when I take my shoes off that I realize I seem to have trodden in something indescribably disgusting and carried it all the way back home from Mucking.

Once showered and changed, I sit down and tell Jane about my day.

'You should have seen it,' I say, a little breathlessly. 'This is the sort of thing schoolchildren should see. It really hits home how much effort we must make to reduce our waste.'

After I've been through the day's events, Jane agrees that we should take the first steps to change our wasteful ways as soon as possible. I want to order a wormery to help us cut back on the amount of compostable waste we throw out each week. Jane is less enthusiastic. In fact, she is verging on the hostile, given her hatred of all things wriggly, but she does express an interest in changing from disposable nappies to washable ones – something that all the auditors said would make a huge difference to our weekly output.

So we draw up a list of things to do over the coming weeks:

- Get a wormery
- Try washable nappies
- Cut back on plastic bags
- Cut back on highly packaged food
- Try to stop as much junk mail as possible coming through our door.

Then we look at each other and laugh. Without a thought, we've just used a brand-new Post-it note to write our list with a disposable ball-point pen.

4

THERE'S A KNOCK AT THE DOOR. 'Hello, would you mind signing for these worms, please?' Relieved of his responsibility for their welfare, the delivery man hands me a large, heavy package which contains plastic trays, lime, 'worm treat', coir – and over a thousand earthworms. We are now the proud owners of a Can-O-Worms wormery.

Jane isn't keen, though. Ever since the auditors raised the idea of a wormery, she's argued continually against giving a home to these slimy specimens and I sense she will do anything to discourage me from setting up their home outside the back door.

'Won't they escape and wriggle into the kitchen?' She peers tentatively inside the package. 'Won't they attract vermin? Won't they smell?'

'Let's just give it a go,' I reply. 'The worms will eat our kitchen waste, Esme will find it educational when she's a bit older – and you've always said you wanted pets.'

Jane forces a smile through gritted teeth.

I have been really looking forward to the arrival of the wormery, which seems to mark the true beginning of our journey. We now have something tangible that I hope will start making a difference to the amount of waste we send to Mucking each week. According to the manual, we should be able to 'harvest worm casts' and use them as compost in the garden – perhaps even on some home-grown vegetables. I love the idea of this cycle: food waste turned back into food again. No more food miles, plastic packaging, landfill emissions, trips to supermarkets. Well, that's the dream anyway.

It takes me about an hour to get the wormery up and running. Standing outside in the garden by the back door, I first clip four legs and a small tap into the '100 per cent re-cycled' plastic base tray. The first of three trays, each with dozens of tiny holes in them, then sits snugly on top of this base tray. This is where I empty the bag of worms, after putting down some cardboard and a two-inch-thick layer of sodden coir (the tough fibre that surrounds a coconut). The manual says that this acts as a permeable barrier, helping water to pass through the wormery without drowning the worms. Finally, I place a snug fibrous 'duvet' over the worms to help keep their temperature and moisture levels constant.

It's a little disconcerting opening your post to find a wriggling tangle of worms. But they don't smell, as Jane thought they might, and they are protected by some compost – presumably to keep them cool, damp and well fed during transit. I'm amazed that worms can just be popped in the post. Where, I wonder, is the cut-off point? Can you send insects in the post? What about fish? Are there laws for this kind of thing? The headline 'JAILED: MAN WHO CAUSED WORM MASSACRE BY USING SECOND-CLASS POST' springs to mind.

As I slowly tip the bag upside-down, I watch the worms slide in clusters on to their coir bedding. They don't seem to be too fazed by their long journey and quickly start to burrow under the coir to gain cover and escape the sunlight. I start to pile the kitchen waste on top of them that we've been saving up as a welcoming meal – potato peelings, old salad leaves, apple cores – before covering everything with a hemp moisture mat and, finally, the plastic lid. I stand back and admire our new wormery with a warm glow of satisfaction. For the first time since the auditors arrived, I really feel that we've done something positive.

I also feel as if we are joining a community. Over the past few days I've started to receive emails and letters from across the world, having posted the first account of our family's experiment on the *Guardian*'s website. I'm amazed by the response, and am keen to solicit advice from others who have tried similar lifestyle transitions. Wormeries, it seems, are not as easy to manage as I first thought . . .

Dear Leo,

Best of luck with your wormery! We ordered ours some time ago from wigglywigglers.co.uk and put it in our basement under-pavement storage vault, which is accessible from our kitchen. Even though the lid was on, the worms managed to explore extensively. The lucky ones now populate the storage vault. The unlucky ones wriggled under the kitchen door and either dehydrated on the kitchen floor or were eaten by our cats. We decided to relocate the wormery in the light well at the front of the house, but even this didn't entirely solve the problem: visitors were surprised to find worms crawling up the wall next to our front door.

Yours, Catherine Regan

Dear Leo,

I'm a Brit, living in Silicon Valley, California. I have been here for ten years. I try to live ethically too, but it's not so easy in this land of excessive consumption. I have a worm bin myself, but I keep it in the garage. In fact, I think you will have trouble getting good results with an outdoor bin, since the worms do much better with consistent temperatures. Last year I had it outside in a shady spot during the summer, but it is so hot here that a lot of the worms died. That might not be such a problem in Britain, but they may well freeze during the winter.

It's best to put the bin in the cellar, if you have one. Nice cool consistent temps. Barring that, perhaps you have a shed that would be more sheltered than the plain outdoors.

Another tip – you need a source of fibre to add to food that goes into the worm bin. I recommend you get yourself a paper shredder, and shred all the junk mail you get. You then soak this in water,

squeeze it out until it is just damp, and add it to
the bin, putting food under the paper. Kills two
birds with one stone, since you now have less
paper to throw away.

Generally, the worm bin is a bit tricky at first. It
took me three batches of worms before I got the
environment stable and they didn't die on me. But
don't give up, you will get the hang of it after a
while. And the worm compost is great on the
garden and in plant pots.

John Grogan

Die on me? Reading this freaks me out a little. The manual
makes it look so easy to keep worms. And I won't be telling
Jane about how they can escape and climb up walls. However,
one person did advise me to go online and join one of the
many vermiculture (the fancy name for worm keeping, I've
learned) discussion groups. And I've also got Wiggly Wigglers'
worm hotline to turn to should I have any urgent queries. So
I'm hopeful that I won't fail my worms.

The second delivery of the day is a water butt. The auditors
advised me to get one to help reduce the amount of tap water
we use on our few potted plants in the garden. When they
first mentioned this I didn't think we'd have enough room for
one, but after looking online at some measurements I soon
realized that we could actually have a rather large water butt –
enough, in fact, to 'harvest' (there seems to be a lot of
harvesting going on today) forty-one gallons of rainwater,

enough to keep all our plants happy for a week or more.

Another tip I had from the auditors was to ring my local council and ask if they offered subsidized water butts. Many councils apparently now try to encourage people to install water butts (and compost heaps and wormeries too) to help reduce the type of excessive water use in gardens that can lead to hosepipe bans in the summer. I doubt we fall into that category of user, with our small decked garden – but I liked the idea of using all the rain that falls on our roof, so I rang around and, after discovering that our council doesn't subsidize water butts, found one for £35 from a firm called Blackwall Ltd.

Now that it stands before me, I must admit it does seem rather large and unsightly. But it's very easy to install. I just stand it by the downpipe next to our back door and then, with a little hacksaw, cut a four-inch section out of the plastic down-pipe to make room for a diverter valve, which not only lets rainwater pour into the butt, but also acts as an overflow pipe for when the butt is full. All we need now is some rain.

As may already be clear, Jane doesn't take well to being told what to do. I have enough trouble convincing her to watch something on telly I like the look of (admittedly, what I like the look of usually lasts about ninety minutes, with the plot centred on a ball), so persuading her to adopt some of the auditors' lifestyle recommendations has been a bit like trying to use a keyboard and mouse with chopsticks. But I assume that what they had to say about Esme's toys, clothes, toiletries, nappies and food would be the perfect catalyst for change.

Hannah, Mike and Renée step into Esme's nursery.

Glancing at the Pampers, baby lotions, talcs and wipes, Mike comments that we seem to have every baby accessory available.

'In our consumer-led society, babies have become the champion consumers,' he says. 'There is a special baby product for every occasion and parents are encouraged to buy. And because we want the best for our children, we tend to succumb. But you don't always need to buy brand-new things. Babies grow so quickly that they rarely wear out their clothes – or other equipment such as baths, cots and pushchairs. Talk to friends and family to see if they have stuff you can use – and then pass on your things to friends when you don't need them any more.'

It's a message echoed by Hannah. 'A fair amount of Esme's stuff looks new – the cot, car seat, baby bouncer and baby alarm.'

'Hopefully, we'll be having more children, so they will all get good use,' I say, trying to deflect some of the criticism.

'Fair enough. But most parents are discouraged from buying second-hand things,' responds Hannah. 'It's a shame, as it is really just a matter of checking that the required safety standards are met that counts.'

All the auditors are concerned about the amount of synthetic chemicals we seem to be exposing Esme to. Everything in her room is a potential threat: the fresh paint on the walls, the toys, the carpet, the cot linen, the nappies, the baby toiletries.

'Because babies' organs are still developing, they are not

well equipped to deal with toxins,' says Renée. 'Babies today
are exposed to complex chemicals from the moment they are
conceived, within the womb and even through breast milk. It
is imperative to give them the healthiest start possible. Less is
more. A lot of the junk out there just isn't necessary. Most
babies don't need lots of creams and gadgets. Just because
shops sell them and other mums are using them doesn't mean
they are a good idea.'

Jane and I are not naive; we know we are going to receive
a mauling for using disposable nappies. So Jane holds up one
of Esme's Pampers and invites castigation.

'The nappy question poses many ethical dilemmas,' says
Mike. 'You have opted for convenience at the expense of the
environment by using these. Disposable nappies are a major
waste problem, with eight million nappies thrown away every
day in the UK. Ninety per cent of these end up in landfill.
Disposable nappies can make up half the contents of a
family's bin. You should try using reusable terry nappies
instead. They may not be practical all the time, but you will
save money. The Women's Environment Network estimates
that using terry nappies instead of disposables can save five
hundred pounds over the nappy-wearing lifetime of a child.'

The thought of battling with big safety pins and having
large pots of soiled nappies on the boil doesn't really appeal
to us. Life's just too short. To be fair, we have considered
washable nappies but, to date, we just haven't got round to
investigating them further.

'Washable nappies have come a long way,' insists Renée.
'They are easier to use nowadays, don't clog our landfills and,

as Mike says, save you money. Companies such as Green Baby offer a large range of different types, and sample packs are available so you can try a few before buying in bulk. When you do need to use disposables, you should make an effort to avoid the chemicals you find in most brands. Artificial chemical absorbents such as sodium polyacrylate form a gel that can end up on your baby's skin as well as in the earth.'

Renée picks up a box of scented nappy sacks that we use to discard Esme's soiled nappies in. 'I have a real thing about these,' she says. 'Nappy sacks mean yet more non-biodegradable plastic – sometimes used with every nappy – and they have a "special odour-neutralizing fragrance". Come on. Nappies don't smell that bad, and you can bet that fragrance is made of synthetic chemicals. When you change Esme, just fill a small bowl with warm tap water and wash her with cotton balls, preferably organic. The last place you want chemicals and poisons is on that cute little bottom.'

Hannah suggests we go a step further with the overhaul of our disposable-nappy habit. 'Realnappy.com advocates biodegradable gauze liners, with unbleached organic nappies with cloth ties rather than Velcro straps, preferably bought second-hand. Eco-nappy soak or a solution of borax are good for home disinfecting, but nappy-washing services are worth considering as they use 32 per cent less energy than home washing, and 41 per cent less water.'

But Hannah is keen to move on to the subject of the multinationals that service most of our parenting needs. She pulls out a bumper pack of Pampers.

'Procter & Gamble, the makers of Pampers, has been

criticized for conducting animal experiments for the development of pet food, although it does claim to be committed to eliminating the need for all animal testing of products and ingredients for human use.'

She then holds up one of our many Avent bottles that we use for feeding Esme expressed milk. 'In 2001, Avent was cited by the International Baby Food Action Network (IBFAN) as having violated the rules of the International Code of Marketing of Breastmilk Substitutes in relation to promotion to the public and inadequate labelling. For example, IBFAN said that Avent labels in the United Arab Emirates, Italy and Malaysia had made comparisons between its products and a mother's breast with claims such as "Just like mother's breast" and "Your baby's natural feeding companion up to thirty-six months". Fortunately, Esme is enjoying the benefits of breastfeeding, rather than feeding off one of the baby-milk corporations with reputations for aggressive marketing strategies. Nestlé, for example, has been singled out as a boycott target for this reason. It is a remarkably effective boycott campaign, given that Nestlé's annual promotional budget totals more than the combined government expenditure of twenty-eight countries.'

Meanwhile, Mike is looking through the pile of toys on the floor. I'm pleased about this, as the question of what toys to give Esme interests me, given that I still get excited about Lego or Scalextric.

'Steer clear of plastic toys that Esme may put in her mouth,' says Mike, 'especially if they are scratched or damaged. Manufacturers can no longer use plastic softeners called phthalates in teething toys for babies, but you never know which toys children are going to chew.'

Renée explains why it is so important to avoid phthalates. 'Studies are showing links between these chemicals and cancer and kidney damage, and they may interfere with development and the reproductive system. The Swedish and Danish governments are now restricting the use of PVC, which can contain such toxic chemicals. With a bit of thought, it can be avoided.'

But it's Hannah's last point that alarms us most. 'With the human population expected to grow by a quarter in the next twenty years, there has never been such pressure on the Earth's resources. Some people now feel that remaining childless, or adopting, is the single most effective environmental decision they can ever make. But of course there's no "correct" choice. Parents considering having just one child might be interested to know that single children score just as well if not better than those with siblings in measures such as co-operativeness, generosity, number of friends and occupational success.'

Jane doesn't surprise me by not taking kindly to what the auditors said about how we were raising Esme, but her views on what Hannah had to say about procreation are even less sympathetic.

'Are they seriously proposing that we restrict the number of children we have for environmental reasons?'

'I guess so.'

'So if we want another child, we are meant to adopt or foster instead?'

'It's just a suggestion, not a rule,' I say. 'But over-population is a problem in the world and adding another mouth to feed, particularly one that will live in the West, is certainly a responsibility to bear, it seems.'

'I appreciate that, but it still seems a little extreme to me.'

I'm never going to win this one, I think. What surprises me, though, is that it's a subject that people have already started to send me emails about, even without any prompting.

> Having children is the most unethical thing you can ever do, so try ceasing that for starters.
>
> Neil M

> My situation is I find myself the mother of three children in a very short period (my eldest is five). I have gone from being a reasonably ethically based individual to running a household for five people that consumes so much stuff I am appalled. I am that woman you see pushing the absolutely overloaded trolley around the supermarket, trying to balance ever more stuff precariously on top. I am horrified that this is my life (well, horrified at the consumer I have turned into, but I feel I have to mention here that I actually do like my kids).
>
> Best of luck, Deirdre

To have kids or not? This is one that I've wrestled with over the years. It was in the *Guardian*, as I recall, funnily enough, that I read a piece on the costs of raising a child in the UK. To do the job well, to high middle-class standards, the article suggested, would cost around £125,000 over the child's lifetime. (This was at 1996 prices, and not including the costs of college and tuition fees!) I gawped a bit and wondered how many children I could sponsor in a Southern country for that sort of money. I think it was at that moment that I decided I would rather not have children, and send my £125,000 to a country more in need of it, where indeed it would go much, much further.

I don't want to judge anybody who feels it is their right to have kids, or whose biology tugs them inexorably into procreation. I know many loving, ethical people who have chosen to have kids and do it very well; indeed, they tell me it's helped them to become more thoughtful and selfless. But – allowing myself an open door to change my mind in future – at this moment, my opinion is that a Northern life creates so much more waste and pollution than a Southern life, unless we change things radically. To raise a kid sustainably in this country is difficult at best and can seem cruel at worst (how can you refuse a child new trainers or a holiday to Disneyworld when all their classmates have them?).

Best wishes for your experiment, Rachel

(NB. I should just point out here, if it isn't clear, that when Rachel uses the terms 'Southern' and 'Northern' she is referring to developed and developing nations. She's not saying that people in Newcastle create more waste and pollution than those in Newbury. I hope.)

> Should irresponsible breeding practices be rewarded by absorbing unwanted offspring through adopting children from other countries? If so, what is the net impact on the environment when surplus mouths are guaranteed a slice of the pie? For every extra slice of pie allocated, there must be a corresponding increase in fertilizers and pesticides produced and distributed; an increase in farmland and food production space carved from stressed ecosystems; more fossil fuels produced and consumed in the transport sector.
>
> The overall solution to the dilemma of ethical living is fewer mouths. When humans are barely surviving day to day at a stable population number, then the planet will be at true carrying capacity. Probably this is around one billion people consuming at Chinese levels, or 100 million consuming at American levels.
>
> **Jeff Schneid**

I'm not too sure what Jeff is suggesting here. Does he mean that the world needs to adopt a *Logan's Run*-type system whereby people are simply exterminated at the age of thirty to keep the world's population under control? Or are people to be forbidden from having children unless under tightly controlled licence, for which you would need to meet certain criteria such as wealth or genetic distinction? Or maybe it would need to be a global lottery, where you stand a slim chance of winning the ultimate prize: the right to have a child. It's all science fiction, of course, but, seriously, Jane and I do wonder whether there will ever come a time when we see such measures being considered by governments. I can't imagine it being much of a vote winner for at least a few decades, though – not if the number of parenting manuals on sale is any indication of how popular making babies is today.

Harmonious agreement, at last. We are now the proud owners of twenty washable nappies for Esme – and not an ill word has been spoken of them between us in the two weeks since we started using them.

We had both agreed that the first thing we needed to do after the auditors swept through Esme's bedroom was to change her nappies, so to speak. The thought of their effect on the environment concerned us, but to be honest, we were also attracted to the idea that washable nappies are considerably cheaper in the long term than disposables. A friend put us in touch with the local 'nappy lady' and we shortly received a delivery of sample nappies.

Not being a connoisseur of such things, I hadn't realized that nappies could come in so many shapes and sizes. All were made from a brushed-cotton terry towelling, but the range of fastening devices was quite varied – poppers, Velcro, clips. They all seemed to be shaped like disposable nappies, except that they had a towelled liner inside and a waterproof wrap outside to secure the nappy. My fears of battling with safety pins and squares of muslin cloth evaporated.

But it was Esme who held the casting vote on whether we would adopt these nappies, so we put her into one and waited for nature's good work to be done. We watched her nervously out of the corner of our eye for an hour, occasionally lifting her in the air to sniff her nappy. Still no developments. The nappy was noticeably more bulky than a disposable one, but Esme seemed happy enough.

Then, finally, the moment of truth – a grimace, a gurn, a smile, then a look of puzzlement from Esme. We laid her down on her changing mat and apprehensively peeled off her clothing to reveal the nappy's wrap. No sign of leakage, so we un-popped the wrap and unfastened the nappy to find that, without wanting to embarrass Esme too much, all our questions had been answered satisfactorily.

A couple of days later, we had a bucketful of soiled nappies waiting to be washed. We had been sprinkling a few drops of tea-tree oil into the bucket as the nappy lady had advised, to keep the pong down to acceptable levels. We had also been following her advice of wringing out the nappies under a hot tap rather than leaving them soaking in water, as some other converts had recommended to us.

Although the auditors had told us not to wash anything over 40ºC for reasons of energy efficiency, we stuffed all the nappies, liners and wraps into the washing machine and washed them at 60ºC. Having smelled these nappies, we were convinced that this was the very least they should be washed at if they were to be cleaned thoroughly. Once the wash was finished, we examined the nappies to see if all the stains had gone. Thankfully, they had.

A week later we were still managing well with the washable nappies, so we decided which nappy out of the trial set was working best. We settled on the one made by Mother-Ease as the poppers had been the easiest to use and it seemed to fit the most snugly around Esme's legs and belly. So we went ahead and ordered twenty more at a cost of about two hundred pounds. It was a big financial hit to take, but considering that disposable nappies can cost upwards of a thousand pounds in a baby's first year, we justified this considerable initial outlay as a long-term investment. We were comforted further when we asked the nappy lady how long they can be expected to last and she said each nappy will take at least two children through to potty training.

A good start then, but we are now starting to realize the first pitfall: we don't seem to be having much success with them at night. With Esme largely sleeping through now for about twelve hours, the washable nappies just get too wet. We have tried some 'eco-disposables' instead – nappies made with fewer toxic gels and more biodegradable materials – but they still don't seem to do the job for Esme, who woke up soaked from head to toe. So we have now reluctantly opted to return to conventional disposables at bedtime. However, we console ourselves with the thought that the number of nappies we throw into the wheelie bin is now down to single figures for an entire week compared to the many dozens we would toss out before. We can proudly notch up our first true success of the experiment.

It's been particularly heartening to read that others had similar experiences to us – and to receive their advice.

Howdy Leo!

As a father of three, ranging in age from one to five, I have a Ph.D. in nappies (or diapers, as we say in America).

When our first child was born, we bought about twenty-five cloth nappies for about eight dollars each. They are not the old-fashioned, plain white squares; they are different colours, contain a moisture-resistant barrier, and have Velcro closures. They're just the same to put on as disposable.

For all three children we've used the cloth nappies almost all the time, using disposables when travelling, and, as the children get older, at night. (The cloth ones get too wet overnight on a toddler.)

I find the cloth ones to be generally more convenient than the disposables. You never have to run out to the shop in the middle of the night, and we own a nice washer-dryer, so it's no trouble to wash them. We do go through a lot of bleach – not sure what the external environmental impact is, but it certainly improves our internal environment!

I don't care what figures the diaper companies come up with, it's far cheaper to use cloth. The cheapest I can get diapers here is about $0.25 each; that's about $2 per day for one child – more than $700 per child per year. For the cloth ones we spent the initial $200, and then whatever it costs to wash them. And we've used these for all three children, for more than two years each. We also pay for trash disposal by the bag here, so we've saved the cost of getting rid of all those disposable nappies as well.

Good luck!

Ed Hartnett, Nederland, Colorado, USA

Dear Leo

This year I pledged to try to make our lifestyle greener, whilst hopefully avoiding becoming a complete obsessive, but actually it's quite hard.

Am expecting our third baby any time now. Used washables with number one, gave up with number two but used greener 'sposies', and am now reverting to washables for this one. And you can now get hemp nappies, which are greener because the production uses less pesticides than cotton. I'm planning to use washable wipes as I've discovered that the throwaway ones are actually plastic! At the moment I've been buying various different sorts of nappies to see which works best, but have decided to make sure that they are all British made and that most of them come from 'work at home' mums. Love the idea of giving them my money rather than Pampers or Huggies. There is also a strong second-hand market for them, so you can recycle them too.

I've also switched to washable menstrual products (or will once baby arrives). Again there is a huge range out there, and although I'm sure as a bloke you'd rather not touch on this one, your wife should think about it as they are really comfy and come in gorgeous fabrics. I've even had my husband (who was initially horrified at the idea) trying to find new ways to clip them to our clothes airer – we thought about hanging them on the guy ropes when we went camping recently!

Katherine, Buxton, Derbyshire

Comfy . . . gorgeous fabrics. That might appeal to Jane, I think, upon reading Katherine's enthusiastic words.

'Why don't you start using washable tampons?' I suggest, still buoyed by the success we've had with the nappies.

Never have I misjudged a moment so badly. The look I receive is a combination of shock, bewilderment and outrage at the sheer indignity and brazenness of such a question.

'Sure. If you're prepared to wash them.'

I know when I'm defeated – I don't even bother to show her Katherine's letter. Now is not the time to persuade her to try and bond with her 'common sisterhood'.

Fate predictably determines that within hours of the Washable Tampon Debacle, I receive another letter raising what is now a taboo subject.

> My girlfriend uses cotton sanitary towels that she washes and reuses (some she bought, some she made herself). It's the same issue as disposable nappies, I suppose. She's quite proactive about them, having converted a few other people, and I'm sure she won't mind me mentioning them to you. She gets really annoyed by those Always adverts 'with a cotton-like top sheet' . . .

> Matthew

Needless to say, I never even consider telling Jane that some women choose to *make* their own sanitary towels, let alone wash them. Life lessons are coming thick and fast at the moment.

5

ANYONE WHO KNOWS south London wouldn't naturally associate Loughborough Junction with locally produced, organic food. It's a place where you try to walk with purpose, keeping your head down to avoid eye contact. Estate agents describe it as 'up and coming', a backhanded compliment if ever there was one.

But tucked away in several adjoining units on a business park just south of the railway station are the offices and distribution centre of Abel & Cole, one of the country's most successful – in terms of both sales and awards – organic box delivery schemes.

I would never have known it was there if I hadn't typed my postcode and 'box delivery schemes' into a search engine one day soon after our unsuccessful post-audit trip to Sainsbury's. Astonishingly, we had a highly rated scheme within a mile or so of our front door. Excellent, I thought – that means low delivery miles. Such good fortune was spur enough for me to ask if I could come and see the operation up close.

Jane and I have heard about such schemes and even have a couple of friends who are enthusiastic converts. But, like visiting the Pyramids and finishing off the photo album, signing up for a box scheme has been just another thing added to our long list of life aspirations.

It's the convenience that sounds so appealing. The fact that all your fruit and veg for the week is handed to you on your doorstep without your having to shoulder-wrestle your way to the weighing machine in Aisle Three, or ask a stroppy teenager for a new roll of plastic bags for your button mushrooms. It seems like heaven.

We all have a mental image of what a farm should be like. For some it's moulded by experience, but for lifelong urbanites it's more likely to be inspired by *Emmerdale, The Archers* or 'Old McDonald'. There's the loyal sheepdog walking close to his master's side; the chickens scratching underfoot in the yard; the mugs of tea and homemade cake accompanied by market-town gossip beside the warming Aga; the communal rush to bring in the crops at harvest time – a bucolic idyll that many still fantasize about giving it all (the large mortgage, the commute, the office politics, the irritating neighbours, the school waiting lists) up for.

I'm still a sucker for the fantasy – even though I actually grew up in Cornwall and so learned about the ebb and flow of the seasons. (I mean the difference between the tourist season and winter shut-down, of course.) So when I pick up a bag of potatoes or carrots at the supermarket I still associate them with muddy tractor wheels, tarpaulin-covered piles of silage and doing the 'farmer's vault' over wooden gates.

I suppose I'm expecting a taste of that rural idyll as Jane and

I walk through the traffic fumes of south London to the doors of Abel & Cole. It's disappointing from the outside. The anodyne business-park setting gives it the look of – and I'm scrabbling for dull business stereotypes here – a photocopier-cartridge merchant or toilet-roll distributor. Only the half-squashed courgette on the Tarmac outside gives any clue as to what kind of business goes on behind the large sliding doors before us.

Keith Abel, the firm's co-founder, meets us and, before we embark on a tour, fills us in on the background behind Abel & Cole.

'We started well over a decade ago to make money as students by delivering potatoes locally,' he tells us. 'Now we have over four thousand customers in Greater London.'

Keith explains how the firm takes great care to source organic, seasonal produce, grown in the UK wherever possible, keeping food miles down. Food is never flown in from abroad – contrary to what all the supermarkets are doing, he says. If produce is sourced from overseas, such as bananas, it will always be shipped in to help keep related emissions to a minimum.

But it's the relationship he's built up with the farmers that he cherishes the most. He believes in returning to trusted suppliers year after year, thereby helping them to plan ahead with their crops – in stark contrast to how the supermarkets treat their suppliers. It soon becomes apparent that Keith sees the supermarkets as the farmers' nemesis.

'Just last week I had a lettuce farmer we use a lot ring me up and ask me if I wanted his entire crop of lettuces. He was desperate. The supermarket which had verbally committed to buying the crop had pulled out of the deal at the last minute. And I mean last minute. His workers had been picking and packing the lettuce through the night to meet the order when he received a call at midnight to say the deal was off. They had overestimated their needs, they said. No compensation. Nothing. He was left with thousands of pounds' worth of lettuce, soon to be worthless unless he could quickly find a buyer. Luckily our box scheme allows for flexibility, so I bought the lettuces from him at the same price as the supermarket had promised to pay. In fact, we had so little time to get them to our customers that they went out still in the supermarket's bags.

'He was lucky, but I hear this kind of story all the time. Many farmers are being screwed by the supermarkets. What we try to do is reconnect the farmers with the people who actually eat their produce.'

Keith beckons us towards a door that leads to a large, hangar-like room where dozens of people are packing open-topped cardboard boxes with fruit and vegetables. Radio One is blaring and the staff start joking with Keith as we walk in. This isn't how I'd imagined organic boxes would be prepared. I'd visualized a handful of people leaning over a trestle table filling boxes with muddy root vegetables and an apple or two. I suppose it's that 'worthy equals dour' stereotype from the seventies that's hard to shake off.

What we actually see are staff speedily packing cardboard boxes that are cleverly compactable so they can be easily stored and reused by both the customer and the company. And it's not just the carrots, turnips and spuds of box-scheme lore being packed up, but a huge range of organic produce, including fruit, bread, eggs, beer, dairy goods, sausages, chicken, fish and pasta. I even spot Ecover washing-up liquid and dishwasher tablets on the storage shelves nearby. It seems that if we really wanted to, with some forward planning we could largely eradicate supermarkets from our life.

Naturally, talk soon moves to cost. I ask Keith whether, honestly, an average-income household could ever afford to buy their weekly shop exclusively from a firm such as his. This can't come cheap, I suggest.

'I'm certainly not claiming that we are cheaper than non-organic produce in supermarkets,' he says. 'But I do say that like for like, organic product for organic product, we match supermarkets, or are even cheaper. And we deliver free to your door – in an LPG-powered van.'

I ask Keith which of the many box options Abel & Cole offer we would need to keep us in fruit and veg each week. He recommends the mixed organic box. It costs £12.80 and in the week we visit includes a cauliflower, a bag of spinach, half a dozen Fuji apples, eight Milva potatoes, a red pepper, a brown bag of Santa Rosa plums, half a dozen carrots, a bag of white mushrooms, four white onions and a bag of yellow peaches.

Keith says that new customers generally take a month or so to acclimatize to a box scheme. He always advises customers to make the transition from supermarket to box scheme slowly, otherwise the change could prove to be too much of a culture shock. What new customers can find hard to adjust to, he says, is that the produce within the boxes is seasonal. This means that you need to get used to not having the same staples in your fridge every week. Instead, you will find new produce that will often require some fresh thinking about how it should be prepared and eaten. Furthermore, customers need to be aware that some produce is only available for just a few short weeks a year and needs to be seen as a treat. Asparagus is a classic example, as are broad beans.

Keith says that unfortunately the general public needs to be re-educated about the seasons and the different foods we produce in this country. Box schemes can be a great tool for doing this, and he thinks they will get more and more popular as people become increasingly disillusioned by the supermarkets.

Esme needs a feed, so we conclude our tour in Keith's office. We have a brief chat about the highs and lows of having a wormery (not your usual man-to-man banter, admittedly) – he admits to not having had much joy with his and has now moved on to a proper compost heap – before he passionately argues the case for organic farming.

'For me, the way bananas are grown is one of the most alarming things about conventional farming.' He glances at Esme. 'I would never want a baby holding such a banana in its hand – let alone eating it – when you know what they spray on them. It's just common sense to want to eat organic food, in my view.'

He's a master salesman, if nothing else. We sign up for a weekly mixed box.

The following Friday our first box arrives, accompanied by two pints of milk, a bunch of bananas, an extra box of mushrooms, a loaf of bread and half a dozen eggs – the organic extras we estimate we'll need at first, until we establish the pattern of our consumption.

Unpacking it, we speculate on the impact it will have on our meals. Even though the box scheme allows us to express our dislike for anything and have it automatically replaced with something else, we realize that we are going to have to create meals out of what we're given rather than relying on the ever-available supermarket ingredients of old. Abel & Cole has anticipated this anxiety and encloses a weekly newsletter with its boxes that includes recipes and explains where the produce has come from and how the farmers are faring this season.

> This week's hispi cabbage comes from Andy Johnson of Buckfastleigh. He planted a large crop of cabbages this year, but did so with some trepidation. Last year, leatherjackets devastated thousands of his cabbages. Andy is extremely relieved to report that this year's crop has been virtually untouched by leatherjackets. He says he didn't do anything differently this year, other than laying fleece after planting. Perhaps the leatherjackets just felt like a change after all the cabbage they ate last year.

I don't even know what a leatherjacket is, so look it up in the dictionary – the larval stage of the daddy-long-legs, I learn. And it's highly unlikely we would have chosen a hispi cabbage ourselves, having never heard of them before. And we certainly wouldn't have known the name of the farmer who grew it.

The box is an immediate hit. Jane and I are both really enthused by the whole experience: the visit to Abel & Cole itself; the sight of the delivery van pulling up outside our house; the anticipation about what we'll find in the box; the stories and recipes that we read in the newsletter. And this is before we've even tasted anything.

Once we've unpacked the box, we look at all the food laid out before us and speculate about what we should cook up first. It doesn't even strike us that the contents of the box happen to be rather mundane. We have a head of celery, some Chinese leaf, hispi cabbage, two large courgettes, an iceberg lettuce, six vine tomatoes, ten carrots, ten new potatoes, ten golden plums, ten Helena apricots and five kiwi fruits. Let's face it, a pretty poor cousin to what we'd normally pick up at the supermarket. The flash South African seedless grapes and exotic Thai mangosteens of old make the salt-of-the-earth celery and humble carrot seem fairly lacklustre in comparison. But we are delighted with our new arrivals and, it seems strange to say, find them almost endearing in their simplicity and lack of fanfare. We lovingly set about putting them all away, thinking of things to cook with them all. This is already an advance on our old life: unpacking the shopping was always, to me at least, yet another chore to dread.

After all the build-up, the first meal constructed with the contents of our box doesn't deserve the hype. We simply have omelettes with salad. (Although isn't the true test of a chef his omelettes?) But it tastes great, no doubt helped by the positive mindset with which we are eating it. Soon, though, our confidence starts to build and by the end of the week the hispi cabbage has been used in a chicken soup and the Chinese leaf transforms our usually rather uneventful stir-fries.

And several boxes later, the enthusiasm remains un-diminished. This small connection with how and where the food we eat is grown – in particular, the weekly newsletter – enthuses us so much that we start to eagerly await the box's arrival each week. Just to whet the appetite, the Abel & Cole website also provides a list of what next week's box is likely to include. This means that we can look up recipes that feature forthcoming produce and then shop for, or order, additional ingredients as required. We start enjoying our cooking more, rather than just seeing it as a chore to face at the end of a long day. It helps too that, without question, the produce really does taste much better than our shopping of old. (Try – as we did – the definitive taste test: mashed potato made with organic spuds versus generic supermarket spuds.)

We have now started to wean Esme, too, which has increased our concern about what we are all eating. And because the food in our organic box is so tied to the seasons, our diet seems to have effortlessly ended up being much more varied. The seasonal shift in produce available is noticeable even after just a few weeks – we've just started to receive the first treasures of early summer: broad beans, asparagus and strawberries.

With the wormery now up and running and the organic box scheme in place, I feel the next step is to tackle the garden – which the auditors said had much potential for positive change.

When Jane and I were house-hunting, a garden, in addition to a spare room for our imminent new arrival and shelf space for the books, featured high up on our wish-list. Having spent the last ten years living in flats bereft of any outside space, owning a garden had always been a fantasy – long sunny afternoons spent meandering among the flowerbeds, cool drink in hand, sniffing roses and admiring the topiary, that sort of thing. Reality struck hard on the cold November weekend when we moved in.

Stepping out of our back door for the first time, we were greeted by a fifteen foot square of barren garden decking – not a plant in sight. We'd forgotten that the previous occupants would have taken their many garden pots and plants – so attractive when the estate agent showed us round – with them when they moved out. But at least we would have a clean slate, we said. We'd now be able to enjoy building up a new garden from scratch.

The garden decking had also seemed appealing – low-maintenance and safe for children, said the estate agent temptingly. Staring at it in the cold November rain, though, without any garden furniture or plants to adorn it, was simply depressing. But a few months on, despite the onset of spring, we still had not got round to tackling our garden. Esme had just been born, so planting laurels and hardies were not high priorities for us. All we had managed was one trip to the garden centre for a token handful of bedding plants. By the time the auditors arrived, the garden was still an inspiration-free zone.

After a brief discussion about the pros and cons of removing the decking from our garden, the auditors agree that for the time being we should just make the best of it.

'Ripping it up would be quite disruptive and expensive,' says Renée. 'I suggest using potted plants to make it greener and create softness against the walls. Climbing roses and fruit trees placed around the perimeter would give colour, fragrance and food, and you could use different pots to transform what is quite a barren space into a lush haven.'

Hannah is bending down to examine the decking more closely. 'I can't tell what timber has been used,' she says, 'or whether it has been treated with pesticides or other wood treatments that could have leached into the soil, but it is unlikely to have been certified by the Forestry Stewardship Council. Hopefully, it is a British-grown hardwood or European softwood from a managed forest, and not from the tropics. This is because at the current rate of deforestation, the world's rainforests will vanish within a hundred years, taking with them the majority of plant and animal species on the planet and creating havoc with the global climate. Widespread loss of tree cover is one of the major environmental threats of our time.'

'Struth, that's quite a lot of guilt to carry, isn't it?' I say. 'Those garden makeover shows have got a lot to answer for.' We all step up from the low trough by the back door on to the main raised area of decking.

'What really excites me,' says Renée, 'is putting together a very simple, low, large, rough-hewn wooden box for a vegetable garden. Or, of course, you could just buy something similar from the garden centre. Not only could you then grow your own organic vegetables at home, but it's also exciting for children to watch plants grow and bear fruit. If you need inspiration, you should read the Soil Association's *Little Book of Organic Farming*. And if you have pest problems in the veggie patch or with the fruit trees, the Soil Association can also help with suggestions for natural pest control.'

Hannah is keen for us to grow some organic vegetables too, but adds that it is important, especially in a city, to sow plants that attract wildlife. 'Choose any new plants carefully to suit the condition and aspect of the garden, but also to begin creating a bio-diverse haven for wildlife, and for Esme to play in. Urban areas are increasingly important to the survival of British wildlife. Even using only pots and planters, you can attract a mass of invertebrate life, including natural predators that will avoid the need for chemical treatments on so-called problems such as greenfly. There are lots of organic gardening sites on the web that can advise you.'

Hannah says that if vegetables seem a bit daunting at first, we should try growing some herbs to start with. 'These will add an extra sensory dimension to the garden and keep the kitchen supplied with fresh leaves. If you get the bug, branch out into other crops. Organic strawberries are expensive to buy in the shops but amazingly easy to grow yourself.'

However, one of the most satisfying things to do can be to attract birds other than the odd bedraggled pigeon to our garden, says Hannah, particularly when the population of wild birds such as sparrows is in such decline. 'Changed farming practices mean wild birds are increasingly dependent on our domestic gardens. You could install a bird table –

keeping it out of reach of cats – a nesting box or two, and maybe start some thick creepers up the fence to provide extra nesting potential. And why not plant a new fruit or nut tree as a symbol of hope springing from the deathly influence of the decking?'

Mike agrees that herbs, tomatoes and strawberries are probably the best starting point for people who have never gardened before. He's particularly encouraged that we have a south-facing garden.

'But make sure you avoid peat-based soil products,' he warns. 'Peat is a precious natural resource which forms in peat bogs over thousands of years. Industrial peat-cutting is destroying these valuable wildlife habitats to supply garden centres and horticulturists with nutritious soil. These rich lowland habitats are being ruined, contributing to global warming. But peat-free alternatives are available – and nothing is quite as organic as some fresh manure.'

And where exactly do you buy that in central London? I wonder to myself.

'Avoid using chemicals to kill pests, too. Common garden weedkillers can contain risky chemicals. Beer traps are a much more environmentally friendly way of tackling slugs than slug pellets, which not only poison the poor slugs but the soil too – and used coffee grounds will also keep slugs at bay. But don't forget that some birds feed on slugs too, so attract as many birds as you can. Flowers attract butterflies, especially cottage garden and wildflowers, and long grass provides a haven for insects.'

Hannah adds that much of the garden furniture and

barbeque charcoal we buy in the UK is also responsible for various environmental crimes. 'Try to find garden furniture and barbeque charcoal certified by the Forest Stewardship Council, which means it's come from sustainable woodland. Cheap charcoal made from treated and painted old wood products can give off choking chemical fumes when you first get it burning. Cheap furniture may have been made in the Far East, where there's an acute problem of manufacturers using virgin wood and exploited labour.'

Talk of organic herbs, bird feeders and peat-free soil aside, both Hannah and Mike believe that one of the best uses of our garden space would be for composting. 'Recycling organic matter by composting kitchen waste is one of the most ecologically sound things you can do,' stresses Hannah. 'Organic household waste should be composted, instead of allowing it to rot away in landfill sites where it generates methane, a potent greenhouse gas. A wormery made from recycled plastic, or a compost bin dug in below the surface of the decking, would also solve the peat problem as compost makes great potting soil.'

Mike illustrates how composting could reduce our waste output. 'Kitchen and garden waste counts for around 35 per cent of the typical household dustbin, so composting would drastically cut the amount of rubbish you send to landfill.'

Jane and I now feel ready to start work on our garden, especially as we've developed quite a nice little routine with our wormery. We keep a large Tupperware box by the kitchen sink for peelings and plate scrapings, then once every day or so I

(Jane still doesn't like to go near the worms) take it outside to empty into the wormery.

At first I couldn't resist peeking in a couple of times a day to see how the worms were faring, but now I've grown less curious. The whole process still fascinates me, though. Like children, they eat their favourites first and leave stuff they don't much like till they're really hungry. Lettuce leaves and apple cores first. Orange peel and onion last.

I wish they were a bit faster at eating, though. I've noticed that they just don't seem to be able to get through the volume of food we are giving them, and some of it is beginning to rot. As instructed, I've recently started to add a handful each of lime mix (to help keep acidity levels down) and worm treat (looks like cheap muesli and adds extra fibre) to the wormery each week. And acting on the advice of my readers, I've also started to add shredded newspaper and cardboard. I'm not yet achieving the correct balance of food to worms, but I'm determined to succeed.

No such trouble with the other new addition – the water butt. Sod's law meant that we had to wait nearly two weeks before the first downpour, but once it did rain, it only took one night before the whole butt – all forty-one gallons of it – was full to the brim.

As chief plant-waterer in our household, it falls to me to remember to water everything. This used to be done – even though we had hardly any plants – by attaching a hose to the kitchen sink. Now I can just fill up the watering can from the butt without worrying that I'm going to cause a nationwide hosepipe ban. Even better, the blurb that came with the water butt said rainwater is better for plants than tap water, which contains lots of additives they prefer not to consume.

The one thing neither of us feels at the moment is a sense of being alone. The gardening advice that has been pouring in as a result of my *Guardian* diary has really spurred us on. Out of all the issues I've tackled so far, gardening – unsurprisingly, perhaps, given our nation's addiction to bank holiday queues at garden centres – seems to have provoked the biggest response.

The smallest water feature will attract frogs and give them shelter for the summer. Last year I made my own with a washing-up bowl, three water plant bulbs and some compost. Despite only one plant actually growing there was one frog resident within two weeks and two in a month. These undoubtedly contributed to the lack of slug damage later in the growing season.

I also overlooked an infestation of blackfly and greenfly on a large shrub, but a local swarm of hoverflies chomped through them in just over an hour one afternoon. It was fascinating to watch.

My garden is a regular haunt for birds, including the usual sparrows, starlings and blackbirds, but also blue tits, great tits, wrens, chaffinches, greenfinches, goldfinches, robins and a sparrowhawk. They come to feed on seeds and nuts, but also to bathe in the tray of fresh water I provide. Of course the sparrowhawk comes to feed on the other birds, but usually misses.

In short, whatever space you allow, whatever food you provide and whatever shelter you give, wild creatures will take advantage of your hospitality. You will gain great pleasure and your child will gain knowledge from your garden. Have a great time with your experiment and I hope it sets you up for a lifetime.

Sincerely, Graham Smillie, Barrow-in-Furness

If you ever get around to ripping up the deck and get your soil tested for heavy metals, you might want to experiment with biointensive gardening. A fifteen by fifteen plot would yield potentially great results. In case you haven't encountered biointensive methods before, read *How to Grow More Vegetables* by John Jeavons. The official website is www.growbiointensive.org. The idea is that with double digging, intensive crop spacing and attention to soil amendment, an individual can grow his yearly vegetable needs in a hundred-square-foot space over eight months. Cool stuff and a timely idea that deserves to be spread around.

Best, Rick Fonda, Philadelphia, USA

Living in a big city with a small town garden, I decided to grow veg in containers on my flat kitchen roof. Result: fresh veg for two from June to October (and with a bit of protection you can grow salad greens in a window-box all the year round). Downside: there are only so many mangetout peas you can eat at once.

Don't use peat (a bit difficult in Belgium, where peat-free compost seems to be unknown). Don't use chemicals of any sort; aim for a natural balance. Result: fantastic garden full of birds, bees, butterflies, frogs, bats (yes, even in Brussels). Only downside: slugs and snails, though with fond memories of Brian in *The Magic Roundabout*, I can't help being rather fond of snails.

Michele Bailey, Brussels, Belgium

The water butt arrived just in time for our first foray into buying some new plants. Our relative failure with indoor plants over the years has probably been hindering our confidence somewhat – umbrella and rubber plants were about as adventurous as we got – so anything as complex as rearing roses or propagating seeds seemed best left to the Dimmocks of this world. I once tried to grow some rocket from seed, but a weekend away one hot summer left us with a potful of wilted seedlings. An avocado I grew from the stone about five years ago is inexplicably still alive today, despite many near brushes with death through over-watering, under-watering or lack of adequate daylight. It's not surprising that it hasn't grown more than two feet high or sprouted any new leaves for about two years now. I claim it to be my very own avocado bonsai, but others may view it simply as flora abuse.

So, taking the auditors' advice, we are aiming low and starting with some easy-maintenance garden herbs. After stumbling on a rather inspiring organic herb stall at a local fair, we purchase two carrier bags full of herb plants, including oregano, green basil, mint, purple basil, tarragon, thyme, coriander, flat-leaf parsley, bay and chives. Back home, I fill two disused window boxes we had in the garden with peat-free compost bought earlier from the nearby garden centre and plant them all.

We're having quite a hot spell at the moment, so I'm watering them every evening. This seems to do the trick as most of the herbs become quickly established (by this, I mean they are still alive), and ironically, we find that we can't eat them quickly enough.

My one failure, however, is the green basil. Within a couple of nights of planting it out, the tell-tale signs of slug attack become apparent. Within a week, the whole plant has been nibbled down to just a few stumps. The slugs also adore the damp, dark sanctuary of garden decking, which means our garden is now the neighbourhood's most buzzing nightspot for molluscs (I'm calling it the Slug and Lettuce until I can come up with a better name).

Before, I might have just bought some slug pellets, but I now find myself wondering how to repel these unwanted guests in an ethical way. Not wanting to kill them – they provide food for other wildlife and help organic garden matter to decompose faster – I'm loath to try some of the 'final solution' methods favoured by many gardeners, such as beer traps, buckets of salt water or trails of dry bran.

I have tried raising the window boxes up on bricks in the vain hope that this might prove too much of an obstacle course. But the slugs soon return.

I've read online about many ingenious deterrents – baked crushed eggshells, sheep wool, seaweed, chopped brambles, cut hair from the salon floor, watering in the morning rather than the evening, even patrolling for slugs with a torch at two a.m. – but in the end I've just re-potted the basil and moved it to the kitchen windowsill far out of reach of the slugs.

But the herbs also seem to have encouraged other more welcome visitors. Our large pot of apple mint, in particular, has attracted lots of insects and, most pleasingly, some small pale-yellow butterflies. And whether it was the lure of our herbs or our resident slugs I'm not sure, but one evening as I was watering the garden a frog leaped out by my foot, before disappearing beneath the decking. To be in the centre of a vast city and to have created a welcoming enough environment for a creature as shy and sensitive as a frog left me with a broad grin on my face.

I am already planning ahead for next spring: I've just received a catalogue in the post that sells organic seeds, and am considering having a go at peppers, French beans, tomatoes and new potatoes. And both of us are keen to install a nesting box on the tall brick wall at the end of the garden. Anything to help more wildlife prosper in our small corner of south London.

6

I'M TERRIBLE WITH NAMES. Before I've even finished shaking hands with a new acquaintance I'm desperately rummaging through the dusty attic in my head to recall their name. But, strangely, I'm not too bad at remembering facts and figures. I was that child geek who wanted the *Guinness Book of Records* for Christmas every year. And who now takes pub quizzes a little too seriously as a result. I think I've worked out, too, how my mind remembers all that useless trivia: it uses that old revision chestnut of putting an image, song or ditty to each fact. I once tried to remember the sequence of all the elements in the periodic table by making up an improbably long mnemonic. I think it helped me as far as the first of the noble gases, but I forgot it all as soon as I'd scraped through whatever exam was dominating my life at the time.

However, it's a trick I still use today, though mostly subconsciously. And I think the subjects I now choose to help me remember things say a lot about my key interests – music, sport and travel. I tend to link things to favourite songs that were in the charts that year, to who won the FA Cup, and to what holidays I went on. The year Thatcher was toppled? Easy, that's 1990: the Happy Mondays sang 'Step On', Manchester United beat Crystal Palace, and I crossed America by Greyhound bus.

Music and sport are, and I suspect always will be, permanent daily fixtures in my life. (We're talking listening and watching, not participating.) Travel, on the other hand, is something that I enjoy just a handful of times a year, but still it occupies much of my thoughts and aspirations. It's one of my few regrets that I don't get to travel more often, even though I have been lucky enough to clock up more miles than average over the years.

My childhood trips were largely restricted to two-week summer holidays in Europe (which usually meant France). In essence, they involved long drives, a ferry journey, a hired holiday home, and travails with funny foreign food. Whether it was in the car, on the ferry or after visiting a restaurant, someone being sick featured at some point.

But even though I enjoyed all my holidays, I was always slightly jealous of classmates who returned from far-off trips to exciting-sounding places such as America or Australia. And other members of my family always seemed to be speaking of their own exotic travels. When I was twelve, one of my aunts was involved in an expedition to Antarctica that concluded with the support ship – which my aunt was on at the time – becoming trapped in pack ice and sinking. The whole drama, in which all the crew were rescued by US helicopters, was reported on the *News at Ten*. This was all tremendously exciting in my eyes and was certainly the seed of my wanderlust today. My mother (who I didn't live with) also travelled widely, and would talk of countries she'd visited that sounded so interesting and other-worldly to me. She encouraged me to take a year off before going to university to travel around the world. I spent a long, impatient summer working in a bar, saving up for the big trip.

The trip itself – during which I travelled alone, to the great concern of much of my family – took in a coast-to-coast journey across America, followed by visits to Fiji, New Zealand, Australia, Indonesia, Malaysia, Singapore, Thailand, India and Kenya. I enjoyed every second of it and largely dreaded my return home, not relishing the prospect of three years stuck in the same small coastal town at university. Ever since that trip, a part of me has always wanted to relive the experience.

Luckily Jane, who I met at university, shared the same desire to travel, and not long after graduating we spent three months in India, Sri Lanka and Nepal. Ever since then, we have tried to have at least one trip abroad a year. Our holidays are one of the highlights of the year – which is why they help me to remember dates, because they leave such an indelible mark. Jane and I will discuss holiday destinations many months, even years, before any bookings are made and always using the same criteria – cost, weather, local cuisine, culture and the variety of activities. We also have a couple of rules: no repeat holidays and no package holidays.

In recent years we've been to New England, Western Australia, Morocco, Rome, Greece, the French Alps and Andalusia. The pattern is usually the same. We'll get a place into our head and start looking on the internet for cheap flights, usually with a budget airline. If we find some, we'll buy a guide book, work out an interesting itinerary, then start ringing recommended hotels to check availability and prices. Lastly, we'll book a car rental.

Once we arrive, the holiday will usually be a mix of touring in the car across the countryside and staying in cities of interest, or by the coast. Where possible, we try and stay in small, local hotels, but occasionally we'll splash out on something a bit more luxurious and live above our means for a night or two as a treat.

I'm explaining all this because I want to stress how important travel is to us. I believe my life would feel considerably impoverished if I didn't have the prospect of foreign travel on the horizon. Jane cherishes and looks forward to our trips just as much as I do. Before the auditors arrived, we both agreed that any suggestion of tempering our holiday habits would be hard to swallow.

The auditors ask us where we've recently been on holiday. I feel a little self-conscious and showy listing all the destinations, particularly as both Mike and Hannah don't seem too impressed.

'You really need to kick your fly-drive habit if you're going to green up your holidays,' says Mike. 'In recent years I reckon you've clocked up nearly 20,000 kilos of carbon dioxide emissions each. And that's without including the driving.'

Hannah is pleased to hear that we don't take regular short-haul mini-breaks to Europe or package holidays with the large tour operators. But whatever holidays we take, she says, we are helping to fuel the world's largest industry.

'Global spending on international tourism reached $453 billion in 1999 and has kept on growing since – despite the fact that only 4 per cent of the world's population travels abroad each year. The worst problems are associated with all-inclusive resorts, where most of the money spent is quickly repatriated to Western countries via the owners. Meanwhile, the local community servicing the holiday suffers a wide range of negative consequences, which can include the destruction of nearby coastlines, or even the loss of indigenous cultures through the creation of neo-colonial dependence on low-paid, low-status service jobs. In fact, a recent survey of UK-based operators found only half had responsible tourism policies, many of which were judged to be "virtually meaningless".'

But Hannah also backs up Mike's point about the polluting impact of aviation. 'It's the fastest single growing source of greenhouse gas emissions,' she says. 'It generates nearly as much carbon dioxide each year as all human activity in Africa. A return flight to Florida produces as much carbon dioxide per passenger as a year's driving by the average British motorist. Aviation is also predicted to account for half the annual destruction of the ozone layer by 2015. However, one reason why air traffic is increasing at four times the rate of road traffic is because of the featherbedding of the industry: it pays no tax on fuel or VAT on the purchase of planes, servicing or air fares. Just taxing aviation fuel would leave the UK's coffers £7 billion better off and help cut projected demand by 33 per cent.'

At this point I meekly stress that foreign holidays are

really important to us, and that we are reluctant to cut back on them. I receive support from an unlikely source.

'You have had some great holidays and are gradually exploring the world,' says Renée. 'And I say good for you. I don't worry about ethical travel too much – although I always respect whatever land I am in. Being on holiday for me means letting my mind relax and not worrying. Or, more to the point, not thinking about everything like I do when I'm at home. So I don't agonize too much about how I get there or if I need to rent a car while I'm out there, but I do follow the same principles I live by in England. So if I'm with my family in a hotel, we use our towels several times. Or if we're in a villa, we don't waste water, and so on. Wherever we are, we try to find an organic store to buy provisions, and of course we buy and eat the local food.'

Renée does add, however, that she blanches when she hears about how certain countries are being ruined by the negative impact of tourists. So she urges us to consider 'eco-tourism' as an alternative. It's something that Hannah is keen to expand on.

'Over three-quarters of British package tourism is controlled by four companies – Thomson, Airtours, First Choice and Thomas Cook,' she says. 'You should avoid lining their pockets at the expense of, say, local businesses at your destination. But if you ever choose to holiday in a developing nation, you should first consider whether the local people even want you visiting them. For example, tourist money is used to prop up the Burmese regime and opposition leader Aung San Suu Kyi has pleaded for tourists to stay away. The best starting place to find out about where you are welcome is Tourism Concern's *Good Alternative Travel Guide*. After this, contact the Association of Independent Tour Operators, whose 150 or so members have signed up to responsible tourism guidelines. And why not pledge never to fly within Europe? If a longer flight ever seems unavoidable, make sure you properly calculate the impact.'

Mike agrees that, where possible, it is best to travel by train and not to travel too far. In fact, it's preferable to stay within the UK. Jane gives him a bit of a scowl as bucket-and-spade holidays in the rain spring to mind, but Mike suggests activity holidays. It does nothing to appease her.

'Cycling and walking holidays can be good options,' he says. 'Hiring a cottage or camping can also be sustainable ways of spending a holiday. And take the chance to support local pubs, restaurants, shops and markets, thereby putting money into the local economy.'

Mike doesn't have many good words for staying in hotels, though. 'Living it up in a hotel tends to be quite resource intensive. Remember, you don't need clean towels every day. Sending them off to the laundry uses up lots of water and energy. If you do want to pamper yourself, look out for hotels that offer local and organic food – more and more are springing up – or hotels that advertise themselves as being "green".'

The auditors seem to have managed to make travel seem not only unappealing but impractical too, and so we've been putting off the decision about where to go on holiday this year.

Matters are complicated by the fact that we now must factor in travelling with a baby who has just started weaning. And who now wears washable nappies. I'm starting to wonder whether it would be easier just to stay at home and get the deckchairs out.

'They're nothing but boring spoilsports,' grumbles Jane, as we mull over the thought of life without our usual type of holiday. It's the news that we've got to start by stripping away flights and car hire that leaves us feeling that the sun is setting fast on the chance of ever enjoying our two weeks away again. And with the 'no plane' rule, vast swathes of the world have been eliminated as a potential destination, leaving just continental Europe. Not exactly a poor option, of course, but it still leaves the quandary of what type of holiday to go on and where.

Another problem is that, for us, the word 'eco-tourist' throws up images of clearing shopping trolleys from canals, or attending African-drumming workshops. That's to say, not really our idea of fun. We're at a complete loss as to what sort of holiday we should try to organize. All we know is that we would still like to go abroad, if possible, if just to get some nice weather.

Despite our misgivings, I decide to see what kind of holidays eco-tourism has to offer, so I contact ATG, an Oxford-based travel operator that has recently won two major international eco-tourism awards. First, I look round its website. Since 1979, I read, ATG has specialized in the most environmentally friendly trip possible – the walking holiday. But what sets ATG apart is that 10 per cent of its pre-tax profits go to a trust that funds various local projects, such as restoring ancient pathways and local cultural artefacts. In addition, 65 per cent of the price of the holiday is guaranteed to be spent at source, so benefiting the local economy. Also, ATG only advertises by word of mouth, to keep the cost of its holidays down.

I phone them up and explain that we'd like a foreign touring holiday, but without using a plane or a rental car. We must also have as minimal an impact on the local environment as possible, and see that as much of our money as possible is left in local hands. But we must – and I stress this point – come away from the experience feeling like we've actually had a holiday too.

The saleswoman is quick to suggest their six-day walking trip across Umbria in Italy. The holiday itself, she says, meets all our criteria – no rental car, low environmental impact, and enjoyment (i.e., no digging of wells or such like). Sounds lovely, I say, but how on earth do we get to Italy?

Most ATG customers do fly to their destinations, she admits, but going by train is a possibility. I don't need to look at Jane, who's listening on speakerphone, to know that we're both thinking the same thing: 'But we've got a baby!'

Our memories of long train journeys are dominated by our three-month trip across the sub-continent, and, needless to say, putting a baby into that equation doesn't seem to compute too well.

But a call to Rail Europe, Europe's largest train travel agent, starts to put our minds at rest. With an extensive and swift rail network serving most of Europe, the logistics of getting to Italy by train, even with a baby, aren't a problem. And although going by rail still clearly causes pollution, per passenger kilometre it is estimated to be at least three times less polluting than going by plane.

The only problem is the price. Book a return flight with a budget airline a few months in advance and you can fly to Italy for well under a hundred pounds. Go by train, though, and depending on the class you travel, prices can rocket up towards a thousand pounds per person. A clear conscience comes at a high price, it seems. But I'm still keen to work out exactly how we can get to the town of Todi in Umbria, where ATG's walking holiday starts.

First we would need to catch the Eurostar to Paris, where we would then need to get from Gare du Nord to Gare de Paris Bercy to catch Artesia's sleeper train to Florence. Once at Florence's Stazione Santa Maria Novella, we would then be able to catch a fast train to Perugia, and travel the final leg to Todi on a picturesque, privately operated line. This amounts to three changes and twenty hours of track time each way – a considerable commitment, considering a flight, check-in and transfers would have probably totalled less than ten hours each way.

As our days of spending overnight train journeys struggling to sleep on a couchette are now hopefully over, I'm keen to book a berth on the sleeper from Paris to Florence, especially as we will be taking Esme and all her accessories. By treating ourselves to a first-class cabin for that leg – the only way to ensure privacy, which we feel is important both for us and for others, bearing Esme in mind – the total return price for all three of us from London to Todi just tops eight hundred pounds. If we choose the cheapest tickets throughout – i.e., no beds for the night – the price is about £440. Still a lot more than by plane. I say I'll ring them back once I've talked it all through with Jane.

Now that we've actually heard the details, the thought of the train journey sounds quite appealing, romantic even. It's just the prospect of the walking holiday that doesn't leave us too enthralled. It's not so much the walking itself – that sounds fun – it's the thought of having to carry Esme all the way. It feels more than a little cruel to put a baby through that. But we convince ourselves that we're just being precious, mollycoddled Westerners: babies are hardy little things and Esme will no doubt benefit from all that fresh air. Somewhat hesitantly, we book the holiday.

I'm always relieved to actually get out of the front door and start on any journey, given that we've missed flights and trains before. There's the frantic, gone-midnight packing (made worse by Jane's insistence that every last thread we're taking must be ironed; it only gets creased in the suitcase), the constant checking that we've got the passports and tickets, the panic that the gas might be left on, the fight to get VideoPlus working to record the soaps, and the struggle to remember that we need to order a taxi, put on the timer switch for the lamp in the sitting room and tell the neighbours we're going away.

But this time we've got new anxieties. A major one is whether we should try to persist with Esme's washable nappies while we're away. We're in a bind as to whether to just have a holiday from them for a couple of weeks, or lug them around with us and have the headache of trying to launder them. It does seem like an act of self-flagellation to have to stick to the washables – and a number of people writing to me confirm it would be madness. So, with a few pangs of guilt, we choose to leave them behind.

I'm also worried about what to do with the worms and our new plants. I dread the thought of returning to find wilted herbs and, worse, a wormery that looks like a mass grave of limp spaghetti. The plants aren't too much of a concern as we can arrange for someone to come over and water them, but I hesitate to ask anyone to tend the worms too. The manual says that they should be fine for a couple of weeks unattended as long as they have enough food and are protected from the weather. I'm still a bit nervous about leaving them for so long, but I fill their tray up to the brim with about three days' worth of kitchen waste, and I even make sure that they have their favourite food to hand – some lettuce.

The taxi question arises, too. Can we use any form of car or petrol-driven vehicle on our holiday, we wonder? We would normally get a taxi to the airport, or at least to the station, from where we would get a train to the airport. But this time we're not sure what to do. We've got Esme to carry, our luggage, her pushchair, her luggage – it seems madness, if not impossible, to struggle all the way to Waterloo on the bus or Tube. But then again, it doesn't seem the most auspicious of starts to set off in a car, even if it is just a taxi.

'Stop being ridiculous. We've made enough compromises already,' says Jane, as I loiter by the phone wondering whether to ring for a cab. 'I'm sure the odd taxi journey can be justified.

Are you really prepared to heft all this stuff on the Tube to Waterloo? If you are, then Esme and I will meet you there as we're getting a cab.' Keen to avoid the traditional pre-holiday row, I call a cab.

As soon as the train pulls out of Waterloo, Esme does the decent thing and falls asleep. She remains that way virtually all the way to Italy, bar the odd nappy change, feed, or squeal as we whoosh in and out of ear-popping tunnels. The main advantage of travelling by train rather than plane becomes clear as soon as we enter our cabin on the night train in Paris – there's enough space for all of Esme's paraphernalia to be on hand at all times, rather than stuffed in an overhead locker or packed in the hold of a plane. As this is our first trip away with her, we weren't sure how much bumf we'd need, so we've brought the lot just in case: pushchair, bottles, countless out-fits, sling, parasol, the list seems endless. But at least with our own cabin we don't have to attend to all her needs in full public glare and earshot. And, after a disappointing meal in the dining car, we get what must be one of the best nights' sleep in transit ever – with bunk beds to hand, we are all rocked soundly asleep as soon as the sun sets over the French fields speeding past our window.

There's a sharp knock on the cabin door at six thirty a.m. and, after a breakfast of coffee, orange juice and croissants (we don't try to ask in Italian whether they are fair trade or organic), we're told Florence is 'trenta minuti' away. There's even time for a quick shower in our en-suite bathroom. But there's no danger of depleting precious water supplies, it seems, as the water pressure isn't even strong enough to wash the sleep out of our eyes.

It's another two train journeys and four hours before we reach Todi, the starting point of our walking holiday. And as it's now 34ºC outside we fall into our hotel room and, without a thought, immediately flick on the air conditioning. It's only ten minutes later, once we are freshened up and ready for a stroll around the town in search of lunch, that we debate our use of the air conditioning.

'We shouldn't really have this on,' I say, pointing at the thermostat by the door.

'Sod that, we're not going to risk Esme overheating.' Jane is a tad irritable after our long journey in the heat.

'OK, maybe when it's really hot, like now, but at night perhaps we should just leave the windows open instead.'

We agree to give it a go, but as we head off for lunch I realize that on any other holiday we would have instinctively left the air conditioning on so that we'd come back to a really cool room. We would even sometimes leave the ceiling fan on.

Todi is a hill town close enough to Rome to have become a weekend retreat for the capital's media and arts crowd. It offers Renaissance churches, Roman ruins and a scattering of art that would catch your eye in any museum, as well as the ubiquitous streetside cafés. We spend the afternoon wandering around, struggling over the cobbles with Esme's pushchair. The views down into the valley and across to the Monti Martini, the hills on the horizon, from the Piazza Garibaldi, the town's main square, are striking.

After an early supper of pasta on a restful garden terrace just beneath the Piazza Garibaldi, we return to our room defeated by the combination of travel, heat and excessive amounts of carbohydrate. As I brush my teeth, I'm reminded of how wasteful we normally are with the linen, towels and all those little bottles of complimentary hotel goodies – the ones we normally stuff into our bags when we leave. Many hotels we've stayed at restock the room completely each day, even if we're just staying for a couple of nights. But this time we've brought all our own toiletries and make a point of not using the freebies on offer, instead putting them in a corner so they can be used again. We don't need to ask for our sheets and towels not to be needlessly replaced, as we're only staying one night, though I'm tempted to tell the hotel staff anyway.

But the question of the air conditioning soon rears its head again as we try to settle for the night. The long, hot day is followed by an airless, humid night, and just leaving the window open rather than resting under the cool blast of a fan leaves us tetchy and restless by the morning. Despite the relief of a few illicit ten-minute blasts with the air conditioning to lower the temperature in the early hours, it's not an ideal start to a day in which we will have to traipse thirteen miles across Umbrian countryside.

When we wake up, however, it is clear that the heat is going to be too much for Esme if we're out walking all day. Jane reluctantly decides to opt out; she and Esme will get a lift with Toby, our ATG route manager, who has arrived to meet and greet us and to transport our luggage to the next hotel, so allowing us to walk without the added burden of huge rucksacks. We are both disappointed that we haven't even started walking yet and already we've had to fall back on the convenience of a car. Armed with a packed lunch of ham, tomatoes, bread and cheese that I've bought from a local shop, I say goodbye to the others and set off down the steep hill out of Todi.

The walking on this first day is relatively tough, but it concludes with a fantastic trek up and over the grassy rises and ridges of the Monti Martini, then down to the mountain village of Giano dell' Umbria. The ascent over the summit is accompanied by an exhilarating thunderstorm in which I fear that I'm going to be fried by way of my umbrella. I don't pass another soul, bar the odd cow munching soporifically on the lush grass underfoot. I haven't walked this kind of distance in a day since tramping across Dartmoor on school camping trips and I wonder why we haven't thought of doing this kind of thing before. It seems ironic that we're trying it now, just when we have a young baby. We could have done this freely at any point in the previous decade, but instead we largely chose car hire, beaches and exciting cities as our default options. Why has it needed the auditors to open our eyes to all this, I wonder. As I descend into Giano, I reflect on what our lives had been like before the auditors' visit – fewer guilt-trips, less hassle, fewer groans from Jane. I can't decide whether I preferred things as they were, before I'd heard what they had to say, or whether it was better to know more, but to have to contend with the associated guilt as a result. Ignorance is bliss? Or knowledge is power? I really can't decide.

The next day's planned walk is much shorter – just seven miles

– but much hillier, and we all set off together from Giano to Montefalco, another hill town, this time labelled the 'balcony of Umbria' due to its panoramic views across the Vale of Spoleto. It is another steep descent into the countryside below the town, but even though it's not yet nine it is already getting worryingly hot. I reach for the umbrella to keep Esme in the shade.

The question of who carries Esme soon becomes the topic of the day. We set out with the intention of alternating between carrying Esme in her sling and carrying the small rucksack filled with a packed lunch, bottles of water and Esme's changing gear. However, we soon realize that the rucksack is actually the more heavy and cumbersome of the two so I offer to take it, leaving Jane to carry the lighter load. But this seemingly practical solution has an odd effect on the various locals we pass once we start to enter farmland.

Whether it's the sight of us carrying a baby under an umbrella in the midday heat along the *strade bianche*, Umbria's dusty country tracks, or whether it's the fact that I have left Jane to carry the baby, we're not sure, but we receive more than a few scowls along the way. It's only when a lovely old woman comes out of her porch with a look of deep concern to offer us a seat in her front garden and some water that we learn – via hand gestures and pigeon Italian – that it is traditional in Italy for babies to stay largely indoors with their mothers for the first year of their lives. The scowls start to make sense.

What puts us at ease, though, is that Esme appears to be really enjoying her morning in the sling. She's bright eyed, fascinated by all the new sights and sounds. And she doesn't seem to be too hot, in stark contrast to her parents. We must be quite a sight – baby in sling, umbrella in hand – traipsing past fields of broad beans, olive trees and corn, through to the cooling oak woods and shallow brooks that lie beneath the rise into Montefalco. We arrive just in time for lunch.

Aside from the town's famous fresco cycle by Gozzoli, which shows how little the Umbrian landscape has changed in the six hundred years since it was painted, the highlight of our night's stay in Montefalco is the visit in the afternoon to one of the town's celebrated vineyards. The sangrantino grape is grown on the slopes leading up to the town and is used to produce a red *passito*, or dessert wine, that costs about fifty euros a bottle. We spend a couple of delightful hours tasting samples at the organic Paolo Bea vineyard. After taking us on a tour of his vines, the proprietor, Giampiero, tells us how he grows vines without the need for pesticides or chemical fertilizers, and has an ingenious method to improve exhausted soil that involves planting globe artichokes directly under any sickly vines. What's more, artichokes are one of his favourite foods. Nature always has the answers, he says, before topping up our glasses with another 'sample'.

The next morning we descend out of Montefalco and walk the five miles down to Bevagna, where Toby has promised we will be able to see the ATG-funded local restoration project. In the town's museum we find the once neglected but culturally important thirteenth-century wooden crucifix that has now been restored by the ATG trust to its somewhat garishly coloured and unsettlingly primitive former self. After lunch we venture out in search of Bevagna's other promised delights, which include the Teatro Torti, a nineteenth-century theatre, and the Chiesa di San Silvestro, a Romanesque church that has the humbling sight of the architect's signature carved into the stone by the door, dated 1195. We talk of all the history that has passed since then – the wars, the revolutions, the art, the technology, the exploration. Seeing such sights can't help but stop you in your tracks and make you ponder your own insignificance and mortality.

A further day's walking brings us to Spello, a Roman town that straddles a thin ridge at the base of Mount Subasio – the mountain where St Francis is said to have talked to the animals. As has become routine now, we spend most of our afternoon here, enjoying the cool escape of the town's two principal churches, both of which contain excellent frescos by Pinturicchio. Once again, we carbo-load on pasta and pizza (it seems fruitless trying to ask if ingredients are organic – besides, the waiter assures us it's all freshly made with local ingredients) in preparation for the next and final day's eleven-mile walk up and over Mount Subasio into Assisi – Umbria's proud ecclesiastical, architectural and cultural epicentre. Toby has told us it is now totally back on its feet after the 1997 earth-quake that caused so much damage in the area.

Over dinner, with Esme asleep under the table in the car seat that we've ironically brought with us to help transport her around, we discuss what we think of the holiday.

'I'm actually enjoying it,' says Jane. 'Much more than I ever thought I would. I think Esme is, too.'

'I agree, but I'd hate to never be able to go on a plane again. I don't want to be restricted to Europe for the rest of my life. Some of our best holidays together have been in far-off places.'

'I know,' says Jane. 'I can't stand the thought of Esme not being able to experience those countries as she grows up. I think eliminating air travel from our lives for ever is taking it too far. Restrict it, fine, but banning it just seems too extreme for me.'

'What about car hire?' I ask.

'I can understand the argument against it, but I think we'd really miss the flexibility hiring a car offers, especially now we've got Esme. I think we should restrict both flights and car hire wherever possible, and certainly use them a lot less than we have in the past, but to rule them out for ever is just too much.'

'Why don't we try to alternate our holidays?' I propose. 'One involving a flight. One without. And it would be nice to get to see more of Britain. Anyway I suspect that from now on our holidays are likely to be largely determined by Esme, and any other children we have. I doubt we'll be able to afford to keep jetting off all over the place even if we want to.'

It's a four-hour climb to the summit of Subasio. I set off early, just after breakfast, but Jane and Esme get a lift to the top with Toby. As I puff my way up through 4,300 feet of olive groves, then pine forests and grassy pastures, I keep hoping that the next visible summit is the last. I'm shattered by the time I finally reach the top, where I discover Jane and Esme serenely munching on lunch. After a quick photo of us astride the summit, we all begin the five-hour descent through the wildflowers and butterflies into Assisi, just visible below us.

As we drop down the mountainside, the views continue to extend for at least twenty miles all around, but it is especially pleasing to look back over to Monti Martini and retrace our steps. We would never have got such satisfaction if we had driven, or flown.

During one water break about two hours after lunch, we joke that it's no wonder St Francis started talking to the animals – he must have been nearly delirious with fatigue from trekking over this mountain. And it is here that we witness our own apparition of sorts – the golden arches of McDonald's. No, we don't succumb to a Big Mac and fries, but as we walk through one particularly *Sound of Music*-esque expanse of wild poppies, more than half a mile from the nearest path, we stumble across a discarded McDonald's carton nestling among the flowers. We are stunned. Who could have left such a thing here of all places? We stuff this unhappy meal into our rucksacks and carry it off the mountain.

When we get back to London, we act on the advice of the auditors and investigate the possibility of 'neutralizing' the carbon dioxide emissions that our journey to Italy would have created. Future Forests work out how many trees we would need to plant to neutralize the emissions our holiday produced, based on the fact that trees absorb carbon dioxide. They calculate that we have travelled 2,620km in total and that if we had chosen our traditional method of transport – i.e., plane and rental car, we would have produced 1.56 tonnes of carbon dioxide. But by travelling by train and largely walking once there, our total has been reduced to 756kg. To neutralize this, Future Forests say we need to plant one tree at a cost of just £8.50. I'm not sure whether this is just a fancy way of buying off our guilt, but it seems a fitting end to a memorable holiday.

7

SOMETHING JUST ISN'T RIGHT. I'm starting to have major doubts and anxieties about what we're doing. Ever since we got back from Italy – and, in particular, since my lone, contemplative walk over the Monti Martini into Giano – I've been plagued by constant thoughts that this experiment isn't progressing at the pace or in the direction anticipated before the auditors arrived.

I'm happy with much of what we've tried – the box scheme, the wormery (which survived our absence, by the way), the washable nappies – but I keep having moments when I struggle to feel that we've achieved anything truly meaningful. After all, what effect are all our efforts *really* having on the wider world? I can't help feeling that we're just minnows swimming against the tide. Why do I now feel so annoyed by other people's seemingly selfish acts, such as dropping litter or even driving cars? I don't like this feeling boiling away inside me. Shouldn't it all be about Zen and forgiveness? Part of me is becoming a grumpy old sod bemoaning everyone else as they press on with their 'thoughtless' lives.

Jane has become a worry, too. I just don't feel as if she is on board. For much of what we're trying to do, I feel as though she is being dragged along, usually grudgingly. If she's on the road to Damascus, then she hasn't even reached the M25 yet. And I really don't want it to be like that. She has certainly grown into some things after an initial scepticism, but there's still a friction there between us. I understand why she isn't as enthusiastic as I am – no one likes to have someone else's agenda thrust upon them, least of all by strangers – but I feel frustrated that she doesn't want to embrace things to the same degree as me. Before we started this experiment, I never considered for a moment that one of the hardest aspects would be making it work and progress within a relationship. I'm at a loss what to do. The more I try to persuade her, the more she recoils. Yet I don't want to do all this without her by my side. Should I just leave her to work out her own course and determine her own level of engagement, even if it leaves me frustrated that we can't advance at the pace I want?

The degree to which we should grasp each aspect of the experiment is also leaving me in knots. Of course, I want to try to succeed at everything the auditors have advised us to do – what they had to say makes sense to me, even if much of it seems unrealistic at first, and I feel compelled to act on as much of it as I can – but I'm starting to feel a little over-whelmed by how much there is to do. There seems to be no sight of a finishing line. Life is largely full of goals and aspirations – buy a new TV, get a better job, have a child, lose weight, buy a bigger house – that are, by and large, obtainable, even if they might involve a lot of effort. But much of what we are working towards at the moment seems to be totally unattainable. It's a lot to ask of two adults and a baby in a mid-terrace house in south London: reducing climate change, global human suffering, toxic pollution, unjust trading practices, globalization, excessive corporatism. It's quite some to-do list and I feel insignificant in the face of it. Isn't what we're doing simply futile, given the odds and the direction the rest of humankind is heading in?

But then I hear of people who are incorporating this sense of ethical focus into their lives to a much greater degree than we are. The letters I have been receiving are full of stories of how people have been able to change their lives and feel great about the transition; they feel they have really made a difference. But I am struggling to find that sense of reward and satisfaction. Much of what we have done so far, no matter how hard I try to convince myself to the contrary, sometimes strikes me as being nothing more than a bloody great chore. Is it really worth all the hassle? Are we just lightweights? Maybe it's just not in our blood to be these caring, thoughtful beings 24/7.

As a result of all this angst, I'm seeking more and more solace and advice from the letters I've been receiving, even if some of the holier-than-thou ones do make me feel increasingly inadequate, angry even. I'm gaining particular comfort from the significant proportion of people who say they have also had these same feelings – the 'is it all really worth it?' sentiments – and explain how they have come to terms with them. It's been good to hear that I'm not alone.

I have decided to gather together some of the letters that have either rocked or settled me, as I want to show how their words, in combination, have been a help. I think they need to be read in full to get a sense of the journeys most of these people have been through, wherever they are in the world and whatever their circumstances. Most, it seems, have reached very similar conclusions.

> Boulder, Colorado, where I live is filled with people concerned about recycling, organic food, living green, animal rights, etc. They worry about every morsel they ingest, while ignoring homeless people on street corners. These are some of the most provincial, self-absorbed people on the planet.
>
> I think the essence of ethical living is caring about others: it's exemplified by a teacher who takes a few extra minutes to talk to a troubled student; a protestor demonstrating against war or injustice; a researcher analysing the same; an activist helping the poor through donation, political work or direct personal action.
>
> A little more abstractly, there's the whole idea of living with integrity, which I'd define as pondering the consequences of your actions and doing the work that comes to hand well, whether it's baking bread, raising children, keeping accounts, running a business, policing the streets or waiting tables.
>
> Juliet Wittman

Where we live, in north central Texas in a small town in the country, what you call 'ethical living' is almost non-existent. We've been here five years and came here committed to recycling. Unfortunately, our fellow citizens and our local government are not. While we have diligently taken paper, aluminium and plastic to the town's recycling centre, the town has made it very inconvenient for us. The bins are not emptied frequently and are often overflowing, so sometimes we can't leave all we bring in the bins. We then have to leave it in bags next to the bins, which could mean it either gets bunged in the rubbish or is potentially harmful to animals.

It has been suggested to me and my husband that a lot of what is left in the recycling bins often gets tipped into the rubbish heaps for one reason or another. So, basically, while we've tried to be good citizens of the earth, our efforts have been mostly fruitless because the town just doesn't care.

We've tried to make people care, but in Texas rubbish flows freely from the beds of pick-up trucks and out of cars on to the highways – you see plastic bags ensnared on barbed-wire fencing and McDonald's paper cups strewn about. Our house is on a main road and we often have rubbish blowing about the front yard, residue from careless drivers and passengers who throw their cups and hamburger wrappers out of the windows when they're done with them.

So what's the point? The point is that ethical living is a wonderful goal and a noble endeavour, but you need to have the support of others around you or it just doesn't work. Come with me to WalMart one day and notice how many diesel engines are left to run while their owners go inside to shop. We live in cattle country and don't eat beef – how many cows have I saved? I'm not sure that I've saved any, but I'm hopeful! We still recycle in the hope that some of what we take to the centre is sent on, but as a friend of mine said, 'Do you really think they're going to pay some guy to separate out all that plastic?'

Marcy Tanter, Stephenville, Texas

'Ethical' means so much more than buying Ecover, cycling to work and remembering to put out the newspapers every Friday for recycling.

The brand of 'ethical' that is sold (I choose my words carefully, you understand!) to younger people these days is a pre-packaged, off-the-shelf solution that certainly seems to provide the customer with value-added feelgood.

I would contend that 'ethical consumerism' is far removed from genuine ethics and the way of life demanded by them. It is a bandwagon simulacrum of the real thing. The current trendy brand of 'ethical' as a personalized lifestyle choice is little more than a lucrative heaven for auditors and market researchers: lots of tick boxes and bipolar semantic differential scales quantifying nothing but human desires, which are, by dint of this measurement, then manipulable and controllable with the right PR mix of guilt-trip, sentimentality and everyone's-doing-it cool. Thus, another organic aisle goes up in Sainsbury's, another half-million-pound ad campaign for 'green fuel', another bus lane adding further to the degradation of urban communities by restricting access to small/family businesses and fuelling the growth of out-of-town, car-accessible-only retail 'parks'. Ah yes, they sell lots of things with green-industry-approved stickers on in those places, don't they? And every single penny of the profits goes out of town and, increasingly likely these days, out of the country.

At the very bottom of all this rush to achieve an 'ethical lifestyle' is the barely admitted sense of emptiness we each feel in Western, money-focused and consumption-driven societies, where consuming (anything as long as it serves to alleviate this emptiness, even for a short time) is now touted as the only panacea. My essential point is that if you get the 'people thing' right – that is, if people feel truly valued and cared for, treated as precious and not themselves bought and sold as units of economic production – then the 'environment thing' resolves itself as a natural byproduct of people treating their surroundings well because they themselves are treated well. We

**are very dangerously out of kilter with these
proven principles and so will remain so extremely
ethically challenged until we stop this rampagingly
out-of-control consumer mindset – ethical or
otherwise.**

Candida Weston

What I've been taking from most of these letters so far is
simply that I must work out my own interests myself. It's fine
having the auditors kick-start my interest in ethical living, but
there's no point rigidly sticking to their advice if it is making
Jane and me unhappy, or worse even, distancing us more and
more from each other as well as from the original aims of the
whole experiment. I still feel the need to try everything
the auditors recommended, but need to reserve judgement
until I've digested what impacts – negative and positive – there
might be. There's no doubt that I've been too cavalier, blindly
accepting what they said to us and taking their word as gospel
– which has made Jane more resistant to the experiment than
she might otherwise have been. Even though I don't really like
the tone of Candida's letter and feel she is being perhaps a bit
too cynical about the current interest in 'ethical consumerism',
I think she is on to something with her point about the
need to get the 'people thing' right first, and then the rest will
follow.

The road to hell being paved with good intentions, I must admit I am often extremely cynical about people who tell me how I should be living. It's a bit overwhelming at times – trying to be good can induce the kind of external pressure I am trying to live without. 'Ethical exhaustion' seems preferable to apathy, though.

Ultimately I want a free and simple life. Have you read *Walden*? There is a line in there about living 'deliberately' and being free from artificial wants. Aim for this. I'm not in a position to go off and sit by a lake for a year, though. Like my city comforts.

Chiefly, I am concerned with living in a way that doesn't impact adversely on the environment, and will instead enhance it; a lifestyle that helps rather than exploits people; and that benefits my physical and mental health. I am a single middle-class white feminist who likes travel but likes shopping more. I could never choose between Felicity Kendal or Penelope Keith as the more appropriate role model in *The Good Life* and still harbour crushes on both Jerry Leadbetter (nice plaid pants and witty banter) and Tom Good (cheerful *and* can make his own methane-powered electricity generator).

Japan (where I'm living) is nowhere near as sociable or charitable as Australia (where I'm from) and I find myself astounded at the casual way plastics are burned and the homeless are shunned (in the Edo period, however, Japan was a sustainable society). Cultural differences and strange local laws are really complicating many changes I am trying to make to my life. I figure if I can live ethically here I can do so anywhere.

When I moved out of my house last year I collected cardboard boxes from a local supermarket to ship stuff home in (reduce, reuse, recycle). When I took one to the post office they took one look at the whisky logos printed on it and politely wrapped it in brown paper. What a waste! I once bought a watch here and to save packaging I told the sales assistant I didn't need a bag, I would wear it home, and as I was putting it on she took out a small brown paper bag and put the receipt from the cash register in it.

There is a different idea of how to help others here. The attitude seems to be that you look after yourself so that you won't be a burden on anyone. I came to Japan to earn money to buy an apartment in Sydney (almost any Australian with an Arts degree teaching English in Japan is here to advance plans for property ownership). Gradually the dream changed to building a sustainable house (like Michael and Heather Mobbs in inner-city Sydney: see www.abc.net.au/science/planet/house/default.htm)Now I'm thinking of donating my savings to charity and living in a tree, but I think that may be the culture shock talking.

I have a friend who was made redundant while the ink on his mortgage papers was drying (after years of commitment to his ungrateful company).

I want to avoid such a situation. It's like that saying from *Fight Club*: sooner or later the things you own end up owning you.

I am not sure I want kids, but I enjoy sharing what I have with the exploding world population. I resolved this year to spend an equal amount of money on charity if buying something extravagant. I am enjoying the extra sacrifice of going without some unnecessary things to help out others. Volunteer work and giving money away to charity has become a bigger part of my life, especially as my job is so unsatisfying. I want a life, not a career – as Oprah would say, no one lies on their deathbed thinking, 'Gee, I wish I spent more time at the office.'

When the war in Iraq was brewing and anti-war marches were not being reported on the news in the US, I felt completely disenfranchised. I figured if the war was about oil, I must try to stop using it and help others stop using it; I feel outraged that my government is chasing oil. Its consumption is causing environmental damage and we keep fighting wars to maintain supply. I don't drive, which makes me a pariah in my Australian hometown, but I have no wish to learn. Oddly, the most common response to this back home is the question, 'But what will you do when you have kids?'

Walking, cycling and Japan's super-efficient trains get me everywhere I need to go.

Composting was easy – and it meant I spent less

time taking the garbage out. And some vegetables grew out of what I had composted. Nice surprise. I spent weeks, and considerable yen, cycling to the local garden centre buying A4-sized blocks of grass to lay down. Grass always looks sick here. I also approached the town hall officials to see if I could make a garden in some vacant space at the local train station, but was turned down.

I once challenged myself to throw out as little rubbish as possible, and got it down to one small plastic bag for two months or so. No mean feat in packaging-obsessed Japan. To do this you need to practise 'precycling' – buying products without packaging or with packaging that is reusable or recyclable. I had stopped eating a lot of meat at that time so that meant less styrofoam came into the house. I brought plastic trays to the local grocery shop to collect tofu instead of using the plastic bags provided, and of course I always brought a cloth bag to carry my shopping home in.

I have found that living ethically by saving energy can lead to a more pleasant lifestyle. I don't buy clothes that are high maintenance (i.e., that need to be carefully ironed or sent to the drycleaners for washing) and thus I don't need to spend time, money, energy or use a lot of chemicals to keep them presentable. Ironing is a horrible waste of human life. Likewise, I'd rather get a goat (quiet, cheap, biodegradable) than a lawnmower (noisy, expensive, polluting). Or have a water-saving low-maintenance Japanese rock

garden instead of lawn. There are always
alternatives.

I love clothes shopping, so I have had to seek
out ethical alternatives. I buy second-hand a lot.
You can't go wrong with the St Vincent de Paul,
Salvation Army or Smith Family 'pre-loved'
clothing stores in Australia, because everything is
dirt cheap and even if you don't wear what you
buy, the money you spend often goes to help
needy people. And the sales staff are much
friendlier than in other places. I started shopping
here when I was a student, mainly out of necessity.
A lot of pub-crawl costumes came from here. I
give clothes to charity and pass them on to friends
and relatives (or back to charity stores) when I
don't need them any more.

Alternatively I buy fair trade, though it is
expensive. I volunteer at a fair-trade company
started by an English woman in Tokyo. I
sometimes make my own clothes, which, while
rarely cheaper, makes me feel happy and proud, if
a little crooked at the seams.

I believe in thinking globally and acting locally
and don't expect the world to change overnight. I
am irritated by angry people who stand on
soapboxes and point their fingers accusingly at
others. I don't believe in social change that is
expensive, difficult or dependent on other people
changing their habits to suit you. I prefer to lead
by example than nag, even if it means I am
sometimes laughed at or sneered at by redneck

relatives. Changing my life has been liberating and empowering. I'm proud of my choices and actions. I feel significant.

Being unable to understand the TV here helps. Here's a good tip: try living without television. You will have more time, save energy and feel less stressed.

On the language-barrier thing, I also started making my own cleaning products (using vinegar, lemon juice, baking soda, etc.) because I couldn't read the kanji on labels here and sometimes the pictures are confusing. Some things work better than others – there are loads of websites that deal with this.

I can send you a washable, reusable dishcloth crocheted from acrylic wool. Makes washing-up time fun! A friend brought me one she collected when she attended a meditation course in Kyoto. It was my New Year's resolution last year to learn to make them. Because it is acrylic it is slightly abrasive, so good for cleaning plates. When it gets dirty you can throw it in with your other laundry and when clean reuse it.

The thing that has sustained me has been the support of my friends and the knowledge that other people are out there trying to make a difference. Even managed to convert a few people, which builds confidence.

Good luck with your project.

Yours ethically, Christina Reitano

Some letters just seem to stick in my head, and this is one of them. I haven't taken her up yet on her kind offer to send me one of her crocheted dishcloths – I'm still in shock, to be honest, that anyone would even think of making their own dishcloths – but her letter continues to warm the cockles each time I read it. What I have gained from it is the sense that she is on a journey. She's tried many things with varying degrees of success, but has ploughed on because she is so confident in her convictions and knows that she is headed in the right direction. The difference between me and Christina, I feel, is not only that she is much further down that road, but that she is effortlessly weaving past obstacles she encounters, whereas I'm finding myself snarled up in traffic without any sense of when or how fast I'm likely to be moving forward. 'Not waving, but drowning' is the expression, I think.

> For me the key to ethical living is not to replace everything that is unethical with things that are, but to change your lifestyle altogether. For me it is the consumption that is unethical. For example, I no longer use deodorant, I have a shower every other day, the only cosmetic product I use is soap and I only flush the toilet when absolutely necessary. Luckily, I do not have a high-powered job, so I can afford to scrimp on personal hygiene and clothing. The problem is that people are not prepared to change or make sacrifices in this way because our Western society dictates a certain lifestyle. Until we educate people that they don't have to go on holiday five times a year, have

extensions built on their houses and own lots of
cars to achieve a happy and fulfilling life, then they
will continue to consume, and live unethically.

Heath Davies

Dear Leo,

First of all, good for you – it's really worth it.
   These are my tips:
1) Eat vegan. It's cheaper, much better for the
environment in terms of production and waste,
and you will feel amazingly healthy.
2) Boycott supermarkets, with the exception of Co-
op (though I am still having an ongoing battle with
them to get them to use less packaging). Find
local wholefood co-operatives. I live in Oxford
most of the time as a doctoral student and I've
found a little co-operative near the centre of town.
I live in Cambridge during the summer vac and
there's a great place called Daily Bread
(www.dailybread.co.uk) that's also a co-op.
There's bound to be something like that near you.
3) Public not private transport. Bit of a nightmare
this one, given the state of the public-transport
system. I tend to cycle everywhere now after
investing in a good bike, good dayglo nerd-style
jacket, and good helmet. It takes me twenty
minutes to cycle into the centre of Cambridge from
a village six miles out; a nice peaceful ride along

the river whilst everyone else slogs it out in the traffic jams. The downside is winter dark and strong winds, but if you've got the right gear it's not so bad, as I found out after cycling twenty miles to work and back last winter. I gave up on buses a long time ago after a bleak experience at Bedford bus station. Trains are OK for longer journeys, though I'm rapidly losing faith in the network. Otherwise I rely on parents and friends with cars.

4) Change your bank account to the Co-operative. I tried to open a student account with them and they turned me down, so I wrote back saying that I wasn't going to take no for an answer because I wanted to invest in an ethical bank. I haven't had any problems with them since the account was opened.

5) Cosmetics: companies like Honesty and Green People are great. My only downfall is perfume – I end up putting money into the coffers of YSL etc. I haven't quite reconciled this with my conscience yet. But I smell great.

6) Clothes: second-hand shops. This is a rule I break from time to time, I have to admit. It's a toughie. My gran knitted my dad and his three brothers some fantastic woollen jumpers in the sixties that she never threw out, so I wear those in the winter. They're a bit holey but warm.

7) Never buy women's magazines again. This probably won't apply to you, but I will tell you about it anyway. As far as I'm concerned, reading

these magazines damages the self-esteem of women and girls. They are out to convince their audience that luxury products are necessities, through the manipulation of wants and desires – harmful to people and environment. Instead, there are magazines like *Ergo*.

8) Recycling is a cop-out and a salve for the conscience – aim to reduce at source, i.e., don't buy products that are wasteful.

9) Buy fair-trade wherever possible. (I am going to be honest though and admit that I have the biggest weakness for Caffè Nero's black coffee: two shots of espresso . . . mmm.)

What I have learnt after making these changes in my life:

1) I am always going to be frustrated with my parents/boyfriend for not respecting my lifestyle choices. I can argue with them for eternity on why they should change, but if they don't realize it for themselves it'll never happen. In that respect, it's a lonely and disheartening thing.

2) It is only a lifestyle change, and ultimately it doesn't do very much to address the real problems. Ethical living is OK so far as it goes, but it only goes so far. I know that were I really living ethically I would no doubt be clapped in irons for direct action. I've found Gayatri Chakravorty Spivak interesting on this aspect of it all: as a woman championing the rights of 'Third World' women and campaigning for the global justice movement, she nonetheless has to use a

discourse steeped in the inequalities of the globalized 'First World' in order to make her point. She knows she works at a remove. Perhaps she's been able to reconcile this intellectually. I haven't been able to do so.

Useful reading: George Monbiot: *The Age of Consent*, Paul Kingsnorth: *One No, Many Yeses*; Spivak.

3) I should have studied economics, not English Literature, so that I could understand how the system works and make a change from the inside. It's all about knowing how to assume power in order to make lasting changes that have beneficial repercussions, ethically speaking. And at the moment, that means the IMF, World Bank, etc.

4) Anonymously sticking up satirical pictures of George W. Bush in the workplace is never a wasted effort.

Good luck, all the best, Laura

Hello,

Several years ago I noticed that I was spending money just to spend money. Then, about a week later, I noticed I spent more money a week on extras – food for spur-of-the-moment recipes, cosmetics, jewellery, hair products, magazines, coffee, etc. – than I was giving away each week in the church plate (called a pledge in the States).

I once heard someone say that if you give money away, you should give away at least what you would spend on a vacation. I decided to see if I could stop spending money every day. It took me about a month to get from going without buying for one day, to four days consecutively. If I needed gas for the car or grocery shopping, of course I spent the money, but I tried to discipline myself so that the act of purchasing was not market-prompted, nor psychologically driven (like a need for chocolate), but simply an act of subsistence. I did not then save the money I didn't spend, but gave it away. I found that I became more aware of the inequalities between people and between populations. This has made everything about daily life much more complex, much less comfortable.

If bliss and happiness are the goals, I don't think ethics will serve. If becoming mature is the goal, I think the practice of ethics (in contrast to the practice of morals) serves very well. I would say that the whole experience could have permanent effects on the way you live after you give up the experiment. The sure way to make it all fail and to embitter yourself or entrench a cynic's point of view is to start too large and guarantee failure. Smaller efforts (say, using vinegar to clean the bathroom mirrors instead of a chemical product) teach you how to adjust to the changes.

Charlotte Weaver-Gelzer, Lancaster, Pennsylvania

I am, like you, attempting to make changes to my lifestyle that would make it more environmentally friendly. Maybe I should start off by introducing myself. My name is Seong. I'm not a native of the UK – I grew up in a rural Malaysian fishing village that was lovely to live in before all the environmental problems took over (Asian brown cloud, etc.). So your project is something close to the heart, if you like. I now live in the UK as a permanent resident, and am working as a hospital doctor. I'm also a working mother so my lifestyle is somewhat hectic. These are some of the changes I've put in place: recycling paper, plastic containers, aluminium cans, tin cans and cardboard boxes; switching over to unit-e (a renewable-energy supplier); volunteering at a community garden centre that promotes environmental issues; supporting Ecover products; supporting the 'Stop Esso' campaign by boycotting Esso; buying from farmers' markets; buying as much organic produce as I can; saving up for an LPG car (because, unfortunately, I need to use the car a lot in my line of work); and using biodegradable nappies (available from Sainsbury's, would you believe). The one thing I find about this lifestyle is that it's always evolving.

Yours truly and good luck, Seong

As a long-time utilitarian, I long ago abandoned 'right' and 'wrong' for 'worse' and 'better' – otherwise you go mad in the knowledge that the forty-five minutes you spent watching *Buffy* could have been spent repainting the local play area, or helping underprivileged kids to read, but actually, if you spent the evening stacking shelves in Tesco and gave the money to Oxfam (directly through payroll giving to make it tax effective) then that could pay for a new water pump that could save the lives of twenty children in Somalia . . .

Penny Heal, South London

Take the toilet-roll test. When it runs out, do you replace it with a new roll? It takes time to unscrew the holder and hang the new roll in place. My guess is most people will leave the new roll resting on the floor or near the flusher. And why? Because in the loo you can retain your anonymity and not be held responsible.

Real ethical living has to do with actions that you believe in, rather than doing something because you fear consequences.

Alicia Peyrano

I've tried it all. The crunch came for me when I found out that my carefully separated bottles and cans all ended up in the same dump. I used to think I was being an advanced thinker as I sorted the smelly stuff into various piles and containers, until total disillusionment came. I've tried organic food, but it not only tasted awful, it looked spotty, diseased and flea-bitten and I had to give it up. I've spent hours shopping around for the best clothes bargains, but got tired of the hassle and ending up feeling just poor and cheap. I tried coupon clipping and that lasted about a week. I even bought the little purse to keep them in, but always forgot to bring the damn things with me when I went shopping. I shopped around for the cheapest gas, but why bother for the sake of a buck or two per fill-up? I even bought a little Japanese 'rice burner' car to conserve gas. Since I drive eight hundred miles each way to see my kids in Florida once or twice a month, I could not stand being shoehorned into the little car, so I changed it for a big ol' Buick nine-passenger wagon. To heck with the ethics, I needed the comfort to stretch out.

I'm not convinced that all the ethical living pays off, either financially or psychologically. Maybe it's me. Maybe I don't have the 'guilt ethic' that's needed. Maybe if I had a more developed social conscience. Maybe I'm hooked for life on good-looking waxed oranges, polished apples and genetically engineered tomatoes. Maybe I don't

give a damn (but I really want to). Maybe I'm too
damn conflicted thinking about it all. God help me,
but I tried. Failure goes down hard. I'm truly just a
rabid, wasteful, no-good, torn-with-guilt
consumer and I know the Golden Gate will be
slammed In my face when all this selfish and
careless living finally kills me.

Vince Hennigan, Atlanta, Georgia

I'm strangely attracted to Vince's nihilistic, cynical and
resigned view on the merits of ethical living. I think I'll save his
letter for those bleak days when I need reminding that other
people feel like they're sinking too. He seems to have been
unlucky with his organic food supplies and choices of car, but
there have been times – and surely will be many more – when
I've also been mighty tempted to say, to hell with this, I'm
going to have a cola and packet of crisps and I don't care that
it means I'm supporting a multinational corporation or consuming evil processed food. It's simply not possible – for me at
least, even if some of these letter writers evidently feel they're
near to attaining sainthood – to operate at Defcon One on the
Ethical Living Index of Righteousness every waking minute.

But doesn't thinking like that still suggest that I see this all as
a slog, in which I hanker after brief but frequent periods of
respite? When am I going to start instinctively living as the
auditors suggested, and not having to consciously keep
reminding myself what needs to be done all the time? I feel like
an eager and fresh-faced pupil in one of those corny martial

arts films, who can't wait any longer to be told by his master that he is now ready to strike out alone. 'Be patient,' says the wise one. 'You will know when you are ready.'

I, too, decided to make a conscious effort to be more ethically aware. However, my attempts to be more 'world-friendly' are completely at odds with my current job – I work for Esso. Yes, Esso, subject of the 'Stop Esso' campaign, rapist of Mother Earth, with an executive board that's allegedly home to more than one crooked American politician.

Ever since joining the company, I have felt pangs of guilt when walking past 'Stop Esso' stickers where I live. So I decided to bring the company down from the inside. I stopped working hard. Was this just a ruse to be lazy? Of course not! As you probably guessed, my attempts to bring the gangsters at Esso to their knees have not even dented the company's earnings.

So, after reading an article in a magazine about the plight of coffee farmers in South America, I decided to boycott Nestlé and other tight-fisted coffee giants, and start buying CaféDirect coffee and tea (available at Oxfam and all good supermarkets). After preaching to colleagues, friends and my parents, I decided to turn my attentions to Esso (or at least the office in which I work). I noticed that the coffee machines use Kenco, so I wrote a letter to the facilities manager, explaining the reasons why we should look for a fair-trade alternative, even directing her to the 'Make Trade Fair' website. What was her response? What bloody response? She couldn't even be bothered to send a courtesy email thanking me for my note! From that day forth, not a drop of coffee from the machine has passed my lips. (And I used to drink at least five cups a day!) A valiant effort.

And so, after months of a guilty conscience, I have now handed in my notice. I'm off to teach English to teenagers in Spain. I feel so much better.

Good luck, Leah Campion

We accidentally got the inspiration to start looking at how we were living when I got Hugh Fearnley-Whittingstall's *River Cottage Year*. I'm still not sure about HFW, but his basic premise of eating seasonally and sensibly struck a chord, and we started getting our veg from a local delivery scheme. As you say, things tend to get obsessive from there on, and we're now wondering if we might need counselling. Or a henhouse. And a bigger compost bin.

We're having a new kitchen put in and ended up making the designer's life difficult by demanding efficient appliances. We've still not worked out whether solid oak doors are really sustainable compared with pine, which grows faster, but anything is better than the horrors of MDF and particleboard.

Unfortunately, I work thirty miles away from home and don't have a feasible public-transport option for getting to work, and my work involves covering large swathes of the country in Tarmac, but we can't all be perfect – especially my wife, who has an aversion to turning lights off when leaving the room. On the other hand, I am more profligate with plastic bags than she is, and put some potato peelings in the kitchen bin rather than the composter last night because it was snowing. Hmm.

Not sure whether any of this is relevant, but we appreciate having a kindred spirit . . .

WP

It is virtually impossible to live completely ethically in the developed world, especially in a city. I live in a flat in Amsterdam, so some things I would love to do, such as growing my own vegetables, are non-starters. If you don't live as a hermit on a mountainside, ethical living is about deciding what is most important to you. Do you want to reduce the impact of your life on the environment? Or ensure some of your money is spent on fair-trade products? Or do you want to support local traders over corporate retailers?

I tend to do a little of all three, while accepting that you always need to make some compromises and some things are not worth the worry. Here's my checklist for treading a little lighter on the Earth.

Eating/shopping

I eat very little meat or fish – only occasionally when I know where it came from and how it ended up on my plate. Locally produced meat and fish are the best choices. Certain former favourites like shrimp and tiger prawns are gone because of the huge by-catch from conventional shrimp trawling and the habitat loss and pollution caused by farming prawns.

I do buy some organic produce, but believe that for some items the prices are inflated and the products aren't worth the extra cost. I always buy fairly traded organic bananas to support small farmers in the Caribbean and Africa rather than the American multinationals Dole and Chiquita, who farm chemically intensive mono-crop plantations in Latin America. I buy fair-trade coffee and chocolate to ensure more of the money goes to the farmer rather than big food multinationals such as Nestlé and Kraft. I avoid Nestlé products because of their aggressive marketing in developing countries and their exploitation of coffee- and cocoa-growers, despite their huge profits.

Products like lettuce, carrots and fruit sustain the heaviest use of chemicals so I try to buy these

organic when available, as well as organic pasta,
onions and flour for bread-making.

Cleaning

I buy everyday products such as washing-up liquid
from the Ecover range. I use conventional cleaners
sparingly and avoid those containing chlorine
bleach because it is non-biodegradable and the
most polluting chemical in home cleaners.

Bathroom

Most of my bathroom products are community
traded products with more natural ingredients
than artificial chemicals. I shower more often than
I bathe to save energy and water. The toilet paper
is recycled and unbleached. The advert says 'soft,
strong and long' but doesn't mention that the
product was made out of hundred-year-old trees.

Household appliances

We have a new energy-efficient fridge and
washing machine. The Netherlands has A–E
energy-consumption labels now on consumer
goods from fridges to cars.

DIY

I use water-based paints when there's a choice.
Less polluting, healthier and less smelly! I avoid
tropical hardwood in furniture and construction or
spend extra on sustainable Forest Stewardship
Council hardwood products. Choose softwood such
as pine over hardwood because it is more likely to
have come from an abundant European pine forest
than an illegally and destructively logged
rainforest. PVC (vinyl) products in flooring, pipes

and shower curtains etc. are best avoided because the material is polluting to produce and dispose of: it is made of chlorine and leaches nasty chemicals into your home during use. Ikea (a multinational, but Scandinavian so more progressive than most!) excludes ancient forest products and PVC from its stores. Wooden floors are healthier for your house – easier to clean and with fewer chemicals than modern carpets. Investing in good insulation cuts the energy bill and helps keep us warm!

Clothes/presents

Most presents come from the Fairtrade shop – even if they're unwanted the money goes to a good cause. I try to avoid the major clothes and shoe brands because of their poor labour policies. Unwanted clothes and shoes go in the Amnesty clothes bank.

Recycling

Dutch recycling figures are much better than the UK's, but there are variations between locations. Amsterdam has one of the few incinerators in Holland so recycling isn't as good as in other areas. Paper and glass go in the recycling bins, beer bottles back to the supermarket. Organic waste goes into the bio-bin down the street. This organic waste accounts for about half of our rubbish each week, so if we miss the bin collection one week the rubbish doesn't smell so much, containing mainly plastic. Old batteries are collected at electronic stores.

Transport
I cycle to work every day and cycle to the shops a few times a week. We recently bought our first car after being car-free for five years. To ease our guilt we bought the smallest and most efficient car we could afford. We try to use it only when it is essential.

Money
I have yet to move to an ethical bank account but it's on the 'to do' list. I'm a member of Oxfam and occasionally buy a homeless paper.

Entertainment/eating out
I avoid chain pubs and restaurants because in smaller places you can see who is benefiting from your custom. Having worked in a poorly paid catering job I like to leave a tip for good service wherever I am. For good street musicians and performers I try to have some small change handy. I haven't eaten in a fast-food chain for eight years.

Holidays/travel
I like to travel and it's part of my job. So lots of flying (big minus points), but I always travel independently and avoid Western chain hotels and restaurants. Hopefully the money I spend benefits the local economy more than spending that money at home or on package deals. The house is full of art and bits and bobs from far-flung places. As none of it is made of tropical hardwood or wild animals, buying it from local traders did more good than harm. When possible I buy my air ticket

through travel agents that give the profits to developing world projects, such as North–South Travel in the UK.

In the days when I had more time and less money I had a few wonderful working holidays – as a volunteer on a forestry project in the US, clearing footpaths in Wales, spending weekends with the National Trust and British Trust for Conservation Volunteers (BTCV). I also spent two months in India working in local communities. You discover more than you ever would as a normal tourist, and put something into the local area – for less than the cost of a package holiday.

So: by no means a perfect, impact-free lifestyle (I own a pair of Nike trainers and there is PVC flooring in the kitchen because it was the cheapest option when we moved in and were broke). However, I like to think my choices do make a difference to what is important to me and the world. Of course, there is always more you could do, but money and practicalities intrude. I'm not even close to being an ethical angel yet, but I do spend all week working for an environmental group so it is good to take a break from work sometimes.

Good luck, Tom

My family and I have lived 'ethically' since 1984, though we mightn't have done if circumstances hadn't conspired to force me. My younger son had just been born, my elder son was six, I was recently separated, and I felt I had to stay at home with my family and not return to teaching.

My younger son and I are vegetarian. We lived in Hammersmith and across the road in King Street was a magnificent organic wholefood shop that was a lot cheaper than the nearest supermarket. Packaging was minimal; you could, for example, take along your own container and fill it with washing-up liquid. I never bought processed baby food. I pureed ingredients in a blender and discovered a wonderful food called Kohkoh – a blend of buckwheat and aduki beans – which I added water to and cooked like a sauce.

In those days Nestlé was the brand to avoid. Since then I have added others, like Procter & Gamble (their products are tested on animals), SmithKline Beecham, Novartis and Monsanto. I don't use any cosmetics or toiletries that are tested on animals, or ones that contain harmful ingredients like parabens or sodium laureth sulphate. For health care, I use homeopathy, herbs and acupuncture. I don't give credence to any medical system or product that is tested on animals or on poor and vulnerable people, as many vaccines have been. I don't see how healing can occur as a result of any product whose development has involved cruelty and exploitation.

I won't buy any fruit or vegetables that have been grown using chemicals that might have harmed anyone involved in their production. Likewise with clothing; more chemicals are used in the production of cotton than anything else, and cotton clothes are also sprayed after being made up. I prefer to buy fairly traded, organic clothing. It's priced more or less on a par with Marks and Spencer. My son also likes the clothes, which are more distinctive than those available on the high street. And because they're that bit more expensive, we are less extravagant.

We always think twice before buying videos or DVDs, or anything else that might end up in landfill. Before buying anything, we ask ourselves if we really need it.

Having a visual impairment, I can't drive. There again, I've made a virtue out of a necessity – we've always used public transport for shopping, outings and holidays. As far as the latter are concerned, we're members of the Youth Hostels Association, and of WWOOF (Worldwide Opportunities on Organic Farms). We joined WWOOF in 1992 and have been on working holidays in France, Italy and Slovenia, as well as in the UK. It's a fantastic way of meeting people and learning about the environment and agriculture, as well as achieving a language fluency not to be gained in most colleges. Imagine being able to say 'That couch grass needs to be got rid of' in seven different languages!

Ethical living isn't a matter of shoulds and don'ts. I feel it's good to do something positive towards making the world a better place – even though one sometimes feels that the odds are overwhelmingly against. I consistently support Amnesty International and an organic gardening organization, and when I can I give some of my income towards medical treatment for torture victims, and a brilliant place in Derbyshire where they help disaffected and excluded schoolchildren to gain self-esteem and self-discipline. I also campaigned, for a long time, against water fluoridation, and organized nationally known speakers to come and address local meetings. I feel that being aware of different issues makes it my duty to do what I can.

Dyana Rodriguez

My wife and I live in the woods of Pine Ridge, Arkansas, on the Ouachita River, bordered by the Ouachita National Forest. It is beautiful here, and we live rather simply. We grow our own organic vegetables every year and are building a cabin from lumber from trees that died in an ice storm a few years back.

We are also actively involved in the fight against factory farming. We have gone vegetarian within the past year and are working our way to implementing more and more vegan choices into

our diets. We have both noticed a dramatic
improvement in our health and energy levels since
we made the switch. We have also found out
considerably more about the damage the meat
industry does to the environment. And, of course,
we spread the word as far and wide as we can
about what we find to help others make the best
decisions they can on the information available.

One person *can* make a difference, as I have
found out. You are definitely making one. I do
believe that if we are not part of the solution,
then we are part of the problem. You are obviously
part of the solution. Have a good day, and keep up
the good work.

VB

The biggest lesson I have taken from these letters, I believe, is
that we each need to find our own way forward. It seems
obvious now, but it seems to be the just-do-the-best-you-can
way of looking at life. There is no right or wrong way to get
there, just so long as we all set out on the journey.

God, now I'm even beginning to sound like the new-age
hippy clone some of my friends have said that I'm dangerously
close to transmuting into. But, seriously, I think these letters, in
combination, have helped to save my experiment from drifting
away from me. I'm now feeling much better about carrying on.

8

THIS IS HOW ARGUMENTS TEND to be sparked in our household. It will be a Sunday afternoon, just as the *EastEnders* omnibus is about to start, when the question is raised. 'When was the last time we cleaned the bathroom? We should probably do it today.'

We both know it must be done, yet the prospect of spending a relaxing afternoon with the feet up is now ruined by the thought of the drudgery to come: leaning over the bath, cream cleaner in one hand, cloth in the other, feverishly attempting to return the gleam to the taps. It is enough to leave us both tetchy and it will be only a matter of minutes before the argument begins about who did it last time, who does it better, and couldn't it just be put off for another few days?

The truth is that I'm usually in the wrong when it comes to the chore wars in our home. Jane is the master cleaner and takes much more pride in it than I do. Therefore, whenever I do it (which, I admit, is less often than Jane) I just know that I'm going to fail the inspection afterwards. I think Jane suspects that I conspire to do it badly on purpose so that I can get out of it by letting her push me to one side in exasperation.

But I do the best I can. I just don't meet her exacting standards.

If this is reflected in households across the land, it may explain why the manufacturers of cleaning products still persist with those slightly old-fashioned slogans such as 'sparkling results', 'effortless power' and a 'lemon-fresh finish' when advertising their wares. They're trying to exploit the fact that much marriage counselling could be avoided if only cleaning the home was limited to a couple of airy squirts of miracle cleaner. And although we all know cleaning is hard work, we still fall for these false claims.

Our cupboard under the kitchen sink is stuffed full of cleaning products – or 'poisons', as the auditors described them. We've got the lot – all-purpose cleaners, oven cleaners, bleach, toilet ducks, scouring agents, surface sprays, limescale removers, window cleaners – any weapon of mass destruction that blitzes germs, leaves a fresh scent and, most importantly, requires as little elbow grease as possible.

But over the years we've periodically turned to the best form of marriage counselling money can buy – a cleaner. I can't think of a better or more satisfying way to spend one's money. You can keep your fast cars, luxury holidays, fine wines – give me a cleaner once a week and I'm a happy man. Luckily, Jane agrees with me on this one – even if she's never felt that any cleaner has ever cleaned our home as well as she can.

Having a cleaner is an addiction, in my view. Once you've taken the plunge, there's no going back. And we've recently succumbed again, having gone cold turkey for about six months while we were moving and settling into our new house. We don't have many vices in life, but relieving ourselves of the chore of cleaning and hence freeing up an extra couple of precious hours a week is a sin we're freely willing to commit. I say sin because when we've told people who don't use a cleaner that we do, there seems to be an equal divide between those who express a longing to do the same, and those who espouse the 'you're just exploiting cheap labour' argument. I must admit to feeling a sense of middle-class, liberal angst from time to time about having someone else scrubbing my toilet bowl, but, to be honest, it's more the shame of being lazy enough to pay someone else to do it, rather than a sense that we're committing some kind of human-rights violation.

'Trying to combat nature can have dangerous consequences,' says Renée, as she looks through all of our cleaning products under the sink. 'For example, we use poisons in farming, creating super weeds, and we use antibiotics in medicine, creating super bugs. Research is beginning to bear out that if we keep our children too over-sanitized, they won't build up resistance to even ordinary colds and bugs.'

Mike nods in agreement. 'Most people like to keep their home environment reasonably clean, especially when they've got small children about. In an ideal world we should be able to do this without polluting the wider environment or damaging our health. But some of the chemicals used in cleaning products can pose a risk, and it can be difficult to find good alternatives.'

The auditors remove some of the cleaning products from the cupboard and examine the labels. 'There are a lot of

Procter & Gamble products here,' says Hannah, and proceeds
to explain how chemical multinationals, more often than not,
have poor records when it comes to animal rights. 'Exercise
your power as consumers,' she stresses, 'and seek alternatives.'

But it's what's in these products that is most worrying,
says Mike, lifting up a bottle of anti-bacterial kitchen surface
spray. 'Nobody likes to think that bacteria are breeding in
their kitchen – especially when you are preparing food,' he
says. 'But anti-bacterial products tend to contain the chemical
Triclosan, which can pose far more of a risk than the bacteria
it kills. After all, we need some exposure to bacteria to help
build up our body's immune system. And there are also
concerns that anti-bacterial products increase the resistance
of bacteria, creating super-bugs. Triclosan is said to build up
in our bodies and may have a long-term impact on our
health. Traces have been found in human breast milk and in
fish. I wouldn't want this product to come into contact with
my food, or even with dishes and plates. But products
containing Triclosan are labelled, so it's easy enough to avoid
them.'

Hannah points out that we also have anti-bacterial
handwash by our sink. 'And you've got exceptionally harsh
cleaning products such as Mr Muscle oven cleaner.'

It's not just about the poisonous chemicals you are
introducing into your home and on to your skin, the auditors
all stress; it's also important to consider what goes down the
drains.

'Many compounds are only partially broken down when
washed away, and contaminants can combine together,

making it even harder to predict their effects,' explains Hannah. 'Raw sewage, containing heavy metals and hormone disrupters, will even continue to be legally spread on a small percentage of UK farmland until 2005.'

OK, OK, I say, I think it has been made quite clear that we need to paint a skull and crossbones on the cupboard door. But what should we do – let our house fester in dirt?

Mike has noticed that many of our products are lemon scented, but most of these contain no lemon, he says. 'Instead they contain artificial musks, which may smell nice but unfortunately are also persistent chemicals that accumulate in our body fat and may have a long-term impact on health, as well as polluting water and affecting wildlife. It can be really difficult to find cleaning products which are not perfumed in this way, but some manufacturers do use natural oils and plant extracts, so hunt for these.'

Hannah has a more down-to-earth solution. 'You can concoct effective cleaning products yourself from white vinegar. You can make a window cleaner by mixing vinegar with water, or it can be used neat as a disinfectant, with a few drops of tea tree oil. Try baking soda as an all-purpose cleaner or scourer, salt as an abrasive for cleaning pots and pans, and lemon juice as an alternative to bleach. Just re-label your old spray bottles to dispense them. You could also pick up a second-hand carpet sweeper to cut down on electricity-intensive vacuuming.'

I give the auditors the best less-than-enamoured look I can muster. Jane makes a much better job of it than me.

I can't believe they're proposing we use lemon juice down our loo instead of bleach.

'If you can't be bothered to make your own products,' says Renée, sensing our reluctance, 'just go out and buy some environmentally friendly ones instead. Ecover cream cleaner, for example, requires a little more elbow grease, but it won't harm you, Esme or the environment.'

You may have noticed that the auditors didn't comment on the ethics of us using a cleaner. That's because, to be honest, I didn't have the courage to tell them we used one. I just knew we would be marked down for it and we were both feeling vulnerable at that point. In retrospect, we should have asked for their view, as we have been debating this issue long and hard since the auditors left and in the end we've decided to keep our cleaner – on the proviso that we pay more attention to the terms of her employment.

How convenient, you cry, but hang on, let me explain. We used to just pay an hourly rate in cash and that would be it. The going rate for a cleaner in our part of London is about seven to nine pounds an hour – well above the minimum wage, but still not exactly a fantastic little earner. This isn't the fee for an agency cleaner, but for someone you might find via a note in a newsagent's window, or by word of mouth – the kind of person who expects to be paid cash each week. So all the normal working 'perks', such as holiday pay, sick pay, pension, safe working environment, etc., would not be part of the package.

Without wanting to draw the undue attention of the Treasury or the Home Office, I don't know whether our cleaner

– let's call her Maria – declares her earnings, has a National Insurance number, or is even legally resident in this country (possibly not, given that up to 97 per cent of domestic workers in London are immigrants). The only thing I know is that Maria – and others like her, because we've employed them in the past – is happy to accept cash-in-hand, menial work on a no-questions-asked basis. It suits her, and it suits us.

Anyway, we would much rather Maria got all the money we pay her rather than see a large cut of it paid over to an agency, meaning that, ultimately, she would probably be earning less. And if we have the means to pay a cleaner for a couple of hours a week, I don't see too much of a problem. But we will strive to improve her working conditions by paying her if she is sick or on holiday – which we've never even considered before now.

I think that employing a cleaner is peculiarly guilt-inducing because of the nature of the job involved. Asking someone else to clean up your mess is never a nice thing to do, which I suppose is why so many of us hide behind notes and instructions rather than talking to our cleaners directly. But there must be dozens of services that we gain from or use that rely on such labour – pubs, shops, restaurants, gardeners, builders – and that don't cause us the same kind of angst.

I'm pleased to read that others have been having the same dilemma.

Hi, Leo

I employ a cleaning person in California. She is
from Mexico. American liberals are often required
to feel guilty about cleaners, but this is what I say
– the labour movement has shown us how to
employ others in an ethical way. This is what I do:

Let her set her own wages and duties and
hours. If she is worth hiring, then she will give
good value for the money and do a good job. If she
is not worth hiring, then you can't make her worth
hiring by watching her and bullying her.

Pay her a salary rather than a wage. Encourage
her to bring along her children when she has to,
and treat them as guests when they are in the
house. Be friendly and welcoming, of course. Make
suggestions rather than demands.

Don't ask her to clean up a mess that disgusts
you. Either help clean it up or clean it up yourself.
I am thinking of dogs and children here. Learn her
language.

For lots of women, cleaning for a decent wage in
a pleasant private home is preferable to other
work that might be available. If we never hire
anyone to clean, then there is a whole category of
workers who lose out on employment that they
might gain from. Since I first hired her eight years
ago, my cleaner has expanded her operation and
hired several others, gone to school to improve
her language and other skills, and established
herself in her community. She drives a nice car.

> For cleaning my house, she gets $200 per week,
> for approximately six hours' work. That's more
> than thirty dollars an hour, but she has earned it
> by organizing her work in her own way and making
> sure it always gets done.
> So, those are some thoughts from California.
>
> Jane Smiley

The issue of what cleaning products to use, however, has proved much easier to resolve. The auditors managed to scare us half to death about the toxic chemicals lurking under our sink. They did an excellent job, too, in playing the Esme card to give us an extra dose of parental concern.

We've been faced with an immediate problem though: what should we do with all these poisons? Pour them down the drain in one go? Put them out with the rubbish, where they will end up in the landfill? Or just use them up, then replace them with safer and more ecologically sound alternatives once finished?

All things considered, we decide it's best to get rid of them as soon as possible, so we've chosen to just throw them away. Better in an already polluted landfill site, we think, than washed down into the sewers, albeit greatly diluted, where energy will be spent at the water-treatment plants getting the water back into a drinkable state. The irony of cleaning ourselves of cleaning products hasn't been lost on us, believe me.

But what to use instead? This whole subject has led to some

letters that, frankly, I'm still struggling to digest. Dinah's letter in some ways speaks for them all. All I can say is that she is taking this save-water-and-cut-out-the-toxic-chemicals thing to extremely high levels – and I mean high in every sense.

> Instead of showering daily, try using the basin and a flannel to wash just the stinky bits – pits, crotch, feet. I've been doing this for a few months because I have dry skin. My skin is better, and my friends haven't complained about BO.
> Use only cold water in the washing machine. Works fine on almost everything, but really gross items might need hot water.
> Brush teeth with a little salt and baking soda. Tastes like !@#*, but works, is cheap, and saves packaging.
> It's amazing how much cleaning you can do just with white vinegar and hot water. Then boil a teaspoon of cinnamon in a pan of hot water for a few minutes, to help disguise the smell.
>
> Dinah Shields,
> Laguna Beach, California

To be honest, her level of dedication to the cause frightens me a little. How many people are out there brushing their teeth with salt and rubbing their 'stinky bits', as Dinah so charmingly describes them, with a flannel? Or is this kind of thing peculiar to Laguna Beach?

Let's just say that Heather's letter seems a little closer to where Jane and I are currently aiming:

> Hi,
>
> About six months ago I started making my own household cleaning products. It's actually turned out to be very easy, cheap and effective.
>
> The basic ingredients are bicarbonate of soda, vinegar, pure soap and borax, plus maybe some tea tree or eucalyptus oil for a nice scent. With these you can make a variety of cleaners for different purposes.
>
> For example, for a general disinfectant, mix quarter of a cup of borax, quarter of a cup of white vinegar and the juice of half a lemon with some hot water.
>
> My home smells better, and the eco-friendly cleaners are just as effective as the expensive chemical products on the market. Plus, the total cost of all the ingredients is cheaper than buying maybe two chemical products, and they last much longer.
>
> **Heather Padden, Australia**

There's no denying that Renée's advice about using like-for-like eco-alternatives such as Ecover seems the most appealing. The thought of standing witch-like over a bucket mixing up cleaning potions ourselves (vinegar, lemon, bicarbonate of soda, eye of newt) just isn't that tempting. However, we've decided to get into the ethical spirit and try out a few homemade cleaning solutions for ourselves.

Cue one of the more embarrassing shopping trips of my life.

After repeated failed attempts to find anything larger than a small 50ml tub of bicarbonate of soda in the local Costcutter (I'm trying to support my local shops, but still can't decide whether Costcutter really counts as a supermarket) I wearily enter the chemist's next door. The chemist does a double-take when I ask him for two kilos of the stuff.

'Two kilos? I don't think we have that amount here. Can I ask why you need so much?' he says.

'I've been told it works as a cleaner if you mix it with vinegar,' I say.

The chemist retreats and starts muttering to his assistant in the dispensary area. They both look a little concerned.

'Is there a problem?' I ask.

The chemist returns. 'We have to be careful, you see, as we've been told to be suspicious of anyone asking for large quantities of bicarbonate of soda.'

'Why?'

'Apparently, drug-dealers often cut it into their drugs because it is so cheap and is hard to detect. But you don't look like a drug-dealer to me. We can order some in for you, if you like.'

Great! Now I'm being suspected of being a crack-dealer by my own chemist. I only want the stuff to clean the sodding bathroom. I place an order, but leave the shop with the paranoid feeling that my name was only taken to be entered into some kind of national drug-dealer watch list.

Jane finds the whole tale hilarious and laughs even more when she sees that I've returned with just a small cooking-sized pack of bicarbonate of soda, a couple of lemons and a bottle of organic malt vinegar. It looks as if I'm about to cook up some fancy dish rather than start cleaning, she says.

I'm curious to know how all these ingredients are going to work, though, so undeterred I go into the bathroom to experiment. Mixing and applying them doesn't prove to be a problem. There isn't a noticeable amount of extra effort required to budge the dirt – scrubbing is scrubbing, if you ask me. The most exciting thing – if you can call cleaning a bathroom exciting – is the reaction when I mix the bicarb with vinegar. It fizzes furiously, just like one of those experiments you do in chemistry lessons. I pour some down the plug hole, which has been a bit blocked up recently, and after about a minute it actually starts to budge whatever was down there – a hairball, probably. Jane pops her head round the door to complain that the house is now starting to stink like a fish and chip shop.

'Would you like lemon with your fish?' I ask, pointing to the fruit balanced on the side of the bath. She's clearly not amused. But the lemons do actually work, as we both see. Without wanting to sound as if I've been involved in a Pepsi Taste Test Challenge, there really is no discernible difference in the results. I try rubbing the lemons on the tidemark around the bath, leaving it for a minute or so, then wiping off the dirt. To our surprise, it works really well. Jane is impressed. She's less impressed by the lemon pips gathering in the plug hole, and says it's probably worth squeezing the lemons first if we're to prevent Maria from wondering what the hell we've been up to in the bath.

I've now started looking up cleaning recipes online – that's how sad I've become. I'm really fascinated by how useful bicarbonate of soda can be. There seems to be a whole sub-culture of people who swear by the stuff. Alone, or in combination with white vinegar (made by performing a secondary fermentation of alcohol, in case you didn't know), it can be used to deodorize carpets, scrub stainless steel, clear drains, remove tea stains from mugs, remove permanent marker from skin – the list seems endless. I've also learned a really great trick for cleaning a showerhead that has become blocked with limescale – you just leave it in a glass of vinegar overnight.

The trouble is, Maria just isn't sold on the idea. She wants to continue using conventional products. I can't blame her really; she must think we're totally insane. I sometimes wonder too, but we've asked her to come to a compromise and try using products made by someone such as Ecover. It's going OK but there have been a few mutinous moments. Products we've all agreed work and that we should switch over to include Ecover Squirteco, an all-purpose cleaner that relies on plant- and mineral-based surfactants to provide its cleaning oomph. We've tried a few others, including some made by a company called Earth Friendly Products (it makes a great parsley-based kitchen-unit spray), but the expert opinion of our cleaner – and who are we to argue? – is that she prefers the Ecover cleaners. I think it is probably because they come in similar-looking packages to our old cleaners, but Jane has warned me off trying to sneak a homemade brew of lemon juice and flaked pure soap I've read about online into one of the bottles, for fear of losing her.

An altogether more vexing question is the issue of what we slap and rub on to our bodies. It seems that similar dangers lurk within our toiletries and cosmetics as in our cleaning products, if the auditors are to be believed.

Before they arrived, we'd thought our bathroom habits were fairly harmless. After all, we both go through a mundane enough routine each morning. There's no aftershave, hairspray, hair dye or other such concoctions in our bathroom. In fact, the routine is about as dull as you can get.

Ten minutes after the alarm sounds each morning, our bathroom door closes and stays closed for about the next half an hour. In turn, Jane and I each take a shower lasting about five minutes, washing with Nivea body-care soap and Bodyshop's ginger shampoo. Getting bored yet? No? After drying off with white cotton towels (I say it now, even in the name of ethical living I am not prepared to start drip-drying after showering), I brush my teeth with Mentadent P and slap some E45 cream on to my face to prevent dry skin. On alternate days I will also have a wet shave, using Gillette shaving gel and one of those double-bladed (or is it triple nowadays?) razors. My bathroom session concludes with a quick spray of deodorant and I'm off to get dressed and have breakfast. Other than moisturizer, perhaps, I've never purchased any 'male grooming' products, although that's not to say they haven't found their way into the bathroom cabinet as gifts from great-aunts and the like.

As the bathroom is about as functional and pleasureless a place as I can imagine, I aim to be in and out within fifteen minutes. Jane, however, performs a few other rituals behind those closed doors, some of which must make use of the numerous lotions and potions (invariably, it seems, made by Clarins) that litter our bathroom. I know that skin toners and eye creams are applied, but beyond that I'm – like most men – not really qualified to say what the contents of those bottles do, or claim to do.

About once a week, on average, Jane will run a bath in the evening, liberally lace it with bath oils or bubble bath, and have a soak. We also run a very shallow bath for Esme each evening to let her have a splash and quick clean. One bad habit I've been unable to break since childhood is leaving the tap on while brushing my teeth. Over all, I would say we spend roughly one-fiftieth of our time and about 5 per cent of the household shopping budget on the bathroom.

This daily drudge barely registers on my radar. I'm only giving it some thought now to help me list our routine. So I'm not really daunted by the prospect of change. But Jane's re-action to seeing Renée in particular castigate the contents of our bathroom cabinet means I have been strategically shunning the subject for fear of upsetting her.

However, our toothpaste tube has almost run dry, as has Jane's deodorant, and I can see we are soon going to have to decide what to replace them with. I'm keen not to push it too hard, but decide to start with the issue of what shampoo we should be using.

Everyone is staring at our loo. 'I see you have the standard who-cares-about-the-water-we-use flush volume,' says Hannah. 'A third of an average family's water use is flushed down the toilet, and it is hugely wasteful that we flush with water cleaned to drinking standards. Why not place a plastic tub of stones in the cistern to reduce the volume of the flush? And why not ask the Centre for Alternative Technology in Wales for advice on compost toilets, or on installing a grey-water system to channel your old bath water to the toilet and garden?'

I feel like I'm beginning to lose the will to live. We live in Brixton, I think to myself, not an eco-commune. What are prospective buyers going to think of a 'grey-water system' when they're being shown round our house? They'll flush the loo to test it, see our murky bathwater, and be out of the front door before you can say, 'What else have you got on the books?'

Mike, bless him, doesn't appear too concerned about our loo. He's actually quite impressed by it. According to him, it's a 'low-level flush toilet'. We had no idea.

But eyes soon divert to our loo paper. Renée notes that we have a jumbo pack of Sainsbury's super-soft toilet tissue. 'Paper is a bit of a minefield,' she says, 'because there are so many permutations when it comes to recycled and non-bleached. But it's easy to switch to recycled toilet paper and tissues, and the quality has improved over the years.'

Hannah is also keen that we change our loo paper. 'Try replacing the paper with an unbleached, 100 per cent "post-

consumer" variety from workers' co-ops such as Suma or
Essential Trading.'

I can't help but think that by 'post-consumer' she really
means second-hand loo paper. Not an attractive proposition.

'Recycled paper production uses 30 to 50 per cent less
energy than making new paper from trees, and reduces
contributions to air pollution by 95 per cent,' she continues.
'To paraphrase an academic from Chicago University: if the
rest of the world required quilted, scented, coloured toilet
tissue, our forests would be destroyed so rapidly that earthly
life-support systems would fail.'

Having now been ethically potty trained, Jane and I
tentatively await the verdict on our shower. Hannah is
surprisingly upbeat at first, but soon depresses us with more
figures. 'It's good to see your shower attached to the bath taps,
and not separately heated. Try to shower rather than bathe –
showers use around a third as much water.'

Renée and Mike, meanwhile, are looking at the soaps and
bottles of shampoo around the edge of our bath. 'The
bathroom can be a real chemical hazard zone,' says Mike. 'For
some reason, being clean has come to mean polluting our
bodies with lots of smelly chemicals. Just as in the kitchen
cupboard, I see artificial musks here, which often appear on
product labels simply as "parfum".'

Renée says she finds people's attitudes to body-care
products confusing. Why do we worry about what we put in
our mouths, but not what we rub on our skin? 'You absorb 60
per cent of what you put on your skin, like body lotion, and
80 per cent of what you put in your mouth, like toothpaste,'

she says. 'Conventional body-care and make-up ranges have
ingredients that are primarily there to make the products
look, smell and feel nice – not necessarily to benefit your skin,
although they make incredible claims. If these claims were
true, surely there would be no one in the world over the age
of twenty-five with a wrinkle? There are wonderful
companies producing organic body-care ranges out there. For
example, Green People is a British company and has Soil
Association approval. It produces everything from sunscreen
to toothpaste.'

Finally, the auditors offer some advice about what to look
for when choosing a toothpaste. Mike repeats his advice
about avoiding the anti-bacterial agent Triclosan. 'Some
Scandinavian countries have now issued warnings about
using it in personal-hygiene products.'

Hannah recommends toothpaste manufacturers such as
Kingfisher, who use tubes made from biodegradable cellulose.
'And don't leave the taps running when brushing your teeth.
It wastes up to five litres a minute.' Ah, I wondered how long
it would take for that old chestnut to crop up.

The internet is becoming quite an ally at the moment. I've
started to become a real label bore and have taken to looking
up ingredients and strange-sounding chemical names on
search engines. Not wholly scientific, I know, but you soon
learn what are the controversial chemicals.

Take our Bodyshop ginger shampoo. One look at the list of
ingredients – which I've never done before – and second from
the top is something called sodium lauryl sulphate. I now learn

that it's a commonly used detergent and emulsifier that is said by some to cause dry skin – ironic considering the shampoo claims to battle dandruff.

But I also read that this chemical has been repeatedly tested and cleared following recent scare stories about its downsides. This kind of mixed message leaves me anxious; my gut instinct is to go with the boffins who say that blind trials have found that it's safe. But this never dispels the 'what if' niggles, nor does it dispel another of my instincts – that repeatedly putting synthetic chemicals into or on to our bodies just doesn't make sense.

On balance, it seems that the best thing to do – especially as I have also found sodium lauryl sulphate in our baby shampoo – is to play safe and try to avoid it.

The trouble is that such concern doesn't exactly lend itself to speedy shopping. Every time we consider a new cosmetic or bodycare product, we're now on the lookout for chemicals such as parabens (preservatives, I've learned, that can cause skin irritation and could even be xenoestrogens – environmental oestrogens that disrupt the normal hormonal processes), methylmethacrylate (used as a nail filler but linked to skin complaints), and mineral oil (a commonly used petroleum-based oil). This is just a handful of the chemicals we're now trying to avoid, but what has really surprised me is just how prevalent they are. In fact, it's proving quite hard to find products on the high street that don't contain these impossible-to-pronounce ingredients.

Speaking to my grandmother about what she used to keep in her bathroom cabinet in her youth, she reels off things such as

rose water, calendula, chalk talc, witch hazel, cod-liver oil –
natural products that are now back in vogue with aroma-
therapists and the like. She also mentions coal-tar soap and
Vaseline – manufacturing by-products that have largely gone
out of vogue now because they seem too base for us, perhaps,
or lack the fancy branding we crave today.

What's the real point in smothering ourselves in chemicals
each morning anyway? As our demand for perfect products
increases – deodorants that work all day long, toothpastes that
whiten our teeth, lipsticks that don't smudge or fade, anti-
ageing creams – so the manufacturers have asked the chemists
to come up with more complex or inadequately tested
alternatives.

I'd be quite happy to strip right back to the barest bathroom
essentials of toothpaste, soap, shampoo and deodorant (no,
I'm not going any further than that). But I accept that Jane still
wants to persist with her lotions and potions. She has been
really keen, though, to find alternatives. I decided the other day
to buy her a small tester box of Dr Hauschka products and she
was thrilled. (Though her response might have been due to the
fact that I'd bought her a present at all, rather than some
organic body-care lotions in particular.)

She's so enthused, in fact, that she's even starting to sound
like one of those 'Because I'm worth it' adverts. I think she
might be going a bit too far, to be honest, but she even told
some friends that her Dr Hauschka facial toner is so fresh and
delicious she could drink it. And she's been heard to say that
her new REN shea butter, jojoba and grapeseed oil body lotion
(I just had to look that up – you don't think I remembered it,

do you?) is the richest and most luxurious she's ever used. She's refusing to give up on her Clarins eye cream, though; nothing keeps crow's feet under control more effectively, she claims. This seems to be one area where she is willing to use whatever it takes to combat nature's advances – chemicals, surgery, bull-dog clips, you name it.

We've been taking the ongoing debate about whether deodorants are linked to breast cancer seriously, however. And with Jane still breastfeeding, to hear that scientists have found traces of deodorant ingredients in babies has really freaked us out, though I was tempted at first to put it down as just another health scare of the red-wine's-good-for-you-red-wine's-bad-for-you kind.

As we normally both use spray-on, aerosol deodorants – which are said by some, we now learn, to cause lung damage and skin irritation – we thought roll-ons would be the obvious alternative. But just one look at the ingredients is enough to put you off. Both the aerosol we normally use and the roll-on we have since tried contain aluminium chlorohydrate – the aluminium salt mentioned in the breast-cancer scare stories. But the other ingredients don't make reassuring reading either. Our aerosols contain butane, propane, parfum and intriguing chemicals with names such as disteardimimonium hectorite (is that a chemical, or an Asterix character?) and cyclomethicone, while the roll-ons contain ingredients such as ceteareth-20.

So I recently did something that I've never done before – I rang one of those freephone consumer hotlines listed in the small print by the ingredients, to ask what these chemicals are doing to us. In this case it was the Lever Fabergé consumer hotline (0800 0852639), as it produces both Sure aerosols and Vaseline Intensive Care roll-ons, the two deodorants we've been using.

'Hello, please can you tell me about this aluminium chlorohydrate that I've been hearing about in news reports – the one being linked to breast cancer,' I ask.

'Yes, you have nothing to worry about,' responds the operator. 'It's just one doctor's claim. Our products have been tested and approved by scientists all round the world. Would you like us to send you a leaflet we've prepared about this subject?'

'Yes, please. Oh, while you're on the line, can you also tell me whether your products are tested on animals?'

'No, sir, our end-result products are not. Would you like us to send you a leaflet we've prepared about this subject?'

Not being entirely reassured by this phone call or the subsequent leaflets, we've taken to extreme measures – we've bought a deodorant stone each, which I haven't even seen since they were briefly trendy when I was a teenager. The stone is rather uncomfortable to apply when you've been used to sprays or roll-ons. You wet it and rub it on. Its principal drawback, however, is that sadly it just doesn't quite meet the deodorizing standards I'm used to – a considerable mental hurdle to clear for most of us. As we both draw the line at rubbing bicarbonate of soda under our arms, as one person has written to me to recommend, we have now started to try another deodorant. I'm trying the aluminium-free woodspice 'Nature's Way' deodorant and am pleased to say that people haven't started to move to the other side of the carriage yet on the Tube (but I will be closely monitoring this in future). Jane, meanwhile, is trying the tea-tree version, but is far less happy with it. She says she feels self-conscious about turning heads and noses. But I'm much more resolved now, thanks to the wave of letters I've received, just to let her come to her own conclusions – even if I do find myself fretting about breast-cancer links and the like.

It's been a similar experience with toothpaste. Again, bicarbonate-of-soda-based alternatives have been suggested to us, but the ones we've tried taste foul and leave your teeth feeling like they've had the enamel scraped off. (And, no, we haven't tried Dinah's suggestion of using salt, which seems to me best left for getting rid of mouth ulcers.) We are persisting, in the hope that we will develop a taste for the bicarb, but I'm not hopeful, especially as Jane has now started to complain about her tartar-coated teeth and says she is afraid to open her mouth in public. No bad thing, I'm tempted to say, but so far have refrained.

Cutting back on how much water we use in the bathroom has produced slightly better results. Other than having fewer baths (or just sharing them, of course) and showering for less time (there's a finite limit to how low you can actually go with this, as I've found), there doesn't seem to be much we can do, without breaking the social norm of washing once a day (as with deodorant, an essential requirement, it seems, for office workers and commuters, such as ourselves). I'm not going to advocate cold showers for the family, but we have tried having not-so-hot showers to conserve energy, although we realize this has to be done by using less hot water rather than simply adding more cold water.

I've just received a great idea for fixing a problem that has also been bugging me:

> **Dear Leo,**
>
> Water is often in short supply here in Madrid and what was bothering me was those first twenty seconds of cold water that you watch go straight down the plug hole before you jump under the shower. Fortunately I have a small garden right outside my bathroom, and by poking the shower head out the window my plants now get a twenty-second regular watering just before I get clean.
>
> **Simon Betterton**

I love the idea of Simon watering his plants out of his bathroom window each morning before turning the shower on himself.

But the mantra that showers, rather than baths, should always be our first choice has also taken a slight knock. I've read online about something called 'toxic showers'. Whereas the fact that showers (though not power-showers) use less water than baths isn't in dispute, some claim that by inhaling a shower's steam you are actually absorbing chloroform, a chemical once used in anaesthesia. It is claimed that the chlorine in our water supplies, when heated, is transformed into chloroform. But to avoid the possible effects of a toxic shower, we would need to install a showerhead filter at a cost of about

£40 (not including installation costs). So we're awaiting further proof before we think about investing in one. The possible presence of chloroform in the bathroom might explain, however, why so many men forget to put the loo seat down after taking a pee. Well, that's my theory, anyway. Jane just thinks we're all lazy.

The sweep through our home trying to purge toxic chemicals from our lives continues with the washing machine. The auditors were surprisingly quiet on the subject of washing powder. Renée did mention that we should try to reduce the amount of liquid or powder we use, because the instructions always tell you to use loads so that you will buy more, but the advice was basically the same as for our bathroom and cleaning products – avoid harsh chemicals. Other than that there was a request to use the half-load setting, even on full washes, and not to pack too many clothes into the drum. All this, they said, would help make the machine more energy efficient.

We still firmly believe in the mantra passed down by advertisers and grandmothers alike that whites should be washed at a hotter temperature than coloureds. So will, we ponder, washing whites at 40ºC rather than 60ºC, while also using less washing liquid, mean our pristine whiter-than-white linen begins to grey? We stuff it all in the machine and cross our fingers.

However, half a dozen washes later we're delighted to report that there's been no noticeable change in colour. We have also been debating whether to ditch our washing liquid altogether in preference for some so-called 'eco-balls'. These, according to the manufacturer, 'produce ionised oxygen that activates the water molecules naturally and allows them to penetrate deep into clothing fibres to lift dirt away. They are reusable for over a thousand washes and cost on average 3p per wash.' They're also kind to skin, they say, and don't require a rinse cycle, and so use less energy.

I'm not an expert on the ins and outs of ionized oxygen in the washing machine, but despite some rave user reviews on the internet, it's an unimpressed friend who has already used them who has been putting us off parting with the thirty-pound start-up cost.

However, a reader has sent us some, determined to disprove our doubts.

Dear Leo,

We would like to offer you some eco-balls, as our contribution to your efforts to go green.

I'm disappointed your friend put you off eco-balls. We've used them for about two years or more, initially for environmental reasons, but also have found they have saved us a considerable amount on washing powder.

They do work. We just chuck the eco-balls in with coloured washes, while with whites we put in a little Persil (non-bio) – about a third of the usual amount – as we found that whites went a bit grey if the balls alone were used. You can use greener alternatives, but we haven't tried them.

We are still using our first set, and don't know
how many hundreds of washes we've got out of
them.
Everyone should use them! Less pollution and
less cost. We've bought several sets to give as
presents and are delighted to send you a pack.
Good luck with your family's ethical endeavours.

Malcolm and Gia Margolis, Pannal, Harrogate

As soon as they arrived, I was really keen to try them, if only
out of curiosity. They're funny little things – sort of mini
plastic spaceships that contain hundreds of tiny white balls.
But I knew that Jane was extremely reluctant, given our friend's
views, so I did something a bit naughty and put on a dark wash
using the eco-balls without telling Jane. She didn't notice the
difference, but I felt a bit grubby doing so, so have now
confessed.

Unfortunately, now that she has started checking each wash
to see if they work (I am principal launderer in our house), she
has pronounced that she doesn't believe they do as good a job,
particularly with Esme's mucky clothes. I must admit that
they're not great at shifting caked-on yoghurt, dribble and
banana, but it seems a shame not to keep trying them with our
normal washes, especially as most of our clothes are only worn
for a day and aren't all that dirty. The situation hasn't been
helped by Hannah saying to us, 'It doesn't matter if your whites
don't look white,' which really riled Jane.

We've ended up with a rather unsatisfactory compromise. If

I want to wash my own clothes with the eco-balls I can, but general washes are to use conventional detergents, albeit in much lower concentrations than before. (We've also tried Ecover laundry liquid, but Jane isn't persuaded by that either, saying that she feels it just doesn't end up as 'fresh' smelling as before. I'm not convinced, but am happy not to push it in the name of domestic harmony.)

Where we have made progress is that we've agreed to run all our washes on the half-load setting. This cuts the energy and water consumption down considerably (although I'm not convinced it's halved) as the cycle takes under an hour to complete as opposed to nearly two.

Sometimes I feel as though we're on a half-load setting ourselves, in terms of how far we've moved from our previous habits in the bathroom and when tackling domestic chores. But at least we've made a start, I suppose.

Cleaning products, cosmetics and toiletries are one thing, but when it comes to truly toxic nasties found in the house it's hard to beat the chemicals I've used to decorate our home in the past. I don't need the auditors to tell me that. I've experienced the red-raw skin caused by washing my hands in white spirit after a long session with a pot of gloss enough times to know that such a liquid is unlikely to be best buddies with nature.

But Jane and I have known since we moved that a round of major building work and decoration would have to take place at some point, given the illogical and inconvenient layout of our house. The only things that have prevented us so far have been lack of funds and the presence of, first, a pregnant woman in the house, soon followed by a newborn baby.

Another reason for delay is that my DIY skills don't exactly fill Jane with confidence. My home-improvement repertoire consists of:

- Changing a light bulb.
- Changing a three-amp fuse in a wall plug.
- Drilling a hole into a wall then hammering in a rawl plug.
- Screwing a screw into said rawl plug then hanging something on it (preferably as close to true as possible).
- Hammering a nail into a creaky floorboard (successfully avoiding central-heating pipe below).
- Painting a bedroom with a roller and tray in under two days (even though, as Jane was keen to point out, I had 'missed a bit' more than once).

However, my proudest moment deserves special mention. Having never before strayed from the above list, just prior to the auditors' arrival I decided to step up a level after receiving for Christmas – hint readily accepted – one of those DIY reference books that are the size of a toolkit. The chapter on 'Shelving with Confidence' spurred me into attempting a floor-to-ceiling MDF bookshelf in the back room. Armed with a borrowed jigsaw, work bench, spirit level, three large sheets of MDF, a sharpened pencil, a steady supply of tea, and live football on Radio 5, I emerged triumphant three weekends later. I can boast that my handiwork is still standing today.

While Jane seemed impressed with the shelves (that's what

she told me anyway), both she and I are wise enough to know that anything more advanced – knocking down internal walls, plumbing, electrics, plastering, drinking over-stewed tea with three sugars – is beyond the realms of my capabilities. We have seen too many of those DIY disaster programmes to dream of going near a sledge-hammer or angle-grinder. This is a job best left to the professionals, we feel.

The auditors' visit coincides with us finalizing plans for how we are going to make the best of the space available in our house. Ever since we moved in we have wanted to reposition our poky bathroom upstairs. At the moment it is downstairs, next to the kitchen, which means that simple tasks such as brushing your teeth can seem like major expeditions. Hardly up there with life's great hardships, I know, but we also crave enough space to have a table in the kitchen, which would transform the way we use the house – especially with Esme.

The trade-off is making the back bedroom a bit smaller to fit in the new bathroom. And with everything to be chopped and changed so much – including the plumbing and electrics – we plan to have new kitchen units and a new bathroom suite to boot. The ones left by the previous owners are more than a little tired.

Mike's first reaction to our plans is 'why'. 'Why do all these jobs need doing?' he asks. 'Could you find ways of making changes that don't involve a complete refit? In the bathroom, for example, does the whole suite need replacing? And couldn't you update the kitchen by simply replacing the work surfaces or changing cupboard doors? Knocking down a wall and installing a new kitchen and bathroom are all fairly major projects, which will involve a lot of work, create a fair bit of waste and demand lots of new material. But taking an environmentally friendly approach is possible, given a bit of careful thought about what really needs to be done and what materials are going to be used.'

Two main themes soon quickly emerge: the toxicity of the materials used, and their sustainability. The principal concern is what materials to use in the kitchen. Hannah stresses that it's important to research what materials are used to make the kitchen units.

'Timber is the second most widely traded commodity,' she says. 'Consequently, half the world's original forest cover has been destroyed in the past forty years, and continues to be depleted at a rate of twenty-six hectares a minute. Every day, rainforest species are lost for ever. Britain's wood consumption is 60–70 per cent higher than what it produces. Therefore, after reclaimed wood – 500,000 tonnes of re-usable wood is thrown away each year in Britain – the next best option is UK-grown timber certified by the Forestry Stewardship Council. Chipboard and MDF tend to be made of waste wood, but low-formaldehyde versions are better due to the air pollution these materials cause. Despite the problems with timber, though, it is the best environmental choice for many jobs. Plastics are highly energy intensive compared to timber and largely un-recyclable.'

That's a relief, as Jane and I are having trouble imagining

a solid-plastic kitchen. But the thought of a solid-wood kitchen isn't too appealing either, given the expense.

Mike puts us at ease by explaining that the FSC does not just certify fancy hand-crafted wooden kitchens, but also items such as flat-pack kitchen units, work surfaces and doors. 'The FSC logo is the only way of guaranteeing that your wood is from a well-managed forest,' he says. 'And if there is a choice, local FSC timber is always better, as shipping timber around the planet contributes to climate change. Look at www.goodwoodguide.com before you buy.'

Renée asks us what flooring we intend to use. 'If you want a timber floor, think of bamboo, which grows quickly, instead of hardwoods that take years and years to establish. There are also companies such as Crucial Trading and Fired Earth that stock natural flooring like coir matting, cork floors and terracotta tiles.'

Jane's expression suggests she has probably already ruled out using either coir matting or bamboo on our floors. She's more concerned about the auditors' talk of toxicity in the home. 'Paints and varnishes can contain high levels of volatile organic compounds (VOCs), which contribute to ground-level ozone and have been linked to allergic reactions,' says Mike. 'It is possible to avoid VOCs by opting for water-based paints, and most paint manufacturers now produce low-VOC products as well.'

But Hannah isn't so sure that we should choose such paints. 'Water-based synthetic paints can contain harmful chemicals like alkyl phenols and vinyl resins, even if they are low in VOCs. The indoor environment can be ten times more polluted than outside due to a cocktail of off-gassing toxic chemicals used in many DIY products. According to the World Health Organization, professional painters and decorators face a 40 per cent higher than average risk of lung cancer. The production of a tonne of ordinary paint also results in ten tonnes of waste, much of it toxic. And all this is exacerbated by the fact that we tend to buy more DIY equipment than we need. For example, up to a quarter of all paint sold is never used and an electric drill gets fifteen minutes of use, on average, in its lifetime.'

'Look for natural alternatives,' says Renée. 'Nutshell and Lakeland produce natural and organic paints and stains with plant-based dyes, solvents and fillers. In general, watch DIY products such as glues, fixings and other general building materials. Plywood, for example, can contain formaldehyde – a "probable carcinogen", according to the International Agency for Research on Cancer. Instead go for soft-, medium- or hard-board that has no synthetic glues.'

Renée had recommended that we find a builder through the Association for Environment-Conscious Building. We duly looked up AECB builders in the London area but there were only three, all of them a long way from where we live.

Furthermore, we'd already gone to the trouble of finding Dave, a builder who had been personally recommended; we'd seen his handiwork in another house, and he had provided a quote that we were happy with. Our view was that rather than going back to square one and suffering the headache of sour-cing a new builder, we should instead try to guide the one we were already happy with towards using the materials and techniques recommended by the auditors.

But Dave just laughed when we repeated what the auditors had told us. 'That's going to cost you a fortune,' he said gleefully. 'But if that's what you want, that's what we'll do.'

So it's with more than a little trepidation that we watch his van finally pulling up outside our house, loaded with burly men and an arsenal of power tools. It remains to be seen whether letting them loose on our home for the next six weeks will prove to be the right choice.

9

'YOU'RE GOING TO HAVE TO get a car now, aren't you?'
This was the general response to the news that Jane and
I were expecting a baby. Well, other than 'congratulations',
obviously. For ten years we had proudly managed without a
car, but how could we possibly continue to do so with a baby
and all the subsequent kit to carry around?

Not very well, we thought at first. The more people raised
the subject, the more we doubted whether we would be able to
continue to be car-free. We were plagued by the thought of
struggling to fold up a pushchair on the bus as fellow
passengers cast us disapproving looks (as we had done
ourselves in those now distant why-the-hell-would-anyone-
possibly-want-to-have-kids days).

But then we would think again of the cost and hassle of
keeping a car in London. After all, that was why we didn't have
one – not for any reason so lofty as wanting to save the planet
or boycott the oil economy.

But once Esme was born, everything changed – just as all the
sages had predicted. My moment of epiphany came as I was
watching TV one night just after her birth. I noticed that

certain adverts were attracting my attention all of a sudden and it truly dawned on me that I was now a parent. Jane may well have noticed this fact after delivering seven pounds of baby girl, but it took a Renault Espace advert to ignite my spark plugs.

Lying on the sofa that night with Esme asleep on my chest, I was instinctively drawn to the sight of a cavernous people-carrier being loaded up with kids, parents, pushchairs and shopping, and thought, 'We *really* need one of those.' I'd slipped effortlessly into that demographic category so prized by marketers – the aspirational parent. It was now my raison d'être to provide and protect – and transport my family around with ABS braking, air bags and roo bars.

By the time the auditors arrived, we had already started to consider how much we could afford to spend on a car and what type would be best for our needs. It was only due to a combination of budgetary concerns (we were broke) and higher priorities at weekends (there was little time to meander around showrooms – we had nappies to change) that we didn't own one already.

At last, some praise. 'You score lots of brownie points for belonging to the 37 per cent of London households that don't own a car,' says Mike, who then asks us how we travel to work. By train or Tube, I say.

'Crucially, you don't join the rush hour by driving to work. Travelling by train is far more efficient in terms of pollution caused per traveller. All motorized transport produces carbon dioxide, but trains are much more energy-efficient than cars. Indeed, carbon-dioxide emissions per train passenger are on average half those of car users.'

Hannah is also really pleased to hear that we don't own a car. 'Despite being the primary mode of transport for only 6 per cent of the world's population, here in the UK cars account for four-fifths of the total distance travelled and dominate one-third of the land area of our cities,' she says. 'Road traffic, which grew by 73 per cent between 1980 and 2002, is a major source of air and water pollution, habitat destruction and global warming. Twenty-four thousand early deaths a year are attributed to poor air quality in Britain's cities, and there are road deaths equivalent to two Paddington rail crashes a week. Transport as a whole now accounts for 26 per cent of UK greenhouse gas emissions.'

I'm starting to feel guilty about my recent fantasies about becoming a petrol-head. I confess that we feel under extreme pressure to buy a car now that we've had a baby. I ask the auditors whether they've ever tried going on the Tube or bus with a pram loaded with a bawling baby, nappy-change bag and shopping. You're going to have to work hard to convince us, I say, that we should continue life without a car.

Hannah, true to form, plays the shame card, trying to disgust us with information about what the multinational car manufacturers are up to besides manufacturing cars. 'Here are just a few examples: Toshiba has been heavily involved in nuclear power, Nissan in agrochemicals, Fuji, who make Subaru cars, with military aircraft. Mitsubishi, another significant arms company, is also involved in nuclear power. In my view, our dependence on the internal combustion engine fuels international conflict and environmental concerns.'

I agree that it all sounds despicable, but say that I still can't see any alternative to getting a car – especially if we were to have another child. No matter how much we try to resist the temptation, won't we ultimately be forced to buy a car?

Here the auditors' views divide sharply. Mike urges us to continue to strive at all costs for a car-free existence – even to the point of cutting down on trips to the supermarket to avoid the need to get a cab home afterwards. 'With careful planning, you could arrange trips around public transport and totally avoid the need to use a car,' he says.

But Renée says we should just do what we feel is right. 'This is an area I don't get particularly whipped up about. I don't have a car because I live in London and really don't need one. I tend to walk a lot and take buses as well as the occasional taxi. I shop locally simply because it's easier. But it's hard to get people to change the way they get around. I believe that I can get people excited about organic food, for example, but getting someone to give up their 4×4 or family saloon is another matter entirely. At my shops, we use bicycles for our local deliveries. Of course, it's better generally to use a bicycle, Tube or train rather than drive. But some people use a combination. As an American living and working in the UK, I have to say that you are lucky in this country, and in Europe, to have such great train and Tube systems. You can actually live here without a car, which in America is unimaginable.'

Hannah suggests that we could try borrowing a friend's

car occasionally, rather than getting our own. If we do decide to buy a car, she suggests we consider various options. 'Co-ownership of a second-hand car would be the best option. A quarter of the environmental pollution and 20 per cent of a car's lifetime energy expenditure occurs during manufacture. Environmental Transport Association inspectors can advise on the enviro-credentials of used vehicles, looking for features such as catalytic converters, low engine capacity and power, high miles per gallon and low top speed. You could also look into alternative fuels such as LPG, bio-diesel and simple DIY vegetable oil. And you should certainly steer clear of gas-guzzling SUVs. If a household owning an SUV exchanged it for a family saloon that did forty miles to the gallon, in one year they'd save as much energy as recycling all their glass bottles for four hundred years.'

Cost is still the overriding factor that has so far prevented us from taking the plunge. We don't dispute what the auditors were saying about cars – that they're evil incarnate and will bring the world crashing and burning to its knees – but the bottom line is they are bloody handy for popping down to B&Q at the weekend. Both Jane and I have always felt quite smug about not having a car, but now with Esme on the scene it just doesn't seem an option any more.

It's not so hard for me. I commute to work on the train each morning and don't much mind walking or cabbing it around when required. And there has never been any question of us getting a car in order to commute to work. Everything –

parking fines, the congestion charge, bus lanes – is, rightly in my view, stacked against cars and in favour of public transport in London. But Jane is still on maternity leave and constantly bemoans the fact that she feels stuck at home without a car, and can't easily take Esme to the indoor swimming pool a few miles away or to see friends living on the other side of town. When she has gone on the bus she has had to experience un-sympathetic drivers and even aggressive other mothers. And a car would certainly make weekends easier when it comes to going out with Esme and shopping.

We've been thinking hard about what we find convenient and what we find a hassle. Take walking, for example. Is it really a hassle to spend an hour walking to the shops? Or is that actually enjoyable? Given that most of the streets around us are awash with choking exhaust fumes and people who'd rather barge past you than kindly offer to make way for your pushchair, it's easy to see which answer we currently err towards. It's only the big OD on our bank statement that's preventing us from spending our Sundays buffing up bumpers with the rest of them on our street.

But even if we had the money right now, we would still find a car hard to justify financially. If we spend £20 each week on taxis (which we hardly ever do), a car still works out much more expensive over the course of a year. Our annual taxi bill, we generously estimate, would be about £1,000, but buying a car and then taxing it, MOT-ing it, insuring it, repairing it, parking it and filling it with fuel each week would very quickly add up to much more.

Mike's argument that we should avoid *all* car use, be it our own or taxis, seems a valiant ideal, but completely impractical with Esme. Public transport is a chore at the best of times, but to cut out taxis altogether would feel like self-flagellation. However, we have decided to continue without a car for as long as possible (a second child would probably tip the balance), relying instead on a combination of public transport and taxis.

To ease the burden a little, we have now started ordering some of our shopping online, such as tins and dry store-cupboard goods, and having them delivered. The delivery charge is almost exactly the same as the taxi fare home. And having the organic box from Abel & Cole delivered each Friday is making a big difference, too.

We are also trying to plan ahead a lot more and get lifts when we can. And as Hannah suggested, we've gone grovelling to friends to ask whether they would mind lending us their car, should we ever need it for a local shopping trip. They have willingly agreed, so long as we cover the insurance extension, but in reality we might find this arrangement slightly awkward. 'Excuse me, can we borrow your car again this weekend?' is quite an embarrassing request to make on a regular basis.

There is one surprising consequence of the auditors' anti-car lecture: we've become more resentful towards drivers. I'm still struggling to work out whether it's because we're subconsciously envious of them, or whether we are morphing into true eco-warriors; either way, we have started to scowl at drivers in the street if they speed past zebra crossings without stopping or accelerate aggressively in residential areas. Jane is taking down registration numbers after discovering in the Highway Code that it's forbidden not to stop for pedestrians at a zebra crossing. I even found myself walking purposely slowly across a crossing the other day, just to prove to the waiting drivers that pedestrians are entitled to use roads, too. It's about as close as I've ever got to using direct action as a protest.

It doesn't fill me with pride, though. Despising one group of people surely isn't what ethical living is all about? Especially when they make up the vast bulk of the country's population. It's certainly not the best way to make friends and influence people. No one likes a Smart-car Alec – not in the circles we know, at least. But some people out there are proving that a car-free life with kids is possible – even if only just:

> My husband and I chose not to have a car in London in the 1960s and, even after the births of our three children, in the 1970s we continued without a car. We travelled by bus and train, and hired cars for weekends away, and taxis for nights out. As a result, we were better off than many of our friends on similar incomes and could afford excellent holidays. Our children were fairly independent as a result and being ferried around was unknown to them. My husband would still happily be car-less, but I succumbed to temptation when our youngest was five, mainly to avoid inconvenient commuting between buildings in the school where I taught. Good luck!
>
> Bron Vinson

It is definitely possible to live with two young children and without a car. My parents managed it just fine. We always walked to school (a good mile or so away) and back, and took buses/trains the rest of the time – even to our Saturday music school with our violins, cellos (yes!), recorders, music stands, lunches . . . I'm now a cellist and still don't have a car – nor do I plan to get one. I think it's much healthier for kids (and you) to get used to walking and using public transport – they get some exercise and interact with the real world. If going to the supermarket is too much of a problem, get the stuff delivered to you; even smaller chains, not to mention my local independent healthfood shop, do home delivery these days. So what's the problem?

Nina D

Leo,

Just hire a car occasionally, this is what I do. I save up the big shopping trips (B&Q, Ikea) and hire a car every couple of months or when I need to do some sightseeing.

The joy is having a range of cars to drive (but not own), possibly hiring a car you've always wanted to try, and if you shop around you get some really great deals.

Keep up the good work, but don't buy a car.

> You'll save thousands you can spend/invest in
> other ways. Plus you'll get bloody lazy.
>
> Dave

All this sounds fine in practice, but we're beginning to realize just how much effort it can be trying to lug a kid (let alone kids) around from pillar to post without a car – as our holiday to Italy proved. That's why letters such as Andrew's below sound much more appealing than the ones above:

> Despite what some self-righteous non-car-owners
> suggest, owning a car is not a problem. In fact it
> can be actually better for the planet for a careful
> owner to extend the life of an old car, thereby
> discouraging production of a new one. Friends
> used to tease me about owning a car but still
> using public transport. They said it cost more per
> mile to run by not using it all the time! Have a car
> because it makes sense, but still decide on how to
> make individual journeys. After the novelty wore
> off I soon realized that a monthly travelcard was
> cheaper, nearly as quick and often a more relaxing
> way of commuting across Birmingham. My car was
> for other uses.
>   You say you can't afford a car. I could have said
> that, having never had a reasonable income, but I
> have always had decent cars. Do not even think
> that a new car is a good idea. Possible faults are
> waiting to be discovered, huge dealer servicing

costs are forced on you in the warranty period and you suffer massive depreciation. I am very choosy about my cars and have some very specific and fairly unusual needs. If you are less choosy, you can get an excellent car for under £1,000. (The price bracket many people buy into, e.g. first car for son or daughter, is around £3,000 and can actually carry more risks than a cheaper car.) The secret is, buy old – old enough to show that it has been well cared for. A reliable (Japanese, basically!) car, circa ten years old, with only one or two owners, sold privately with full service history, is where the bargains lie. A mileage approaching 100,000 should not worry. The myth is that cars become unreliable at a certain age and mileage. This is not really true. It is the fact they are cheap that ends their lives. They tend to be mainly bought by buyers who can't be bothered to service them or who crash them.

Don't think I'm encouraging you to get a car! I'm rather jealous of city dwellers who can have a life without one. In rural Wales, without a car you don't work.

Andrew Currie, Abergynolwyn, Gwynedd

I'm half thinking of contacting Andrew and getting him to help us find a One Careful Owner for under £1,000, but the burden of guilt would be tremendous. I suspect that until we end up having a major row while standing at the bus stop in the rain and finally cave in to temptation, we will make do with public transport, our legs, taxis and the occasional loan of my mum's car.

I choose to go to work by train (or occasionally Tube) because a) it's cheaper than by car, b) it's quicker than by car or bus, c) it's much safer than by bike, and d) I can read the paper. If this choice is also one of the better environmental options then that's just an added bonus.

Just out of interest, Jane and I decide to calculate how many miles on average we were travelling each week on public transport when Jane was at work. We live about five miles from where we each work, so over a five-day week we were clocking up about fifty miles each. With our fortnightly trip to Sainsbury's a couple of miles away and the various extra trips to friends, other shops and the like, it meant that each week we were hulking our 206 bones and 600-plus muscles about fifty-five miles.

Our first task is to work out whether we can reduce this distance through better organization – avoiding two trips when one will do. We soon conclude that, as the bulk of our travel is commuting, this is going to be hard. Working from home, even part-time, isn't really an option, due to company culture – ironic and slightly depressing really, given that we both work with computers and telephones and rarely need to leave our offices on business.

We briefly consider cycling to work – or even walking. If work was a couple of miles away, I would probably cycle – as I have done before in London in the past. But Jane is adamant we don't.

'It's just too dangerous,' she says. 'Esme having her parents alive is far more important than reducing our carbon-dioxide emissions by a tiny fraction. Besides, Lycra doesn't suit you.'

What about walking to work? I propose. It would take well over an hour each way, Jane counters, and would mean walking through some particularly unsavoury areas of London. 'You can walk, but I'm sticking to the train.'

I decide that, on reflection, walking is not really an option. There's not enough time in the day, plus I really do relish the time I get on the train to read. The status quo it is then – despite constant irritants such as regular engineering works, neighbouring passengers' body odour and repeatedly having to endure the muffled basslines of Ibiza Summer Hits compilations.

But I recently chose to act on a bit of advice Mike mentioned to me in passing. Why not, he said, have a 'pollution audit' done to show what detrimental effect cars are having on our health? It might, he added, also show us how best to avoid the omnipresent pollution that we are exposed to, living and working in a busy, dirty city such as London.

Mike recommended I contact Dr Roy Colvile at Imperial College's Department of Environmental Science and Technology. He is the senior lecturer in air-quality management and regularly assesses how exposed a particular location is to 'particulate matter' – that's air pollution to you and me. After asking me questions ranging from whether I tend to sit by the aisle or by the window on the train to work, to whether I habitually burn the toast in the morning or use an aerosol deodorant, Dr Colvile soon had a detailed profile of our family's typical daily movements. He then explained how alternative forms of transport, such as walking or cycling, can expose us to different levels of pollution.

The bad news is that my lifestyle – a daily cycle of sleeping, dressing, eating, commuting, working, eating, working, commuting, eating, and sleeping – is exposing me to, on average, 1,127 micrograms of particulate air pollution each day. And exposure to high levels of particulates, especially PM10s (particles smaller than ten micrometres across), has, I learn, been linked to increased risks of asthma, heart attacks and reduced lung function.

The good news, says Dr Colvile, is that I can do my bit to reduce my family's exposure to pollution. Predictably, perhaps, striving not to add to the three to four million cars that operate within London each year is the most important thing I can do. PM10s are released, in large part, via petrol and diesel exhaust fumes, so it is important to reduce any unnecessary travelling – not just because we create pollution when we travel, but also because we are exposing ourselves to more particulates.

But even if I remain car-free, I am still exposing myself to pollution by commuting each day, he says. Even on the train I am exposed to PM10s – for example, through dust on the seats. Even if I started cycling to work, it is questionable whether wearing a pollution mask would reduce my exposure to pollution.

'Fine particles are able to penetrate very easily through the smallest gap between your face and the mask,' he says. So are all those cyclists in London wearing masks just wasting their time?

It seems so, according to Dr Colvile. I vow to shout that out the next time one cuts me up on the pavement.

There was some encouragement for cyclists, however. 'It has now been proved that cyclists benefit from being able to keep moving at the most polluted spots where other traffic is congested,' he said. 'Though this is to some extent counteracted by the deeper breathing required to cycle vigorously, using parts of the lungs that are not used in sedentary office work. But the main factor determining the amount of pollution inhaled daily is the total time spent per journey. Choice of route can also have a large impact. Of course, if everyone cycled to work, emissions would be less and everyone would inhale less pollution.'

I was also perturbed to learn from Dr Colvile that fine particulates are found in large quantities inside the home too, as I had always thought that exposure to pollution was considerably reduced indoors. Much of it makes its way inside the home through doors and windows, it seems, but it is also created through cooking, log fires, boilers and aerosol deodorants.

Amazingly, Dr Colvile calculated that up to one-fifth of my daily exposure to particulates was actually caused by using a spray-on deodorant each morning. Thank God we've given up the aerosol as this really freaked me out. He also calculated that 12 per cent of my daily exposure to pollution was due to my walk to and from the train station en route to the office or back home – and half of this total was caused by the short wait to cross a busy road near the office.

'Try to wait for as short a time as possible when crossing

roads,' he advised me, 'and try not to run across them, breathing deeply as you do so. Just standing back a short distance from the kerb while you wait can reduce your exposure surprisingly effectively at many locations.'

I asked him what is being done to reduce pollution. There are moves currently afoot in London to create Low Emission Zones which high-polluting vehicles would be restricted from entering, but unfortunately these are still five or more years away. For the first time in my life I get to see a pollution map of Greater London, which clearly illustrates the impact the main road arteries (and, startlingly, Heathrow airport) have on the capital's pollution levels. It all leaves me with an even bigger downer about cars.

It's been a slow process – we've had enough on our plate to be honest, with the wormery, food shopping, our holiday and so on – but we are starting to get more and more conscious about our energy use at home. It's not cold enough yet to be worrying about the heating, but we have started to take note of how much we rely on our gadget- and appliance-filled home.

If a museum is ever looking for items that represent what consumers bought in the 1990s and 2000s, our home would be a perfect starting place. We've got all the big things – dishwasher, washer-dryer, widescreen television, DVD player, video, set-top box, hands-free phone, mobile phones, fancy steam iron, laptop with printer. But we've also got all those non-essential gadgets, particularly for the kitchen. We've got a whole folder full of instruction manuals and receipts that have been collected over the years, just in case.

Having said all that, I don't think we can be classed as overtly wasteful with appliances. Once we have something we want, we don't then dump it for a later model. When we moved, we brought all our appliances with us from our old flat and fitted them into the vacant holes beneath the kitchen worktops. The only thing we didn't bring that wasn't there already was a cooker, so we bought a compact, under-worktop double oven. Incidentally, our kitchen is also home to our rather brutish gas combi-boiler.

The thought of giving all this up is an uncomfortable one. I know some praise the therapeutic potential of washing up, but no one is going to convince me that there's anything to gain by leaning over a sink sporting a pair of Marigolds. Needless to say, therefore, our most treasured kitchen appliance is the dishwasher. We pack it to the brim daily and switch it on when we go to bed, to be lulled to sleep by its comforting hum. Jane believes that life without a dishwasher would be just plain uncivilized.

But a close rival for our affections is the fridge. It's a beast: a kitchen SUV, all gleaming chrome and beefsteak proportions with more storage than our back bedroom.

Surprise, surprise – our fridge attracts the auditors' attention. 'It's well stocked up, Leo,' says Hannah. 'Maximum energy-efficiency is achieved at three-quarters full. However, it is away from the oven and radiator, more than 5cm from the wall and the freezer compartment lies under the fridge, which is the best arrangement in energy terms. I can't see whether the freezer has "Frost Free"

technology – I hope not, as this will use up to 45 per cent
more energy.'

I ask Hannah how else we might refrigerate our food. I
shouldn't have asked. 'The fridge-freezer tends to be a home's
third biggest energy guzzler,' she says. 'A true eco-house might
have no fridge, just a larder and a water-containing pottery
vessel as a cooler.'

Jane's eyes roll. 'But with a weekly shop and expressed
milk for Esme to freeze,' continues Hannah, 'I accept that this
might not be practicable for you, so the next thing I would
ask is how old is your fridge? An energy-efficient fridge-
freezer uses nearly a third of the energy of a ten-year-old
appliance. If there's no pressing need to replace it, regular
defrosting and cleaning of the condenser coils at the back will
aid efficiency. And make sure the fridge temperature is about
3ºC and the freezer around –15ºC – buy a fridge
thermometer.'

Mike is surprisingly positive about our choice of fridge.
'You have bought a modern, energy-efficient one that will
save you money in the long term and reduce your
contribution to climate change.' Feeling buoyed, I tell the
auditors it's made by Liebherr and had an A-rated energy-
efficiency sticker on it when we bought it three years ago.

Mike isn't happy about our dishwasher, though. 'A small
family like yours can't create that much washing up,' he says.
'An old model uses approximately 15p of electricity per cycle
– while a modern energy-efficient appliance, according to the
Energy Saving Trust, will cut this by half. But dishwashers use
a lot of water that has to be treated after use, again using

energy. Washing up only takes ten minutes – especially if you leave the pans to soak. You should give it a try.'

'But we've bought it now,' says Jane. 'Are you saying just get rid of it?'

No, the damage is done, say the auditors, but try using it more sparingly – and stop using those evil dishwasher tablets and rinse aid every time you turn it on.

'The dishwasher won't be such a waste of water and energy if you only use it when full,' says Hannah, 'and if you dunk plates or scrape pots first to avoid the pre-wash cycle. Use eco-friendly phosphate- and chlorine-free tablets, cutting the dose until you find the minimum needed. Employ the "light wash" option, check that the water comes from your heating system rather than being heated by the appliance, and open the door to air-dry the dishes.'

Hannah isn't happy about the name on the dishwasher door, though. Or the ones on our oven door and on the washing machine. 'It's a shame the dishwasher is made by Neff. Its parent company Siemens has supplied components to the nuclear power and defence industries, and the controversial Three Gorges dam project in China.' Hannah explains that Bosch, who made our washer-dryer, is also part of Siemens. She adds that when we come to buy new appliances – hopefully a while yet as most of ours are relatively new – we should pay careful attention to the brands and investigate them first.

We both felt somewhat confused by what the auditors had to say about the contents of our kitchen. What exactly were they proposing? To throw everything away that uses energy? To stop using everything, but leave it in our home so as not to clog the landfill up further? One thing that was clear was that we must try to minimize use of our gadgets and appliances.

As with the washing machine, it hasn't been too hard to adjust our use of the dishwasher. We are now washing full loads on the half-load setting (or the 'eco' setting, as it ironically says on the machine) and stop the cycle before it begins its long and rather wasteful drying process at the end. I try to remember to catch the cycle at the right moment (it's a shame the manufacturers didn't build in a facility to help us do this), when the load is still wet but extremely hot. Within ten minutes or so the whole load has air dried. OK, it's no longer steam cleaned to the same hygienic standards as before, and we have noticed that the new tablets leave a funny smell in the machine over time, but washing up in the sink and drying things with a manky old tea-towel is hardly any better, is it?

This letter has made us feel a bit better about having a dishwasher too:

We had resisted many attempts from family members to purchase a dishwasher. We thought them a waste of energy and resources. However, we have changed our minds:
1. We use a quarter of the water we used to. We had to run a bowlful of cold water before the hot water reached our sink at a temperature hot enough to wash dishes. Whilst the bowl of cold was saved in our rainwater barrel it still seemed a

waste. We used to wash at least four or five times
a day, sometimes more.
2. Each bowl of water needed washing-up liquid –
four or five dosages each day must add up to more
(in environmental terms) than dishwasher
tablets/rinse aid.

I often wondered why, when we went on holiday,
the Swiss used dishwashers – economical water
usage must have been the reason.

Peter and Shelagh Whitby

In the spirit of reducing the amount of harsh, synthetic
chemicals in our home, we have also changed our brand of
dishwasher tablets. We have always bought Sainsbury's own-
brand lemon tablets and rinse aid, but we started using Ecover
alternatives because they were sitting right there next to
Sainsbury's ones on the shelf. They are also available to buy
from the Abel & Cole box scheme, which is handy, too.
Assuming before we tried them that everything, particularly
our glasses, would come out less sparkly, we are delighted that
there are actually fewer minute glass scratches with the Ecover
tablets. Fewer abrasive chemicals, perhaps?

Price, as ever, is an issue, though. It was costing us £4.49 to
buy a box of 44 Sainsbury's lemon dishwasher tablets (10.2p
per tablet). These would last about a month, if not longer. In
contrast, a box of 25 Ecover tablets costs £3.99 (15.9p per
tablet). But as with most of our new purchases, we've had to
swallow our instinctive hunt-the-bargain urges and look to the

label's small print for reassurance. On the Sainsbury's tablets, it says: 'More than 30 per cent phosphate, 5–15 per cent sodium disilicate, oxygen-based bleaching agent, less than 5 per cent non-ionic surfactants, contains enzymes.' Ecover's ingredients are listed as follows: '5–15 per cent oxygen chlorine-free bleach. Less than 5 per cent plant-based non-ionic tensio-active surfactants, enzymes (guaranteed non gmo). Other ingredients: salts, silicate, citrate, polypeptides, plant-based bleach activator, plant-based fragrance.' Not being a scientist, I don't claim to know the subtle differences between these two lists of ingredients, but I instinctively know which one I would rather wash my dishes in – and ultimately release into the sewers.

Elsewhere in the kitchen, though, we feel there is little we can do to change our habits. There are a handful of things we try to reduce our energy use, though.

Upon Hannah's advice, we've now bought a fridge thermometer. Our fridge, like most models, has a thermostat that ranges from 1 (fairly cool) to 7 (near freezing), but it doesn't give an accurate temperature reading. The thermometer has enabled us to maintain a constant 5°C without relying on guesstimates (3°C seemed to be too cool).

We've been feeling quite pleased with these changes, but I've had one letter on the subject of fridges that could only make us chuckle:

Do large amounts of vegetables, rice, whatever, in a pressure cooker, and reheat on the following days in a microwave. It saves energy, and the food stays surprisingly fresh in a pressure cooker with the lid on. I have lived without a fridge for sixteen years now (which in itself must have saved a few thousand kilowatts of electricity), and have not had any upset tummy by doing this.

Cheers, John

John doesn't say where he lives – it could be somewhere as cold as Vladivostok for all I know – but I can't help thinking that having no fridge in your life might be taking things just a bit too far.

Despite all our efforts, the energy we use to cook has increased significantly since we've started weaning Esme. It seems we never stop steaming fruit and vegetables. We hope this is a temporary arrangement (more experienced parents, feel free to laugh now), and that as Esme's meals begin to resemble ours and we can all eat similar foods, we will be able to start cooking our meals together to save energy.

I've also started to use our slow cooker more often. It only uses as much power as a light bulb, according to the instructions. I'd forgotten how convenient it can be for when you're knackered at the end of the day, after work or looking after a baby. You just stick all the ingredients for a stew, or whatnot, in the cooker in the morning, turn it on, and by supper time it's ready.

Our new laundry routine is still ticking along nicely. We've recently vowed to minimize further our use of the tumble dryer – not that we used it much anyway, tending to favour our good old clothes horse or, weather permitting, the line outside. But we now only ever use it if we really need something urgently, such as a clean babygro for Esme before she goes to bed, a state of disorganization we sink to maybe once a month or less. I enjoyed a letter sent to me from China on this subject. It has really made me think about how used we've all become to our appliances. Maybe living without a fridge, as John has proposed, isn't such a crank idea. (I still don't dare raise this with Jane, though. I may be fanciful, but I'm not stupid.)

I live in a city, Beijing, whose skyscape is normally like something out of a *Star Trek* episode. Grey. Blue-grey. Dark grey. Not that London foggy grey, but unnatural bizarre grey. We get about twenty-five days of truly blue sky a year in a city that used to have wonderful air. In China, washing machines are still pretty new, but now standard. Dryers are still unheard of. But, as an American, I dearly miss them. But for six years I've done without and hang my clothes to dry. This takes more time and effort than just sticking them in a dryer, but I realized an unexpected reward: it makes me extremely conscious of the weather and air quality. A blue-sky day in Beijing is a good day for laundry. Rain is bad, of course. But everything in between sucks too – those days when you can't really see a cloud or any natural colour. So when that yucky Third World Grey takes over the sky, it gives me pause: I think, 'Oh, well, these pants won't be dry by sundown on a day like this, so I'll just have to wait

till tomorrow morning to do the wash.' I can feel
the degradation of the larger environment through
my pants.

Chris Barden

One of the vices that I'm particularly ashamed of is my love of
electrical gadgets. If it boasts 'new features', 'latest technology',
or 'upgraded' on the packaging then tear me away at your peril.
If Jane didn't remind me that we have a mortgage to pay and a
child to feed, then I fear all our disposable income would be
funnelled into my gadget habit. I don't burgle houses or turn
tricks – it's not that bad – but I have to be restrained when we're
passing a Dixons or PC World. Jane won't let me near
Tottenham Court Road.

I haven't got it quite as bad as some people I know – I don't
recite Sony model numbers in my sleep – but I do get all
twitchy if I know a new product or technology is on the market
that I haven't bought, or at least handled.

A bad gadget habit is usually fuelled by an above-average
interest in music and films, and I'm guilty on this count too. To
service this interest we have a widescreen TV, a DVD player,
CD players in three rooms, radios in two more, and a master
hi-fi system. For those of you who haven't drifted off to sleep
yet, I also have an iPod and an iPaq pocket PC, both of which
require our laptop to operate.

So, given that we both work in front of computers, we spend
an awful lot of time looking at screens, quite apart from keeping the makers of four-gang extension cables in business.

Hannah has been scribbling down the names of the manufacturers of all the electrical items she's seen in our house. She disdainfully reads out her long list of well-known brand names, then looks up at us. 'One of the major concerns about the electronics sector for me is the number of companies devoting major resources to lobbying for the free-trade neo-liberal agenda – typified by GATT, NAFTA and the like – and against attempts to make their industry more accountable for its social and environmental impacts. It is an industry characterized by short-term thinking, intentional rapid obsolescence and little regard for worker health and safety, union rights or the environment.'

Hannah adds that many electronics companies contract out labour to sweatshop-style factories wherever it is 'economically preferential' with regard to wage costs, tax and enforcement of health, safety and environmental regulations. Workers are commonly found to have elevated rates of health problems, including conditions such as cancer, miscarriage and birth defects. She says that a Mexican economist has commented that tripling wages to just two dollars an hour for workers in the 'maquiladoras' – Mexican assembly plants generally owned by non-Mexican corporations that manufacture goods for export to the US – would vastly improve living standards, while still providing companies with the multi-million-dollar savings in labour costs they crave.

Jane and I are somewhat stunned at the hidden truth behind our gadgets and gizmos. But then Mike compounds things by raising the issue of their impact on the environment.

'Televisions and computer monitors pose a particular disposal problem because the cathode ray monitors contain lead oxide and barium. The good news is that a new European directive means that producers will have to organize free take-back for a range of appliances including televisions, as well as stereos, toasters and washing machines. This is important as some 120,000 tonnes of glass from television cathode ray tubes alone are scrapped in the UK every year. And some 15 million mobile-phone handsets are replaced each year, too.'

But the bad news is that our electrical goods are often treated and made with extremely toxic materials. 'Many are treated with brominated flame retardants,' says Mike, 'which are known to build up in the body and affect the hormone system. Increasingly, electronic waste is being exported to developing countries for sham recycling operations, often where there is little environmental or safety protection. This means communities overseas are suffering from the ill effects of dealing with hazardous components from our electrical goods as we move on to newer, more exciting models.'

Hannah picks up on this point too. 'Electronics is the world's largest and fastest growing manufacturing industry, and "e-waste" is the fastest growing waste stream in the industrialized world. Manufacture itself is highly polluting, with each circuit board producing ten times its weight in hazardous waste. The 315 million computers expected to have become obsolete by the end of this year represent more than a billion pounds of lead, four billion pounds of plastic, and hundreds of thousands of tonnes of other toxic materials. In the UK, around two million TVs are discarded annually, many ending up in landfill. The lead in their cathode ray tubes (aside from the other toxic materials like zinc, cadmium and phosphor) has acute and chronic effects on plants and wildlife if it leaches into groundwater.'

Jane turns to Renée and asks if she has anything to say, as she's been quiet until now.

'This isn't really my area, to be honest, so I spoke to Dan Morrell, the founder of Future Forests, the "carbon neutral" advocates, beforehand to ask him for advice about how to reduce the negative impact of our electrical goods. He said the first step was to consider the power they use. Just by turning off our TVs, stereos and DVD players rather than leaving them on standby we would save between 10 per cent and 60 per cent of the electricity we use. Some even say that if we all did this each night we could shut off about three power stations in the UK. You should also turn off your mobile-phone recharger once the phone is charged rather than leaving it on indefinitely, otherwise 95 per cent of a recharger's electricity consumption is wasted.'

'TV energy efficiency has been improving,' adds Hannah, 'but the rise of digital TV is undermining this because decoders left on constant standby will increase household electricity use by 7 per cent by 2010.'

What do you want us to do? we ask. Give up watching TV?

'Why not?' says Mike. 'Our appetite for electronic gadgets can have a negative impact on our family and community

life. Time spent with eyes glued to the screen of your
television or computer is time not spent on potentially more
fulfilling activities. Trying to avoid buying electrical goods is
also an important step. When you do need them, buying the
most energy-efficient model is not only better for the planet,
but in the long run is better for your pocket as well. Low-
energy items do exist – including low-energy computers.
They may not be as powerful as some other models, but they
will still deal quite adequately with most home needs. Why
not invest in a wind-up radio for starters?'

'And make sure you recycle any old mobile phones,' says
Renée. 'Many people don't realize that up to 90 per cent of a
mobile phone can be recycled. Other things to remember:
when buying computers look for an LCD monitor that is
compatible with all standard personal computers. A 38cm
LCD screen uses much less energy than a standard cathode
ray tube – typically 18 watts as opposed to about 200.'

LCD screens last, on average, three years longer too, adds
Hannah. She also points out that we should look out for
'eco-labels' if buying products such as TVs as they can
indicate better recyclability, fewer bio-accumulative compounds
and a free 'take-back' scheme by the manufacturers.

'Whoa, whoa, whoa, let's not be too rash here.' My reaction to
Jane's suggestion that we follow Mike's advice and try to live
without television, CD players, radios and the like is un-
equivocal. Being the bookworm of the family, Jane is much
keener than me. She also relishes the prospect of ridding our
lives of the tyranny of remote controls once and for all.

But I argue that we should just try it out for a while first. We haven't thought this through properly, I plead. How am I going to watch *Football Focus* without a TV? Jane hardballs, saying that to do this properly we have to enter into the spirit of things. I think she's enjoying this reversal of fortunes.

With more than a little desperation, I play my last card. 'But how are you going to watch *Sex and the City*?'

Pause. 'OK, let's try it for a week. But I mean it, no gadgets.'

Our experiment starts off well. After supper on the first night we sit down to a game of Scrabble (at this point I would normally sink into the sofa, remote in hand, never to rise again until bedtime). Even though we argue for nearly ten minutes about the legitimacy of the verb 'to hoover', we notice two positive things about the evening: it seems much longer without hours spent in front of the box, and we spend longer talking to each other. Which can't be a bad thing. I think.

It does seem odd, though, without any background noise from the television, radio or CD player. I have a real itch to switch on the news. By the third or fourth day it's starting to feel as if we're both trapped in some kind of Edwardian melodrama. 'What shall we do tonight, dear? Play gin rummy again?'

But we do find ourselves getting round to those chores that have been backing up for months, such as putting holiday photographs into albums and sorting out our paperwork. One night we draw up a list of the pros and cons of watching television. On the plus side, we get as far as 'it's educational' and 'it's entertaining' before we draw a blank. I still maintain, despite Jane's objections, that television has taught me many things I would not have learned otherwise. (After all, I can still remember much of what Norris McWhirter told me on *Record Breakers*.) But it's the hours of dross we watch that are hard to justify. And all those adverts, too. Jane loves adverts and has been known to flick channels to watch them, whereas I will always turn over as soon as the adverts start – hence the warring over the remote control. But we both seem to be managing fine without someone telling us every five minutes that their shampoo contains Ceramide R.

Throughout the trial, though, I do *really* miss my television – much more than I thought I would. I realize just how large a part it plays in our lives. In fact, the only time we are ever away from it is on holiday, and sitting at home for a week without putting it on is a real challenge. Esme is too young at the moment to gain anything from television, but we will need to be careful in the future to make sure we don't just plonk her in front of it for long stretches. We're not too sure how long this lofty aim is realistically going to last, but we both agree that we should keep her away from TV as long as we can. Jane never has the television on during the day and is adamant that Esme doesn't watch it. Sticking her in front of *Tellytubbies* is incredibly tempting sometimes, but we've already had one bad experience when she was with other children when she just sat there totally transfixed by them. Her reaction was quite unnerving; for hours afterwards she seemed to be trying to say 'Ubby, Ubby,' although in retrospect it was probably just wind. We'd been trying our best to get her to say 'Mummy' or 'Daddy', but all she could think of was Laa-Laa and Po. They're little more than crack cocaine for kids, in my view. OK, I'm probably beginning to show classic withdrawal symptoms now, but you know what I mean.

It's good to see that others have come to similar conclusions, even if they do have their own unique ideas about how best to suppress the influence of TV.

> I particularly enjoy watching ads, and regard them as essentially providing a free service in what to avoid.
>
> Jim (a single forty-eight-year-old living in a local-authority flat on Tyneside)

> I am not sure if it applies so much in the UK, but as an American I have found that refusing to own or watch a television for the last nine years has made for a dramatic improvement in my lifestyle and (I think) intelligence. It saves a load on electricity, too.
>
> The downside is that I have a nagging fear that I may be on 'Ashcroft's List'. Choosing to remain unplugged from the Borg collective (watched plenty of *Star Trek* in high school) may make me a dangerous enemy of the state, capable of thinking for himself without the help of Fox News.
>
> Good luck!
>
> Brian Sinicki, Laramie, Wyoming

OK, Brian, I do fear for you a little, but I get your point. To go nine years without TV is some achievement. I'm afraid we've – me much more than Jane, admittedly – now started to slip a little and are back to watching the telly again, albeit a lot less. We've vowed to cut the junk, though. No more vegging out in front of dross. What we can't quite work out is whether *EastEnders* classifies as dross. Is it mind-numbing pap, or important cultural and social commentary?

Television is one thing, but we both find cutting CD players and radio from our lives a little pointless. We can't see the harm in playing music around the house, but appreciate the auditors' point about how much energy all our gadgets use up, especially while on standby, so we have started to make a real effort to switch everything off at night. We haven't quite resolved what to do with the digital TV set-top box, video player and radio in the kitchen, which all need to be re-tuned when the power goes. It feels as though the clocks have gone back every morning, going round the house resetting everything, and after a few days of doing this we give up. But we have completely given up leaving the television and computer on standby.

There is one new gadget that we feel we really need to buy – a new computer. (What do you think I'm writing this on now?) We've had the same old laptop for years – nearly a decade, in fact – and it is becoming a liability. It strains and chugs when executing even the simplest of commands.

We dismiss the idea of not having a computer at home at all, as we both need to work at home from time to time. I investigate just having it upgraded but the cost is almost twice that of buying a new PC and I can't justify the expenditure, so with the auditors' words ringing loudly in my ears I vow to source a computer that meets as many of their criteria as possible – i.e., it is future-proof, energy efficient, made by a firm that isn't involved in unethical practices, and contains as few toxic materials as possible.

I start my research by looking into buying a second-hand re-conditioned computer, but despite my eagerness, none of the machines pack enough punch to last more than a couple of years, whereas I'm banking on finding a machine that will last five years or more. I make a list of all my needs – word processing, running spreadsheets, accessing the internet and email, managing my iPod and iPaq, printing and storing basic digital-camera images. I rule out playing games and running memory-hungry image and video packages. I therefore don't need an all-singing, all-dancing multi-media beast, rather a no-frills machine, but one with a powerful engine that includes a good processor, ample storage and plenty of memory. This way it should remain capable of handling most of my needs for the next few years with ease.

Hannah has told me since the audit that *Ethical Consumer* positively rates only a handful of computer manufacturers across its range of ethical criteria. These include Evesham, Mesh and Viglen, so I restrict myself to these brands, even if I do almost choke swallowing my hunt-the-bargain instinct.

I'm particularly keen to find a machine that boasts the TCO'99 standard, which, Hannah told me, is managed by a Swedish office-workers union and ensures that many heavy metals, brominated flame retardants and PVC are banned from computer parts, particularly monitors. It also guarantees that the item is labelled with details about how it can be recycled. I'm not really thinking that far down the road, but the information should come in handy at some point.

In the end I just plump for a computer that meets as many of my demands as possible. It doesn't perfectly match, but I couldn't really find one that did. It turns out to be an Evesham with a TFT-LCD flat screen with a TCO'99 label, but in all truth there wasn't much in it other than price when compared to the other two firms' products.

Ironically, one of the first emails I receive after taking delivery of the new machine is the one below. It only goes to prove that someone out there is always able to try just that bit harder than you. Make that a lot harder.

> I live and work in central London, cycle everywhere (only very seldom take the Tube or bus), am vegan, eat only organic crops and always consider food miles in my purchasing, purchase almost zero consumer products besides food. In these respects I guess I'm like many of the other people who've written to you.
>
> I'm also an active forager; a member of the Refuse Underground, if you like. A friend was kind enough to tell me a few years ago about some of the gems that are regularly thrown out in London. In particular, computer equipment, which I'm well-versed in and decided to seek out for friends and charities. I started to do my own research and found that there was indeed a lot of valuable stuff

being landfilled daily, and all it took to find was the impetus to seek it out, and the sense to get over the stigma we have about rubbish.

I started an Internet community known as ScavengeUK (http://scavengeuk.mine.nu) where people can talk about and exchange items, ideas and knowledge. I began to find I couldn't resist checking rubbish skips each time I passed one. I started to notice household chattels in my travels. I found I could even get food this way – i.e., leftovers at the end of market days. Even all manner of clothing seemed to be provided to those who had no aversion to picking it up off the pavement and washing it at home. My bicycle trailer is sufficient to carry fairly respectable loads – for instance our four garden chairs, working seventeen-inch monitors, file servers etc.

Obviously, the emphasis for me is not on the accumulation of material things, but on the reduction of waste, on the adventure of doing so, and at the same time on saving myself money (keeping my money out of the predominantly unethical economy), which I intend to use one day to buy land for organic farming. Having said that, finding a working four-slice toaster and a breadmaker at the rubbish tip a month ago was fantastic.

Ashley Hooper

I'm just never going to be like Ashley. Before I would have thought him a crank who has spent too much time in the company of tree-huggers, but I actually admire him greatly now. In fact, I feel quite warmed by the thought that there are people like Ashley out there fighting so hard to swim against the tide. Does that make me a crank too?

10

'I MEAN IT. EITHER THEY GO, OR I GO.'

Jane has issued ultimatums in the past, but this time I think she's really serious. She's standing by the chest of drawers in our bedroom swatting away some fruit flies that have emerged from it. The damn things are everywhere: all over our kitchen, in glasses of wine, the bathroom, even Esme's bedroom. There seems to be no escape from them. But finding fruit flies among her underwear is the final straw for Jane.

The wormery is to blame. I've been in denial for several weeks, but there's no avoiding it now. Each day as I open up the lid to drop in some more scrapings for the worms, a cloud of fruit flies emerges. And the rotten stench is getting so unbearable that I've already moved the wormery away from the back door, over to the far side of the back garden. I've been at a loss to know what to do – the worms won't eat everything I'm giving them, and the food they're leaving is starting to rot – so I've finally called the worm hotline for help.

'Hello, I've got a problem with my worms,' I confess. It's not a line I've used before. 'They've gone off their food.'

'Worms don't go off their food,' says the woman manning

the worm hotline at Wiggly Wigglers. 'They live to eat. Just keep loading up the wormery with food, perhaps adding more fibrous matter, such as egg boxes and newspaper, than you are at the moment. Worms need their food to rot slightly first before they tackle it. Maybe try cutting up what you're giving them, too. They take longer to eat their way through large items such as melon skins and the like. Things to avoid feeding them include too much onion, garlic and citrus-fruit skin. Don't forget that it will take about six months before the wormery reaches maturity. Any more problems just give us a call.'

I thank her and hang up, pausing for a moment to dwell on the fact that I've just rung a worm advice hotline. Is this the kind of thing you admit to friends, or do you keep your worm problems to yourself? Either way, it fills me with a bit more confidence and I head straight away to our recycling box to find some card and paper to cut up to help soak up the moisture that seems to be giving the worms so much grief.

A week later, though, and things haven't improved. Sod's law has it that we've been struck by a weekend-long heatwave and each time I open the lid to the wormery I'm afraid that I will find a mass of gasping habitants, or worse. But to avoid the heat they just seem to burrow down deeper into the casts (the network of minute tunnels they create when feeding and where they lay their eggs). Things have got so desperate that I've started to hit the vermiculture discussion groups online. It's obvious straight away that I am suffering a very common worm problem. Everyone seems to be suggesting the same remedy – less food, more fibre in the form of card and paper, and sanctuary from weather extremes. It seems I've failed my 'reds' and 'dendras' (earthworms and members of the Phylum Annelida, I've now learned from my browsing). In fact, judging by what people have had to say about the state of my worms, I've been so negligent that they should probably be taken into care.

My efforts to salvage the worms have just about staved off the threat of Jane issuing a permanent removal order on them, but I've got no defence against the next trial to test us – the arrival of rats.

The first sighting is made while we are outside eating lunch under our sun umbrella. An old, ragged rat, with a grey mangy tail, suddenly scurries along the decking by the fence, making a dash for the drain by the water butt. I am the only one to notice it, but am so shocked that I foolishly gasp and scream, 'Rat!' Had I been less freaked out and more careful with my words I might have been able to prevent Jane from leaping almost two feet in the air and yelling, 'You see, it's that bloody wormery. Now it's attracting rats.'

What can you say to that? Jane's right – logic suggests that a stinking container of putrefying food waste is, sooner or later, likely to attract all vermin within a mile of the house. In fact, I wouldn't be surprised if all of Lambeth's rats have heard about the bounty that awaits them in our back garden.

In under thirty seconds lunch has been abandoned as we make a dash for inside. I'm then sent back out with the only rat-killing weapon available – a gardening trowel – to do battle with the rodent invader. I admit it now: I'm terrified of rats, and even the need to defend woman and child is not enough to stir me into hunting them down. I poke my head out the door, look quickly around and retreat.

'I think we should call in the professionals,' I say. 'Rats carry disease and I don't think I should expose myself to that risk in case it spreads to Esme.' I start flicking through the telephone directory for the number for Lambeth council's rat catcher. It takes me a while to realize that such people go under the slightly less emotive name of 'pest control' these days.

'Four days?! We've got a young baby in the house. Can't you send someone over to us now? We're desperate.'

'Sorry, the next available appointment is four days.'

My provide-and-protect instinct finally kicks in and I rush out to the hardware store to buy some armoury that should be more up to the job than my trowel. I'm pointed towards a shelf that contains an arsenal of poisons and traps. I contemplate buying the lot, but end up with a rat trap (which is basically a conventional mouse trap, but about three times as big) and some glue traps.

Waiting for the rat man to arrive is agony. We feel like hostages in our own home. Each day we peer out of the back window looking for rats in the garden. But the weather is still unbearably hot and the temptation to be out there in the sun is strong. I venture out every now and again just to check that the traps haven't caught anything.

Then on the third afternoon of waiting we return from the park with Esme to find huge great gouges taken out of all the fruit in our fruit bowl in the kitchen.

'Tell me that's a mouse. Tell me that's a mouse,' says Jane in a panic. I look at the size of the teeth marks in one of the apples. They seem bigger than a mouse, let alone caused by one.

'I'm afraid that has got to be rat.' We are both frozen to the spot. We now have a rat inside the house and it's helping itself to our food.

There's a loud scurrying sound behind the fridge and the rat emerges, darts along the top of our radiator and disappears behind the kitchen units. We sprint upstairs, tightly clutching Esme. Jane immediately calls the council again and explains our dire situation. Mercifully, they say they can get someone round earlier than the original booking. But it will still be tomorrow morning.

I pick up six glue traps and creep tentatively downstairs to lay them all around the kitchen floor. All I can think of doing is trying to lure the rat out of its hole and on to a trap. I then retreat back upstairs and wait.

It only takes ten minutes before the plan works. Suddenly there is a scuffle, followed by the loud screeching and yelping of what I hope is the rat, although it is making enough noise to be a cat. I peer between the banisters, but it's only when I venture to the bottom of the stairs that I can see it. A large brown rat is caught prostrate on a glue trap on our kitchen floor. And it is very much still alive.

As soon as it sees me it desperately tries to wiggle the glue trap it's stuck to under the fridge to safety. But I'm too quick. I've already dashed outside to get the spade. I manage to lever the spade underneath the trap, lift it up and carry it out to the garden, with the rat eyeballing me all the time. It has a look that seems to be saying, 'So then, what the hell are you going to do with me now?' It's a good question – I haven't a clue.

I seem to have three options. Toss it over the back wall on to the derelict ground behind us, put it into the wheelie bin alive, or kill it. I know deep down that I'm going to have to kill it, but despite my innate hatred for this thing, I can't help but think about how cruel that would be. It and its mates (this sprightly young thing clearly isn't the rat I saw outside the other day) have been terrorizing us, but I now seem to have a torrent of compassion running through me. I can see Jane in the window beckoning me to whack it over the head with the spade and be done with it.

I raise the spade above my head, close my eyes and quickly strike down on the rat stuck to the trap below. Thwack! I feel terrible and ashamed, but also relieved that the rat is finally dead. But, like some horror B-movie, it isn't. Its eyes may have popped out of its sockets, but the thing is still desperately gasping for air. A sense of bad karma rushes over me. I quickly strike the spade down on it again, this time even harder. Splat! Rat juice squelches out from underneath the spade and spills on to the garden decking. I now have a properly dead, some-what spatchcocked rat before me. I scoop it up and carry it through the house to dump in the wheelie bin at the front.

The whole episode leaves me feeling disgusted, but I know it had to be done. What else was I supposed to do? Apologize and let it free to run wild again? Put it in a cage and keep it as a pet? I shudder to think what the auditors would have advised. I accept that we're all God's creatures – equal partners on Earth, and all that – but sometimes we just have to look out for ourselves, don't we? There was no way that I was going to allow it any more access to our home. It had already helped itself to our organic apples.

The cavalry arrives somewhat belatedly to the battle. The next morning the rat man from the council pulls up outside in his van to assess the situation and to start laying traps. Jane and I hang on his every word.

'Yep, you've got rats all right,' he says, emerging from the cellar. 'Either they've got in through the garden door being left open, or they dug their way in from a broken sewer pipe. You see, these Victorian houses have shallow foundations and are just built on earth, and rats love to dig so they will often manage to find their way into cellars from cracks in sewers.'

He lays some trays of poison throughout the cellar and in the garden and says he'll return in a couple of weeks to see if the bait has been taken. Like a war hero who's just returned home, I breathlessly recount how I single-handedly saved my family from the rat's clutches. The rat man humours me, but explains how he isn't allowed to rely on the useful ally of the glue trap.

'It's the RSPCA,' he says. 'They won't allow us to use glue traps to catch rodents. The trouble is that when rats get caught they panic, as you saw. If they are, say, trapped alone downstairs in that cellar, they would end up gnawing off their legs in their desperation to escape. You would return home one day to find the trap with four bloody leg stumps on it but no body. The rat would have crawled off to some dark hole where it would die. This is deemed cruel, and so we are only allowed to use poisons. These don't start working for a few days so that the rat – which is an extremely intelligent animal, by the way – doesn't associate the place he ate the poison with danger. The reason for this is that we want the rat to return to its nest and die there, not just keel over immediately. This way all of its family will up and move sticks, thinking there is something wrong with the location they're nesting in.'

It amuses me that even a rat catcher goes by his own ethical code. He's like an executioner choosing the most humane way for his captives to die. But I'm still concerned that our worms are ultimately to blame for our infestation.

I point to the wormery. 'Is that to blame, do you think?'

'No, I don't think so,' he says, hopefully staving off the worms' execution in the process. 'A rat could get into that, but you would see teeth marks on its plastic base if it had. No, I think it's your garden decking, to be honest. Rats love decking as it provides sanctuary to them. They can dig and run around freely under there without being disturbed. They don't tell you that on the garden makeover shows, do they?' He chuckles, before stepping out the front door. As he gets into his van he shouts back to me, 'By the way, don't put dead rats in the wheelie bin. You should bury them if you can, to stop the spread of disease.'

Jane and I find the whole experience more traumatizing than we'd expected. But, as ever, we're cheered by an email from someone else who's experienced their own rodent-and-composting fiasco.

Ten years ago I was a stay-at-home mom, gardening in the backyard with a toddler in her little cloth diapers eating only homemade baby foods. I thought composting was a great addition to my commitment to the 'natural' lifestyle. And with the canning season just around the corner, there'd be more than usual to include in my backyard incubation tank.

So I set up a lidded pot in the kitchen for incremental scraps, to be emptied daily on to the pile in the corner of the garden. I'd go out and turn the pile regularly, excitedly watching the leftovers of our vegetable food matter decompose.

My husband never participated (not the yard type, he explained), until one night when he was unavoidably snared by an unanticipated side effect of my eco-friendly experiment . . .

We awoke to three baby opossums in our house! The little varmints seemed to know the exact location of my scrap pot, and some convenient hiding places along the way. After much screaming, chasing, baby-protecting and rodent lassoing (a trick my husband learned from the Nature Channel), we had them all rounded up, unharmed. The next morning he located their mother and some more siblings living between the shed and my compost pile.

As you can well imagine, not only did these new, uninvited house pets leave our lives, so did my compost pile!

I later learned (after a move to a less urban

home with a larger proportion of yard waste) to be very careful about the type and volume of foodstuffs added to one's compost pile!!

I hope you find much laughter in your trials as well!

Best regards,
Anne Manner-McLarty, Woodstock, Georgia, USA

We've certainly found much slaughter in our trials with rodents. We're still waiting for the laughter, Anne.

It's taken us a while to organize – three months have now passed since the auditors visited – but we've just had confirmation that we've finally been accepted into the small but fast-growing group of people who bank 'ethically'. Before we set out to change our bank accounts, we thought the process would be quick – after all, most banks fall over themselves to secure your business. But even though we are both now clutching our new bank cards, the whole experience has been more complicated than we expected.

'Congratulations, you qualify for a £10,000 loan. Fill out the form and apply today.' This is the kind of correspondence we normally receive from banks touting for business. Why they still bother with this kind of advertising I don't know, but the various financial services that try to lure me daily via junk mail or telephone calls receive fairly short shrift. I keep my finances as simple as possible – this isn't down to sensible advice from a personal-finance sage, rather a combination of laziness and a wish to minimize the amount of superfluous hassle in my life. Basically, I like to see what's coming in and going out each month on one piece of paper, if possible living within my means at all times. I don't wish to complicate matters with extra headaches such as personal loans, credit-card debts, extraneous insurance policies and the like. In fact, the only real debt (not counting the odd overdraft) is, of course, the mortgage.

I've had the same bank account ever since I was ten. I chose my bank for no other reason than that it was the one my parents used and because a poster in the local branch promised me a fancy-looking money box. I've never thought about changing banks for the simple reason that current accounts seem fairly mundane and routine to me – they're all the same, aren't they, so why bother? To be honest, I've also never really thought about what happens to my money in the bank; other than waiting for me to come and collect it at the cashpoint machine.

When it came to getting a mortgage, Jane and I had two criteria for lenders to meet: would they lend us the amount we required, and, if so, did they offer the lowest interest rate? And because we like to know in advance what our outgoings are, we settled on getting a fixed-rate mortgage, then shopping around every two years to see if it's worth remortgaging for a better rate. We occasionally shop around in this way for new household or life insurance. The banks have a name for people like us – the polite version is 'fixers'. I can't imagine that we're cherished or valuable customers.

As we both have occupational pensions, it has always seemed

that the decision-making over how or where to invest our pension funds is out of our hands. As the advice has always been that workplace pension schemes are generally better than private ones, we have both been happy to devolve that particular responsibility to our employers. I receive a letter every year explaining how the pension fund has fared in the past twelve months and what my projected pension will be, but because pension day is so distant, I must confess I don't really give it much attention.

Equally shamefully, our pensions are about the only form of savings we can boast of – despite constantly nagging each other that we must get round to putting something aside regularly each month. We have a meagre amount put aside in premium bonds and we have been thinking a lot recently about how to start saving for Esme, but the money that comes in each month has, sadly, largely evaporated by the next. It's a phenomenon we seem unable to prevent.

Jane and I lay our cards on the table – debit cards, that is. We then place our various insurance policies, mortgage statements, premium bonds and pension packs beside them. This is an awkward and humbling thing to do as, together, these bits of plastic and sheets of paper represent many things – our combined financial worth for one, but also our perceived 'standing' in society, Esme's inheritance, our security, even our lives, in many ways. Jane and I are reluctant to show our statements to each other, let alone to relative strangers.

Fearing he's spotted how much we spend at Sainsbury's, I

shudder when Mike holds up my latest current-account statement. 'How many people,' he says, 'would choose to put their money into a firm selling arms to an oppressive regime or into a project which threatens to destroy some of the world's finest wildlife? Very few, I would imagine. But that is exactly where your financial securities are invested, Leo. Both you and Jane bank on the high street, but the high-street banks all invest in companies which often have a poor environmental track record, and some employ dubious ethics, especially in the developing world.'

I am relieved that he's glossed over the finer details of my balance, but am perturbed that Mike thinks my choice of bank could be responsible for the felling of rare trees. 'In a 2001 report,' he says, 'Friends of the Earth took issue with, for example, both Barclays and HSBC for their financial support of the south-east Asian logging company Asia Pulp and Paper, which, the report claimed, is responsible for clearing huge areas of precious rainforest in Indonesia and Malaysia. All the banks and building societies, in fact, invest in companies such as Shell, which has also faced criticism. For example, in 2001, after it stood accused of putting the local people at risk in Pandacan in the Philippines by operating a depot for oil and gas in the heart of the community, it was pressured into initiating a scaledown of the site.'

Changing our current accounts should be easy, I say. After all, we won't lose money – obviously a concern – as interest rates on current accounts are negligible.

Changing mortgage lenders, though, where the slightest variation in interest rate could mean a big difference in monthly repayments, is a much bigger commitment.

But Hannah is keen that we at least investigate some ethical-mortgage-lender rates. She is also keen that we source alternative life insurance. 'Your policy is currently with Cornhill, owned by Allianz AG. But Allianz subsidiaries are involved in numerous controversial development projects. They contributed private finance to the Azer-Chirag-Gunashli offshore oilfield development, for example, which is linked to the Baku–Ceyhan oil pipeline, so they're expected to be involved in this too – though this hasn't been confirmed. The pipeline has put environmental and human rights organizations on high alert.'

She is pleased, though, that we aren't credit-card junkies. 'Neither of you has credit cards, which fits with the sense I have that you don't have an extravagant lifestyle. But it would really boost your ethical credentials if this relatively modest consumption was complemented by the deployment of any spare resources in ways that advantage society at large.'

After the auditors have impressed on us how important it is to consider where we invest our money, I ask them for help in choosing where to reinvest. Renée throws in a few quick-fire suggestions. 'You can begin when selecting investment funds by asking about their social-responsibility criteria. There are now over forty different "green" funds, for example. There are hundreds of credit cards that support charities, meaning that everyday shopping can be a force for the good. Likewise, consider altruistic insurance companies, such as Naturesave Policies and Animal Friends Insurance Services. And when you look for a new bank, remember that "negative banks" just avoid financing or investing in companies and projects that may damage the environment, whereas "positive banks" only finance or invest in projects that have a positive impact. Try ones such as Triodos or the Co-operative first.'

Hannah says that we can go further still. As we both have occupational pensions, we must ask where they are invested – and encourage our colleagues to do the same. Pension funds control more than 30 per cent of the stockmarket, so an aware, concerned workforce has huge potential leverage. This is now made much easier, she says, as all pension funds are obliged to declare their position on environmental and other ethical issues. Mike recommends that we try former mutual organizations such as Friends Provident for pension alternatives. He says that most mainstream providers are, in fact, now offering some ethical pension funds. Norwich Union is one example.

'Sadly, when it comes to remortgaging, I don't think your property would meet the Ecology Building Society's stringent energy-efficiency mortgage criteria,' adds Hannah, when I ask her for any last thoughts. 'This leaves the Co-op Bank or the clutch of building societies which remain mutual and don't undertake corporate lending. In general, mutuals still give better deals than their demutualized cousins, so it needn't even be a compromise financially. They would also be best for general house-related insurance, given that, despite a few brokers making environmental claims for their products, there is as yet no insurer with a comprehensive ethical investment policy.'

I say that I feel a bit ashamed about my rather pitiful efforts to give to charity. Hannah encourages us to try to be more open to the power of wealth redistribution. Carry some pound coins around in your pocket, she says, and toss one into a hat now and again without stopping to moralize. We could also try placing £500 or so in a local credit union or shared interest scheme, which provide cheaper loans to those in need. You will still earn interest, she counters, sensing that I'm about to say that is too much money to give away.

I live in a society built on the exchange of capital, a process largely oiled by banks, so how can I really be expected to extract myself from the murky world of finance? Store my money under the bed? Money will, I hope, always be a part of my life – after all, I still intend to earn it and spend it – so is it really possible to limit my part in the so-called 'evils' the banks are helping to fund?

My scepticism is probably born out of my long-held belief – which I've had to suppress throughout my entire ethical-living experiment so far – that big business and governments will do what they want to do with or without the little guy's approval. Will me moving my money to a new home really a) teach my old bank a lesson in corporate responsibility, or b) help to limit the funding of undesirable firms and projects around the world? Before I began to launder my money, so to speak, my answers would have been a) no, why should they care about losing one of their millions of customers, and b) yes, but only by a negligible amount.

To part company with something that has been a fixture in

my life for twenty years was clearly going to be more of a wrench than just flicking a switch. The relationship between my bank and me had always been civil and workmanlike – we had never come to blows about a thing. So I felt they deserved an explanation about why I was about to jump ship. But the mechanics of leaving a bank are very simple. You tell your new bank your details and when you want to switch, and they do the rest. All you need to do is sign a few consent forms. You never even get a chance to say goodbye before you are spirited away.

So a couple of weeks after filling out the account-switching forms for my new current account with Smile – the online arm of the Co-operative Bank and the one my auditors had recommended – I rang up Lloyds TSB, my old bank, to explain my rapid departure. I suppose I naively thought there would be a distressed manager on the end of the line pleading with me to stay. 'What have we done wrong, Mr Hickman? What can we do to change your mind?'

But, no, when I asked whether they could list the sectors or firms that they chose not to invest in for ethical reasons, I got what I suspect is a stock response: 'For reasons of confidentiality, we do not discuss such matters.' I probed a little further, but still no expansion. 'The only thing that I can say is that we always operate within UK law when it comes to where we choose to invest. Have you read our annual social responsibility report?'

'No, but I will,' I responded. 'So then, that's that. Goodbye . . .' Click. Brrrrr.

I have a feeling that my departure was more emotional for

me than it was for them – I never even received an 'it was nice doing business with you, Mr Hickman' letter – but I did make the effort to read about Lloyds' social responsibility aims on its website, if only to compare them to Smile's own much-promoted ethical policy.

After a short browse I soon noticed a stark difference in tone between the two banks. Their statements speak for themselves. From Lloyds TSB's Corporate Social Responsibility Report:

> Lloyds TSB has had a local presence in Latin America for more than 130 years. By the early 1980s, the Latin American countries who had borrowed heavily to fund economic development found themselves in financial difficulties. Higher oil prices, rising world interest rates and falling prices for the commodities on which they rely for income combined to create these problems. We took the decision that, as responsible lenders, we could not simply walk away from the problem. We believed that if debt was simply written off, those countries would face great difficulty in attracting the future foreign investment so vital to economic development.

From Smile's Ethical Policy:

> Our customers want to see global trade develop in a responsible manner so that companies recognize their duties in the production and marketing of their products and services . . . We will not invest in: multinational companies who do not have a clear commitment to core labour

standards; in particular, if the conditions in its supply chain have been the subject of major reputation criticisms which they have failed to remedy; any company, regardless of size, which is the subject of 'continuing criticism' for not complying with core labour standards which it is in a position to influence; any company where there is no evidence of a genuine commitment to address reported failings in their marketing practices or which cannot supply answers to reported criticisms of marketing practices.

These two extracts reminded me about what Renée had to say about 'positive' and 'negative' banking. Call me cynical, but the message behind Lloyds' statement seemed to be, 'Fear not, stakeholder, despite the market's volatility we're still lending money to developing countries.' Smile's message seemed to be, 'We lend to the developing nations because of, not despite, their suffering.' A big difference, in my view.

Although changing current accounts has been relatively straightforward, debate between Jane and me about whether we should change our mortgage lender has been particularly heated. As our current two-year fixed-rate deal was drawing to a close anyway, we had already been keeping a close eye on the mortgage-rate tables in the newspapers. What has been dividing us is whether we should source ethically sound lenders first, then find the best rates, or find the best rates first, then ask about their ethical policies.

The potential difference in monthly payments was about £100 when we first made comparisons between the best ethical lenders as opposed to the mainstream high-street lenders. Was this too high a price to pay just to ensure our money had an ethical home?

'Yes,' said Jane firmly. 'I will happily switch current accounts, but I'm not prepared to take a £100 hit every month just so we have peace of mind about who is lending us the money. Wouldn't that £100 be better spent somewhere else – say given to a charity, or paying to feed and clothe Esme?'

I admit that I baulked at this figure, too. But it has been troubling me since that there appears to be a cut-off point at which ethical considerations become out-trumped by financial ones. Our gut reaction implies that living ethically is fine as long as you can afford it, but as soon as the financial sacrifice becomes too great, commitment can rapidly wane. Was our reaction confirmation of the oft-cited charge that living ethically is just a middle-class luxury, one that will only be of concern to those who can afford it? I think we have probably partly answered that by opting, after much deliberation, to move our mortgage to a mutual that in the first instance offers a competitive rate, and only secondly boasts an impressive social responsibility policy.

Our pensions threw up the same problem: were we really prepared to move to a more ethical fund if it meant that our final pension pay-out would be significantly reduced? However, in this case, a quick phone call put my mind at ease. I asked my pension fund manager about where my money was being invested – something I had never even thought to do before – and, thankfully, he satisfied me that ethical considerations were at the forefront of his mind, and that, importantly, I could effectively lobby for any issue I cared about in the future as I was a 'stakeholder' in the company pension scheme.

Another problem we have faced when analysing our investments is where to draw the line when it comes to what you consider to be 'ethical' or not. We both agreed on the obvious – no investing in the arms trade, or companies that have been fingered for environmental or human rights crimes – but we found it harder to decide about grey areas that are still being fiercely debated by society, such as investments in GM technology or pharmaceutical advances (which, let's face it, usually means animal testing). Should we just trust these financial institutions to determine what is an ethical investment on our behalf, or should we pick our way through their investments one by one looking for things that may concern us?

Ultimately, the bottom line for us is that there must come a time when you just have to trust organizations with ethical policies to make the correct decisions. There simply isn't enough time in the day to worry about every nuance of their activities. Of course, there is the danger that a firm may just be using their ethical policies or funds in an attempt to seek good PR – 'greenwashing', as the auditors call it – but if they are actually moving their investments away from the murkier and more unsavoury companies then surely that's a good thing, whatever their motives? My only wish is that investing in ethical funds – whether it be through a bank, mortgage lender or pension firm – doesn't have to mean compromising on competitive rates. Can it really be true that you only ever get the most out of your money when it is invested in, say, oil drilling, cluster bombs and vivisection laboratories?

According to one email I've received, the answer is an overwhelming 'yes'. But the author has an attitude that, to be honest, leaves me cold and a little angry, even. I would love to do what he's done and live the idyllic island life – who wouldn't? – but what happens when we all do it? His escapist life is fine for the few lucky individuals who manage to achieve it, but what is he proposing? That we all up sticks, leave our evil Western countries and join him on the beach under the coconut palms?

Hello,

I worked for nine years in the City, before giving it all up and moving to a remote island in the Caribbean (Roatan), where I started to teach scuba diving. I did this because I could not live an ethical lifestyle in England.

It is one thing to talk about changing what you eat, and using a bicycle and eco-friendly nappies . . . but you still have a bank account, credit cards, you read books and you wear Levi jeans. Please don't get me wrong, I am not some anti-government alternative hippy, but the financial world of banks/mortgages/loans and the concern with profits means that while you live in First World countries you will never be able to live an ethical lifestyle.

I now live on an island called the Commonwealth of Dominica, and don't eat fish (the only wild animal people still eat) or meat. This

island is very poor, but very lush and grows
(organically) all its own vegetables and fruit. You
can drink the water from the rivers and Dominica
has the highest percentage of people over a
hundred years old in the world. The people here
live an ethical lifestyle.

I appreciate what you are trying to do, but you
must be careful using this 'ethical' word. The
society you live in is not ethical. Stop worrying
about what you eat and start worrying about all
the people in the world who do not have the
advantages of your wealth and education.

Yours, Kaj Maney

How do you do that then? By teaching them (and presumably
the tourists who jet in to your lovely island) scuba diving? The
vast majority of letters I've received have been so supportive and
helpful, but the odd one from a high-minded, preaching so-
and-so like this just makes me start to resent the whole
experiment. You're damned if you do, you're damned if you
don't. And then I start to wonder if I'm becoming like them,
too. Why is it so hard to try to make these changes to your life
without coming across like Kaj?

While I'm on the subject of money, I have found that the
whole issue of giving to charity can be fraught with similar
concerns. I've always found it difficult giving to charity. Not
because I am necessarily an uncaring, selfish person,
but because I tend to agonize about whether one charity is a

more deserving cause than another. The net result is usually that no charity gains from a donation. It's pathetic, I know.

I think this is why I have been drawn to donating money through my pay packet. For a couple of years now I have been giving a tenner each month to the Woodland Trust, largely because I was promised that by giving in this way my donation would escape the clutches of Gordon Brown. But when the auditors asked why I had chosen this particular charity over others, I couldn't really answer. 'I suppose I just like the idea of there being more trees in the world,' was my rather feeble response. It did make me think, though: what had made me choose trees over, say, the homeless in London, orphans in Africa, endangered species, or derelict buildings of cultural importance? Which is the most deserving cause? It's having to answer questions like this that has steered me away from giving in the first place.

Hannah's solution – that we should just try to give away more to a range of causes – seemed too simplistic at first. But I have decided to treat it as a kind of education. If you are going to give away a tenner, or whatever, each month, why not give a pound to ten different charities rather than giving it all to one, and, in the process, get to know more about them? Having now tried this, even though I feel as if I'm diluting the power of my charitable giving, I have certainly started to empathize with far more causes than before.

I have an admission to make, though: I still find it hard to give to down-and-outs on the street. For right or wrong, I seem to subconsciously place them towards the bottom of the League of the Deserving. Should I give them some loose change because of their ability to, say, play the bongos, the fact that they say they're homeless and hungry, they are pestering me on the Tube and I want to read my paper, they have a cute dog at their feet, or because they smiled at me? No matter what Hannah said about the need to stop moralizing when giving to charity, I still find that little devil often appearing on my shoulder whispering, 'Come on, Leo, do they really deserve your money?'

Part of my reluctance lies in the fact that I have always found it awkward making a public display of giving money to some-one who's asking for it. The art of giving money away without attaching any strings or value judgements is also something I have struggled with. It's hard to detach yourself from the notion that when you 'buy' a charitable act (this is what you are doing, after all) by donating, say, a pound, you should expect a pound's worth of gratitude or self-satisfaction in return. Are the only true acts of charity those that you never hear about – the ones made silently and anonymously, whatever the sums involved?

11

And the flesh you so fancifully fry
Is not succulent, tasty or kind
It's death for no reason
And death for no reason is murder

('Meat is Murder', The Smiths, 1985, lyrics, Rough Trade/Sire)

A S A TEENAGER LISTENING repeatedly to this song on my headphones, the smart-arse in me would always ponder: 'But death for no reason isn't murder; it's an accident or manslaughter at worst, surely?' Whereas many of my contemporaries were moved to flirt with vegetarianism as a result of hearing this one song, I was probably listening to it whilst munching on a Big Mac or scoffing pork scratchings.

While my taste buds may have become slightly more refined since then, I'm still no nearer to becoming a vegetarian, never mind a vegan. I haven't even got to grips with the subtle difference between the two. Why, for example, don't vegans eat honey?

Wouldn't bees produce honey regardless of whether we harvest it or not?

I wouldn't say that I'm an ardent meat-and-two-veg man, but I do seem to believe, subconsciously or not, that a meal isn't really complete without meat. Jane does too. I'm also a huge fan of dairy produce, particularly cheese. Give me the cheese board over the dessert trolley every day of the week. And there's nothing more refreshing than a cold glass of milk.

I suspect the trauma of thwacking a rat over the head with a spade has been the catalyst for my current round of angst about whether we should be eating animals or their by-products. It's not that the thought of eating the rat (waste not, want not, and all that) ever crossed my mind. It's the ease with which, give or take its last desperate gasps, I killed it that has left me thinking about how I never need to experience such sights, even though we eat meat – a dead animal, if it needs spelling out – almost every day. Would I think any differently about eating meat if it was me placing the stun gun to the cow's head, or tying up the chicken by its feet to face the electrodes? I doubt I'll ever know, given that a journalist's skills don't translate too well into those of an abattoir worker (actually, on second thoughts . . .), but it's something that I now feel I should at least witness.

I'm not going to mince my words here (excuse the pun): I love eating meat – always have – but like so many people in the UK, I have been shaken by a decade or more of meat-industry scares, from BSE to foot and mouth disease. Learning about the horrifying conditions in which many farm animals are kept has also disturbed me. I challenge anyone to remain indifferent after seeing some of the images I have been sent showing how hens, in particular, are reared.

I can understand, then, why many argue that striking meat from your diet is an essential part of ethical living – but still I'm eating it. Why? Is it that buying meat today is so sanitized and removed from the truth of the slaughter house? Probably. Is it that I feel a meal is somehow incomplete without meat? Possibly – I suspect that this might become an issue if I eliminated meat from my diet altogether. The fact remains that I enjoy meat.

People convert to vegetarianism all the time, but you need to have a true awakening, I suspect, and I just don't know whether I'm there yet. It's the arguments about the environmental damage caused by rearing animals for meat that have had the most effect on me, not the ethics of whether it's right to eat meat. I'm more moved by just how much food and water is needed to produce meat.

Despite my reservations, I've been proposing to Jane for a few weeks now that we try to go vegetarian, even if, like our no-television trial, it's just for a week – although I doubt it would prove too much, other than that we haven't got a clue about vegetarian cooking. Jane thinks we should first try to follow the example of the 'meat-reducers'. One step at a time, in other words. However, we have both agreed that we should try to stick to free-range or organic meat and dairy produce when-ever possible, as well as reducing how much meat we eat.

Where we have differed is over the issue of what to feed Esme, who is progressing well with being weaned. (We're currently in the middle of that ice-cube-trays-filled-with-blended-vegetables phase.) I have suggested that we should allow Esme to decide for herself when she is old enough whether or not she wants to eat meat, and that in the meantime we should feed her vegetarian fare. But Jane soon brought me down to earth by suggesting I should be the one to prepare all these separate meals each day. As is the tradition in our household, Jane has got her way. Like us, Esme is to be fed on organic meat and dairy produce.

But I still feel unsettled by our decision. I think it's because, of all the subjects people have written to me about over the past few months, avoiding meat has been by far the most passionately argued. It is also the subject that has generated the most letters.

> Don't eat meat. Whether you think it is right or wrong in an abstract sense, the industrialization of the death process for chickens, cattle, pigs, etc. is appalling. It pollutes, wastes and generates a denial process in our own minds due to the remote nature of the killing act. We are no longer related to the death of the meat that we are eating. The process has become so thoughtlessly common that the average diner has no more ethical regard for veal than he does for broccoli; as though meat is generated synthetically in a manufacturing plant somewhere in Iowa. It's the very worst of globalization and industrialization because we are so distanced from the product that we no longer consider the implications of its source.

Don't pussy out. If you want to live an ethical
lifestyle, this is the first step.

Josh Campbell, Prague

For me vegetarianism is an ethical choice on a
number of levels:
1. Being kind to your BODY (the health thing)
2. Being kind to ANIMALS (the compassionate
thing)
3. Being kind to the ENVIRONMENT (the politics-
of-global-agribusiness-and-consumption thing)
   The last point often gets overlooked, I think, in
ethical debates (around the restaurant table).
Giving up meat is more than an 'ethical/lifestyle'
choice; it's a conscious political act . . .
Presumably you're aware of the gross amount of
cereal the Western world grows to feed its cattle –
so we can enjoy cheap burgers. And how much
rainforest is being destroyed, etc. etc.
   Like you, I used to love the taste of meat. But
I've been a veggie for fifteen years or so – and
never looked back. It becomes natural. Organic
meat? A good step in the right direction. But keep
moving! And hey, I love cooking and good food.
Forget the stereotypes.

Cheers, Steve Turnbull

I spent two years as a vegetarian long ago. The decision came because my girlfriend then was a vegetarian. It suited our lifestyle – as a mutual arrangement, of course. My basic rationale was a consideration of animal welfare, intensive farming methods and so on. It was two years of hell.

Like an 'ex'-alcoholic who spends his life trying to stay out of bars, I exhausted vast amounts of mental energy trying to live that false life. I was never truly a vegetarian, though at times, through habitual conditioning, I glimpsed the feeling of being one. Deep inside I was a carnivore, and at the same level I must confess I never really objected that deeply to the natural status quo of a human being at the top of the food chain. My objections were ineffable, ill-formulated ideas about the world which manifested, partly through my immaturity, as a bout of 'me too' vegetarianism to please my peers.

Andy James

I am surprised that you have made such dramatic adjustments without what I consider to be the most important 'non-action' of all – ceasing to eat animals. You obviously recognize the cruelty involved in modern farming but this has not yet connected with you emotionally. Organic meat is certainly a step in the right direction in terms of animal welfare and the healthiness of your diet, but it still assumes that the satisfaction of the human palate overrides the right of the pig/cow/chicken to live. If you doubt the value of an animal's life in terms of the extent that they share our emotions, intellect, family life, ability to feel pain, etc. then there is a wealth of evidence I can point you to which will dispel this.

My philosophy is to live in a way that causes as little pain to others as possible. If humans needed to eat flesh to survive or be healthy then I would do so. But they don't – in fact the vegan diet is widely accepted as the optimum diet for health (providing vegans utilize all the foods available to them). On the taste issue, there are a plethora of meat substitutes that were developed for the millions of people who have exactly your problem. Most say that the substitutes are good to stem the craving and that after several months even the sanitized meat on the supermarket shelves looks like flesh and therefore loses its appeal. However, I absolutely agree with you that if you haven't fully developed your reasons for abandoning meat, haven't imagined the life experienced by a farm animal or accepted their capacity for suffering, then it will be all too easy to give in to your cravings or social pressure.

My advice therefore would be to find out what it's all about. Recognize how startlingly similar animals are to humans and what exactly is involved in the farm and slaughter process – organic or no. Understand the wider consequences

of the meat trade in terms of world hunger as well
as its health effects on you and your family.
Remember that if children were told the truth
about meat before they had developed a taste for it
or absorbed society's norms then they would
reject it outright.

Sally King

I envy these people's certainty. I don't dispute what they are
saying about the ethical quandary caused by eating meat, but I
don't seem to have enough resolve to give it up altogether. Does
that make me a meat addict, or does it just suggest that I'm
uncommitted?

Ironically, however, Jane and I have found that we are now
eating much less meat than we used to, simply because organic
meat is a lot more expensive (at least 50 per cent more, in most
cases). If this is an intentional strategy of the green lobby, it's a
masterstroke. We are hoping that we are slowly starting to
wean ourselves off meat. Maybe further down this road we will
have the momentum to try to go vegetarian, even if it's just for
a trial period first. Veganism, though, is simply not on the
cards.

I have finally undertaken a journey that I have been wanting to
make since the auditors left. I thought it was important for me
to at least look my next meal in the eye, so to speak, and so I
spent a day at Sheepdrove Farm near Lambourn in Berkshire.
It's one of the country's largest organic farms at 2,250 acres,

and has been rearing cattle, pigs, poultry and sheep organically for thirty years.

It took over two hours to tour the farm, sitting with other guests on a trailer behind a tractor as it trundled through the farm's dozens of fields, which are set on beautiful chalk downland near Lambourn's famous horse-racing studs. The first thing that surprised me was the size of the place. I had imagined that an organic farm, by definition, would be similar to a smallholding in scale – just a handful of fields. But Sheepdrove extends as far as the eye can see. It employs forty people and is home to many thousands of animals. I saw pigs (Saddlebacks and Canboroughs), cows (South Devons and Aberdeen Angus) and lambs (Shetland/Poll Dorset cross-bred ewes), but by far the most diverting were the chickens, housed in large transportable hangars spread out across a number of fields. I'm used to seeing cows, pigs and lambs in fields, but it dawned on me that I've never seen chickens being reared on a farm, probably because it is normally done behind closed doors. I was shown the heated sheds where chicks are reared before they are let outside, and saw the chicks standing on their own perches and kicking back in dustbaths – activities, I learned, that they do instinctively in the wild, where they are forest-floor dwellers, but are prevented from doing on battery farms. They even have a CD playing them farmyard and countryside noises (including the sound of low-flying aircraft, since Heathrow is not too distant), to ready them for the great outdoors, where their parents roam around under huge open-sided, marquee-type structures that are regularly moved around the fields to provide new foraging patches.

But the highlight of the day was lunch, hosted by the farm's owners, Peter and Juliet Kindersley. Over a meal of roast pork and vegetables, all produced on the farm, they explained why farming using organic principles is so important to them. Sheepdrove Farm forms a stark contrast to much of our farmland, which is now responsible for creating a monoculture – a landscape lacking any meaningful diversity of flora or fauna. Most farms concentrate on growing one crop or rearing one breed, thereby quickly becoming vulnerable to disease or market-price fluctuations, and reliant on pesticides and fertilizers. Sheepdrove counters this, said the Kindersleys, by using extensive crop and livestock rotation and incredible amounts of compost, which the local council pays it to use as it would otherwise be destined for the local landfill.

Before I left I pored over the produce in Sheepdrove's farm shop, hunting for a gift for Jane and Esme. There were chickens, sausages, lamb chops, even packs of mutton (which I don't think I've ever seen for sale before in a supermarket), but I ended up buying a packet of organic stoneground flour to make a loaf of bread. Renée would have been impressed by my progress from oven-ready Sainsbury's ciabatta to freshly baked brick.

The visit has left me more convinced than ever that organic farming is preferable to 'conventional' farming. One thing that did nag me throughout the tour, though, was the fact that Sheepdrove has only recently started to turn a profit after thirty years in existence. Peter's successes in the publishing industry (he founded Dorling Kindersley) have by his own admission helped to subsidize the farm's extensive running costs. I also feel sad that so many people are restricted from eating organic produce due to cost. It seems such an irony that food produced at such cost in terms of pollution and animal welfare is in fact the cheapest for the consumer. But the visit to Sheepdrove has reassured me at least that eating organic meat is acceptable. Just seeing the kind of life those animals lead – far better than many humans, in fact – convinced me of that.

One thing I'm still keen to experience with my own eyes, though, is the moment of truth in the abattoir. I haven't avoided it for want of trying – it is quite hard, it seems, to get access to one during slaughter for 'health and safety' reasons. But it's certainly on my to-do list. I feel as if a Pandora's box has been opened with regard to eating meat, and that this is now something both Jane and I will forever battle with. I sometimes feel frustrated at the progress and level of commitment we've made, but I'm pleased that at least we've started.

It wasn't too bad at first, but it's starting to get really tedious having to live with builders in and out of the house. There's dust everywhere, the place is a mess and we are desperate for some privacy.

To make matters worse, we've come to the conclusion that trying to get a builder who's very much set in his ways to use different materials or techniques is a mistake. We under-estimated just how entrenched Dave is in doing things his way. I can't really blame him – being constantly told how to do things can grate (as I can testify) – but he tends to routinely laugh off nearly all our suggestions.

A good example was what to do with all the waste that was

created when he was ripping out the old kitchen and bathroom, and the adjoining wall. My intention was to pick through it and look for anything worth salvaging. But I came home from work one day to find everything in a skip outside our house. OK, I thought, I'll go through it myself, but within a few hours local flytippers (is there a secret network of people who spread the word when a new skip is in town?) had got wind of our half-filled skip, which was instantly filled to the brim with old keyboards, tyres and other discarded rubbish before I'd even had a chance to have a rummage myself. All I managed to salvage were some glass shelves, radiators and two doors – I think a passer-by must have nicked the taps and bath, which was more than a little irritating, but at least they would be re-used by someone, I suppose. All the rest – admittedly most of it rubble and splintered chipboard from the old kitchen – is probably languishing in a landfill somewhere.

We've had our successes, but only when we've taken the initiative ourselves as opposed to leaving decisions up to the builder. In the bathroom, for example, we've got him to install a loo with a low-volume flush. We've also resisted the huge temptation to get a power-shower, instead opting for one with a thermostatic valve, ensuring we don't waste precious water trying to get the desired temperature.

In the kitchen, we've insisted that Dave install a dedicated cupboard for the recycling box. We've surprised ourselves, too, by managing to find a kitchen approved by the FSC. Better still, it was also one of the cheapest, extinguishing our fears that whatever the auditors recommend usually proves to be the most expensive option. And we didn't even need to look far for it – we found the kitchen quite by accident on the B&Q website whilst browsing for designs. Right by the price, in small print, was what we were looking for: the kitchen's carcass, doors and worktops are all 'certified to FSC standards'.

Now that the kitchen and bathroom have been fitted we are already running over budget, so we have decided to save money and decorate ourselves. Our intention was to use the eco-paints the auditors had all praised, but they were stupendously expensive. We needed a five-litre pot of paint for the walls in the kitchen, but when we started researching some of the brands we found the prices easily topped £50 a pot – even £80 on one occasion. It just seemed to be too much when we could find a water-based, very low-VOC equivalent for under £20. So we opted for this compromise instead, resolving to avoid oil-based gloss paints for the woodwork because of the fumes they give off and because you need white spirit – extremely environmentally damaging, say the auditors – to clean the brushes. We've also vowed to donate any left-over paint to the local council's paint recycling scheme.

There might be no paint left by the end of the decorating, though, as I had a bit of an accident last week. I was painting the bathroom walls with a white emulsion, then moved on to paint all the woodwork – the window frames, skirting boards and new cupboard doors. I was flagging by this point – it had been a long weekend decorating, I was tired and the light was fading – and didn't realize I hadn't swapped over to my low-VOC gloss. Without the tell-tale waft of fumes you normally associate with gloss paint, I forgot I was still using emulsion. Needless to say, Jane wasn't too impressed to find the bathroom window frames coated in emulsion the next morning and ordered me to repaint them. I blame the auditors for making us try new, unfamiliar paints. Jane blames my stupidity.

12

THE CALL FROM JANE COMES at precisely five thirty-eight p.m. on an incredibly hot Thursday afternoon. I'm sitting at my desk at work.

'I've just called an ambulance,' she says, crying. Her voice is filled with panic. 'Esme's temperature is really high and she's gone all floppy and is starting to fit. I'm really scared, Leo. Can you get to the hospital as soon as possible?'

The journey to the hospital is one of the longest I have ever made. I sit numbly on the train, staring at the upholstery on the seat opposite me, counting down the passing stations which seem an eternity apart. Every medical condition I've heard of – with the worst first – runs through my head. Then I start to think of more mundane matters, such as whether I should go home first to pick up Esme's favourite teddy, or buy some chocolate to keep our energy levels up. I'm irritated that I can be thinking of such trivial things.

As the train pulls into my station I impatiently pull the doors open and sprint up the road to the entrance of the A&E department about half a mile away. The room is packed, but I can't see Jane or Esme anywhere. This only panics me more, but the receptionist points me towards a cubicle where I find them both with Jane's mother, Margaret, who is thankfully staying with us. Esme looks up at me forlornly as she lies in Jane's arms, but it is the best vision I have ever seen. I'm just so relieved to see her breathing and conscious.

Then, slowly, I catch up with the events of the day. Apparently, Esme developed a temperature of 38.5°C in the early afternoon, so Jane gave her some ibuprofen to help bring the temperature down. Worried about the heat of the day, Jane then popped out to buy a fan, leaving Esme with Margaret. But by the time she had returned, Esme's temperature was even higher. Even another dose of ibuprofen couldn't bring it down and soon Esme had started to turn purple and go floppy. When she stopped responding to Jane's voice, they called 999.

Esme has not yet been seen by anyone other than the triage nurse. Yet more ibuprofen has been administered, but we are still waiting for a doctor. Esme's temperature is now up to 39.5°C and we are getting more and more agitated and concerned.

Finally, nearly four hours later, a doctor sees us. She suspects Esme is suffering from a urinary-tract infection, which can be serious in a baby, she says. To confirm this, Esme will need to provide a urine sample, no mean feat for a seven-month-old in nappies. High temperatures caused by infections can be enough to trigger fitting in some babies, which would explain the convulsions.

We spend another two hours waiting patiently for Esme to pee into a small plastic bag strapped on to her by one of the nurses. But nothing. Not a drop. Under pressure to move us out of the A&E department (we later learn that they have to meet government targets about such things), the doctor says we should go home to wait for the sample there, then bring it in the next day for analysis. We head home, exhausted, and get to bed by one a.m. – Jane and Esme in bed together so that Jane can keep an eye on her, me downstairs on the sofa and Margaret on a blow-up mattress in Esme's room.

'Wake up! Wake up! Esme's fitting again.' Only an hour after we'd all got off to sleep, Jane wakes us with the frightening news. I hadn't seen Esme fitting the first time, but the sight of her now, limp and failing to respond to us, is terrifying. We call for an ambulance immediately and it arrives within three minutes. God knows what the neighbours must think, seeing two separate ambulances screech up to our front door in a matter of a few hours.

As soon as we arrive back at the hospital they admit Esme to the children's ward, where, after yet more ibuprofen, we continue to try to get a urine sample. Finally, she delivers and the warm plastic bag is sent off for analysis. It is only at this point that I manage to take in my surroundings for the first time. Except for Esme's birth, I haven't been in a hospital ward for years, thankfully, and the sight of the place really unsettles me. Hospitals have always spooked me. As it's the middle of the night, the lights are dimmed, but I can still see down the length of the ward. At the far end there are about a dozen beds with children asleep in them, and up our end are private cubicles for babies and their parents. The whole place seems very shabby and our cubicle is surprisingly dirty. It still has the previous occupants' detritus lying around – a crumpled tissue on the floor, food packaging on the bedside table, abandoned food in the fridge. It really shocks us, especially Margaret, who is a retired nurse. Next to the cot that Esme is lying in is a small children's bed and a chair. Now utterly shattered, I take Margaret downstairs to find a taxi home, then return to the ward, where Jane and I lie down on the small bed together and attempt to get some sleep.

The bright, searing sun shining through the cubicle's window wakes us from our heavily disturbed sleep at about six o'clock, though we drift off to sleep again until a nurse arrives to check on Esme. She tells us that the urine sample has now been returned from the lab, but that it was contaminated so we will need to do the whole thing all over again. Esme seems much better in herself, but is still very clingy. Desperate for news of what is wrong with her, and suffering from the extreme heat of the room, Jane and I hardly speak to each other, both retreating into our own thoughts.

Margaret arrives later on in the morning with a bag of fresh clothing, toiletries and some food for Esme, and we begin to settle into the routine that will be our life for the next two nights and two days – waiting for the doctor's rounds, taking it in turns to go to the canteen for food, feeding Esme, and trying to find relief from the baking heat of the ward.

That evening, we finally receive confirmation of what is wrong with Esme. The doctor says that she has suffered two febrile convulsions brought on by a bacterial infection, most probably a urinary-tract infection as first suspected. It can be simply treated with antibiotics and ibuprofen. Nonetheless, the doctor wants to keep Esme in for a couple of days for observation and to allow her temperature to fall for a significant period of time.

Sitting by Esme's cot over the next two days with little to do, we find ourselves discussing the various ethical dilemmas of modern medicine. Should we have asked which pharmaceutical company produces her medicines? Was their invention based on animal testing? Do they contain any hidden toxins? Should we have enquired about, and expected to receive, alternatives if we felt the practices of that company compromised our ethical goals? Should we have considered moving Esme to a private hospital – as we did at one low point after an agency nurse accidentally tried to give her three times the prescribed dose of drugs? Is private medical care even ethical? Should we accept the doctors' word without question at all times? Should we be worried at a time such as this that Aspartame, the sweetener surrounded by a waft of controversy and one we are trying to avoid, is listed in the ingredients on the bottle of antibiotics?

But concerns about the drugs' origins evaporate when the paediatrician tells us what Esme needs to take to get better. I admit it freely: we entrust Esme's well-being entirely to the hospital's staff. If one of them had come up to me and said, 'I should inform you that over a thousand rats died a painful death to allow this antibiotic to be here today,' I would still have said, 'Fine, let's proceed.' (The fact that I have a death wish against rats at the moment has nothing to do with this, by the way.)

If I'm honest, all these questions seem trivial when balanced against Esme's welfare, and I can't help thinking that, if forced into a corner, as we have been with Esme's illness, I will always choose the selfish option over the ethical one.

After all, it's one thing recycling more, using less water, eating organic food – all these have been relatively easy lifestyle choices to adopt – but where do you draw the line between living ethically and abandoning it if things become too uncomfortable? Shouldn't I just stop and consider how lucky I am to be able to fret over such things in the first place? Billions of people don't have this luxury, having rather more pressing issues – such as basic subsistence – to confront every day. I've actually started to resent some of the auditors' opinions, particularly much of their stance towards modern healthcare.

'Leo, I'm horrified by what I'm seeing,' says Renée, after opening our bathroom cabinet. She picks her way through bottles and packets of pills, shaking her head.

'Paracetamol, Benadryl, Buttercup Syrup . . . None of these actually restores health, they simply relieve your symptoms. Conventional medicine doesn't focus on curing your illness, but on suppressing the side effects so that you *feel* better – not so that you are better. Benadryl says it relieves allergies, but it really relieves the symptoms, like sneezing, itchy eyes and runny nose. If you have a skin irritation and put a cream on it, like Lanacane, you are treating the symptom, not finding out what the cause is and stopping that.'

Hannah is rummaging too. 'You've got a fairly typical array of off-the-shelf and over-the-counter healthcare products,' she says. 'Painkillers are the most plentiful – there are two brands of paracetamol, Boots' Nurofen and Anadin Ultra Ibuprofen.'

Mike is concerned that the cabinet is 'worryingly full'. I tell him that we're not hypochondriacs – the collection has just built up over a few years. Mike, though, is cynical. 'It could be that you have an unhealthy lifestyle and get sick a lot – or maybe you are victims of pharmaceutical advertising, and have fallen for the lie that the answer to every sniffle comes as a pill or a supplement.' Jane and I are not too impressed by his assumptions about our health regime. Jane, in particular, feels she leads a healthy life.

But Renée agrees. 'Interestingly, the *Concise Oxford Dictionary* defines medicine as "a substance, especially one taken internally, used in the art of restoring and preserving health, especially by means of remedial substances and regulation of diet". I say interestingly, because the contents of your cabinet are far from meeting the dictionary definition of what medicines are meant to do.'

Mike believes that we have got our priorities all wrong when it comes to healthcare. 'The best way to keep healthy is to take a preventative approach, avoiding exposure to environmental risks, such as polluted air, contaminated food and dodgy chemicals in the home. And a healthy organic diet and lots of exercise will help as well.'

He says that the fact that we live in a big, dirty city doesn't help, but it's still no excuse not to be exercising regularly and eating good, healthy food. 'Of course, everyone can get sick occasionally,' he says, 'even with a healthy lifestyle. And, occasionally, medical intervention is necessary. But given our limited knowledge of what we are doing to our bodies, it makes sense to take pills only when necessary – and to follow a doctor's advice.'

Hannah is more concerned that we're buying goods from large multinational pharmaceutical companies. Do we know what the companies behind these popular brand names are responsible for? 'Wyeth, which owns Anadin, is, like Pfizer, a major funder of the Republican party in the US.' Hannah assumes that we will both find this abhorrent. 'Animal testers Procter & Gamble and Unilever have their inevitable presence in your cabinet in the form of Lemsip and Vicks VapoRub, and Vaseline. It is good from a recycling point of view to see that calamine lotion still comes in a glass bottle, unlike the plastic TCP bottle, courtesy of Pfizer.'

So what do you recommend I do when I've got a splitting headache or terrible cold, I ask – just suffer in silence?

'How many people take pills to reduce their blood pressure?' Renée asks. 'Do the pills solve the stress or weight problem or lack of exercise that is causing the raised pressure? No. Do the pills make you healthier? A resounding no. You can bring your blood pressure down by reducing stress, losing weight, exercising and eating a healthy diet based on fruit, vegetables and whole grains. But it's easier for you – and your doctor – to turn to pills. We want and demand quick fixes these days. If that is your choice, fine, but please understand that you are simply relieving the side effects, not addressing the cause.'

Renée says we need to abandon our pill-popping culture and get back to what our ancestors practised: 'Alternative or complementary remedies support the body with vitamins, minerals, tissue salts, herbs or whatever is needed to help the body with the healing process, whether that means increasing your intake of antioxidants or supporting your immune system.'

Hannah is also full of praise for alternative therapies and medicines. With their increasing popularity, she says, it should be easy to source replacements for the current stock of medicines in our cabinet. 'To replace Vaseline, for example, there is petroleum-free jelly available through the Natural Collection catalogue – though beeswax makes this unsuitable for vegans. The catalogue also sells headlice treatment free from organophosphates. In fact, there are plenty of herbal remedies that can replace petrochemical-based products from global corporations. Witchhazel is a natural antiseptic native to the UK, and arnica cream is great for aches and bruises. Beware, though, of preparations made from plants which are endangered in the wild, such as golden seal.'

I tell her that I have always been instinctively sceptical of alternative therapies, especially ones that attract the crystals-and-scented-candles type, but she tells me to try a few before I reject them out of hand. 'When it comes to alternative health systems such as Reiki, flower remedies or homeopathy – there are even homeopathic dentists who can test your fillings to see if they are leaching mercury into your body – it is down to the individual to see what works for them. However, remember that on the plus side they tend to offer ways of supporting local businesses and smaller, more sustainable companies rather than the often unethical pharmaceutical industry. Many big drug firms, for example, are still refusing to give in to pressure to make HIV drugs affordable to the millions of sufferers in Africa. Do you really want to be patronizing these firms?'

The auditors can say what they like, but since Esme's illness I have been of the view that in a matter of life or death, conventional medicine is the only way forward. I know you read inspirational stories of people who have battled against terminal illnesses with alternative remedies, but if it was me, I know which treatment I would instinctively favour. And when it's your baby at stake, you're just desperate for whatever might work.

This isn't to say that I'm rejecting alternative therapies altogether. There must be something in them other than a placebo effect – after all, they form the basis of Chinese medicine and other similar practices. Nature seems to hold the answer for so many other things, why not medicine?

So I have started to try to stop relying so heavily on my usual panoply of drugs – and the large companies that make them – when I get ailments as minor as a cold. Out goes the Lemsip and in comes the lemon, ginger and garlic. If you think you're taking something natural as a cure, it's amazing how restorative this can be just in itself.

But not everything has met with my favour. Neither arnica nor echinacea have worked for me as herbal cures, despite near evangelical recommendations by others. But then, to be honest, neither did many of the pill-based cold cures I tried before.

I have also resolved to get fitter and healthier. I originally wondered what on earth being fit and healthy had to do with ethical living, but when you think about it there is some logic to it. The fitter you are, the less money, skilled labour and energy should be required to make you better, or tend you in your illness. Thereby, you're freeing resources to be used on someone in more need of them than you. Also, the fitter and healthier you are, the less likely you are to cause grief and distress to your friends and family by becoming ill. Being fitter gives you more energy and zip to get up and do something more useful with your life, too.

This is all pious claptrap, of course. Deep down, the real reason why I want to get fitter is to feel better within myself – to make it up off the sofa to fetch the remote control without panting – and to erase the embarrassment of having my waistline measured for new trousers. The trouble is that fitness regimes have never segued with my daily routine too well.

I haven't actually had a full medical check-up since I was about twelve. I like the idea of an MOT for the body, but I don't need a medical degree to know what the results would say. 'In need of complete overhaul – needs new starter motor, poor bodywork, and replace spare tyre.'

I don't smoke, I rarely drink and I like to think that I eat a fairly healthy and balanced diet. OK, so I love a dollop of mayonnaise, a daily milky coffee, the odd Danish pastry and slice of soft cheese, but I don't generally make a habit of eating processed or fatty foods, especially now that we are receiving our box of organic fruit and veg each week.

However, I will admit to being on the wrong side of those

body-mass-index readings that you can get in Boots. Even the fact that I'm 6ft 4in doesn't compensate for the fact that I'm heavy enough to switch from the wing to second row in the scrum when playing rugby. But that's the problem: I don't play rugby. Or football. Or go swimming. In fact, the only exercise I get in life is walking up the stairs at work when the lift isn't working, and picking up Esme.

Whether they're related to my lack of exercise or not, I don't know, but the ailments I have had over the past twelve months are as follows: five colds, one cricked neck, one corn, dozens of light headaches, and a suspected case of food poisoning after a visit to a relative who will remain unnamed. But offer that tally to me for next year and I will take it, thank you.

My pre-audit drill for these kinds of minor ailments was simple. I'd pop into a chemist and dispense with about ten pounds in exchange for a carrier bag full of pills, powders and potions. I suffer from that peculiarly male aversion to visiting the doctor, so only in extreme cases would I join the queue down at my local GP's clinic.

My routine after getting a cold – my most common complaint – is a good example of how I tended to tackle an ailment. I would buy a ten-pack of Lemsip Extra Strong, a box of menthol-infused tissues and some Vicks VapoRub, then retire to bed for a couple of days until I was over the worst of it. I would drink a Lemsip about every three to four hours. If I sounded pathetic enough and sniffled lots I might even get a dose of sympathy from Jane. However, this was rare.

Now I make myself a hot toddy before bed (hot water, fresh lemon juice, a cinnamon stick, some cloves, honey and a capful or two of whisky). I still don't get any sympathy, though. Although, to be fair, I'm not too good at dishing out the sympathy to Jane, either.

I'm still of the view that I'm going to get colds whatever I do. Even if I did a half-marathon before breakfast I would still expect to get struck down a handful of times a year. It's just something that happens. Whether it's out of sheer laziness or indifference to my health, I'm prepared to admit that, like most men, I don't do enough in the way of preventative measures – i.e., exercise. I read all the reports about the importance of regular exercise in combating heart disease and certain cancers, but, again like most men, always file them under 'Mañana'.

However, the one area of my healthcare that I think I do pay enough attention to is my teeth. I am blessed with never having had any fillings – my dentist says this is down to fluoride in the water, my mum says it's down to my lack of a sweet tooth as a child – and to keep it that way I visit the dental hygienist every six months for a scrape and a prod. I brush my teeth twice a day and floss a few times a week, too.

That's about the sum of my health and fitness routine. Since Esme was born, though, we've talked about doing more exercise (I've slurred Jane here somewhat as she does, in fact, do Pilates on a weekly basis, but, still, in my view it's hardly aerobic exercise), and we've had fatalistic conversations about what we'd do if either of us became ill.

But now that the auditors have advised us to think more carefully about our fitness and health, there's a danger that we could actually be put off. Telling me to exercise more is like telling a child to tidy their room – there'll be a flurry of bluster and activity followed by a declining curve of interest and, finally, moody resentment. Since I left school, where I was literally dragged on to the playing field each Friday afternoon by the scruff of my neck (snooker and chess, my preferred sports, are yet to be classified as physical exercise on the school curriculum, as far as I'm aware), I have made a grand total of four attempts in adulthood to take up a form of regular exercise in an effort to 'get fit'. However, after much deliberation, each has been ruled inappropriate.

Five-a-side football was ruled out because it was a hassle to get to the sports hall, I don't really hold a flame for laddish changing-room banter, and, most importantly, I can't play football for toffee.

Yoga (don't laugh) was ruled out after a couple of lessons because, well, I don't need to explain, other than to say that there are few things as humiliating to an unfit man as doing the Downward Dog in front of a class of svelte, toned and smug yoga fanatics.

Jogging round the park didn't last long because it was mid-winter at the time, my CD Walkman kept jumping ('Keep on ru-ru-ru-ru-ru-ru-nning') and it was just plain boring.

Finally, my one flirt with gym membership voluntarily lapsed after about two months when, one morning, I woke up and declared, 'I can't do it any more. No more spin classes, isotonic drinks, personal programmes or locker-key deposits!' Gyms are just not for me. Period.

Needless to say, this miserable roll-call of weak-willed half-heartedness doesn't fill me with confidence that any new attempt to lead a more healthy – and, therefore, more ethical – lifestyle will incorporate any form of exercise. My trouble is that I need to enjoy exercise. Just exercising for the sake of it will never work for me. And so I have been seeking a sport that has a purpose, but, more importantly, is something that I can actually do.

These restrictive criteria leave just one sport – tennis. I played it competently at school, enjoyed it and, furthermore, there are public courts nearby in the local park, leaving me no excuse.

My attempts to gain some, er, net return in my life, though, have so far been hard fought. I'd say, in tennis parlance, it's going with serve and 5–5 in the first set. It started well. I tried to play at least once a week, but even with a sport I love, interest soon started to wane. A month into the new regime and the court bookings are already starting to slip from a couple a week to one a fortnight. The true tell-tale sign that things aren't going too well is that I'm starting to make up excuses for not being able to go. 'Sorry, can't do it this week – been meaning to re-pot my herbs.'

I feel as though I'm hovering on that fine line – not for the first time in my ethical-living experiment – when you start trying to justify your action (or inaction) by saying to yourself that it is 'ethically' the correct thing to do. Lack of logic, reason or even humanity are no barrier to justification, it seems. For example, I have found myself trying to tell myself it is OK to give up exercise because the sooner I'm removed from this mortal coil – i.e. keel over one day due to lack of exercise – the quicker I will stop using up the planet's finite resources. It is better just to burn brightly and quickly in life rather than suffer a slow and rather ineffectual existence (wake, eat, commute, work, eat, work, commute, eat, sleep, and so on ad infinitum) as many of us do.

OK, as I've already mentioned, I've probably watched the film *Logan's Run* (where humans are culled at the age of thirty) a few too many times, but if all of us live as long as physically possible (as our scientific developments are increasingly letting us do), won't we just speed our inevitable extinction as a race, and damage the planet with more vigour as a result? Is pursuing healthcare – whose principal purpose is to enable us to live longer – even ethical when set in the context of the much larger question of the health of the planet? But then again, the pursuit of pain relief and speeding recovery through medicine must be ethical, as suffering is averted or shortened. What is right? Species over planet? Or vice versa? And am I now destined to suffer wave after wave of existential angst?

It's all well and good convincing yourself that the planet would be much better off without us pesky humans, and that healthcare is a species-centric and therefore selfish obsession, but when your child falls ill the fog suddenly clears: give her the best drugs available and give them to her NOW.

Thank God I'm not a healthcare professional. I certainly don't envy the ethical turmoil they must go through every day, as Tim can testify . . .

Have you the time and energy to discover how to avoid the pitfalls that bias contemporary

healthcare? Drug companies that hype products no better, or even worse, than the next drug? The doctors offering a quick fix privately, even if it may not work? Complementary medicine based on hope, disillusion with the modern Western world, and everyone's built-in ability to believe good news?

I'm an NHS consultant, and guilty of the occasional private case (when asked, I'd rather treat patients with my knowledge than expose them to someone else's ignorance), though I refuse to see my own patients from the NHS privately, and find that my local private hospitals can't offer as good a service as the NHS anyway (but faster, alas, yes).

I try hard to use the tested knowledge and experience of my colleagues and predecessors, discovering often that accepted medical practice is based once more on the built-in ability to believe good news and the lucky coincidence of attempted treatment and observed improvement.

In the trade this is called 'evidence-based medicine'. The difficult part is that my patients have to listen, and often to hear that there is no good treatment, and that the cure they have been promised is illusory. The answer, such as it is (and I practise in pain control), is to change lifestyle and expectations.

My own challenge is that by equating ethical practice with an honest appraisal of medical knowledge, I have to simultaneously care for and

frustrate my patients, knowing that it is easy for
them to seek the nostrums and ill-founded
panaceas of medical mythology and the popular
medical press.

Tim P

13

IT'S LESS THAN A MONTH since Esme's stay in hospital on that memorably hot weekend and already the first signs of autumn are upon us. We've started to notice that the produce in our organic box is leaning towards the classic orchard fruits, such as apples, plums and pears. We've also been enjoying our first kale, squashes and sweetcorn. At last, we have a way of noticing the change in seasons other than having to pick up a new train timetable for the journey into work.

The real sign that summer is fast departing, though, is that I have had to start wearing a coat outside. I also turned on the central heating for the first time in months the other day. But then I turned it off. It had been an instinctive reaction to the merest chill in the evening air, but as I stood by the radiator waiting for it to warm, I realized that heating the whole house was completely unnecessary. After all, as my grandmother might say, I could just put on another layer.

It was a mundane observation but it brought home to me that, despite my efforts to adopt a more ethical lifestyle, I am still programmed to do certain things. When you're constantly analysing every aspect of your life you're left feeling as if you've been in a classroom all day long: it is exhausting to maintain such a high level of awareness. But it has made me realize the extent to which I have been living life in cruise control.

But it is now getting to the point where we can't ignore the drop in temperature. Jane and I have very different responses to the merest hint of a chill in the air, and it's been no different this year: Jane will turn to me and say, 'Stick the heating on, will you?' but I usually hold out as long as possible. Probably a bit mean of me, given that Jane suffers from Raynaud's disease (a painful lack of blood supply to the hands and feet), but I do hate to see money going up in flames.

Our differing responses sum up our heating strategy for the colder months – that is, we don't really have a strategy. The best I can offer is that we use a timer on our combi-boiler during the winter. On weekdays during cold spells, the central heating is timed to come on at six thirty a.m. and to go off at nine o'clock once we've left for work. It then comes on again at about five p.m. before shutting down for the night at ten thirty. At weekends, depending on how cold it is, we override the timed setting and instead have it running on 'constant' throughout the day. And with Esme in the house, we now tend to have the heating set slightly higher than normal at about 23°C. We're quite lazy, too, about monitoring which radiators are turned on, so will invariably be heating rooms we're not using.

But it's not all a wanton waste of energy in our home. A few years ago we were tempted by some blurb sent to us by our electricity supplier to sign up for its 'green tariff' – one of the attractions being that we would be sent some free energy-efficient light bulbs. It was one of our few conscious pre-audit attempts to do our bit for the environment.

Mike's verdict after looking around our house is brutal and blunt. 'You're not doing enough to cut your energy consumption,' he tells us. 'You really should do a thorough survey of your energy use and take steps to reduce the amount of energy being wasted through poor insulation, such as your lack of double glazing. Double glazing can prevent 20 per cent of heat loss through windows.'

Mike's not too impressed by our boiler either. 'Your central heating is gas-powered, which is not a bad thing, but the boiler looks old and could be far more efficient. If you're thinking of replacing it, then consider getting an energy-efficient condensing boiler, which could cut your fuel bills by more than 30 per cent.'

Hannah asks us what energy providers we use. She's pleased to hear that we're signed up to a green-tariff scheme, but is less happy about our choice. 'It's a good start that you're signed up to London Energy's green tariff, but other green electricity schemes give greater support to the emerging renewable energy market. Just 0.09 per cent of London Energy's generation is via renewables. And its parent company, EDF Energy, is part of the EDF Group, which is a big nuclear generator in France.'

Mike agrees that choosing the right green tariff by learning the subtle differences between them is important. 'Electricity companies are all obliged to supply some green electricity, but many merely supply the legal minimum of renewable energy. Friends of the Earth has produced a league table of green electricity suppliers which rates companies according to how much renewable energy they provide. You should compare your options on our website.'

I ask the auditors whether it's just electricity that can be bought via a green-tariff scheme, or if gas firms also offer such an option. They say that there isn't really an equivalent renewable scheme on the market for gas, but Hannah suggests an alternative. 'Equigas is a good ethical option. It aims to avoid penalizing low-income customers by charging 1.62 pence per kilowatt regardless of how much you use or how you pay.'

But the auditors don't just talk about our energy suppliers; they also discuss ways to increase energy efficiency throughout our home. As ever, there are expensive options and more palatable ones. We opt to hear the bad news first.

The first topic is whether our boiler should stay or go. I say that I can't see the logic in ripping out a perfectly good combi-boiler, even if it doesn't boast the latest fuel-efficient technology. Secondly, I add, we can't justify the cost. Hannah tries to tempt me by reminding me that they can significantly lower running costs, but fails to convince me to take immediate action. I do agree, though, that when the boiler packs up we will certainly invest in a condensing boiler – one that uses a heat exchanger to heat water with the exhaust gases that typically escape out of the flue.

'But don't forget there's another, much better option,' says Hannah. 'What about installing solar panels? Grants are available towards solar water heating, and up to 60 per cent of the installation cost of photovoltaic roof panels for generating electricity can be reclaimed, too.'

'But we're slap bang in the middle of London,' I say. 'Is that really practical? You'll be asking us to put up a wind turbine in our garden next.'

Jane asks for some more affordable advice. The auditors all insist that there are dozens of simple things we can do around the home that would make a big difference to energy efficiency.

Renée says she draws inspiration from her frugal father. 'My dad seems to have spent his lifetime turning lights off in the house. Although it drove me nuts when I was a kid, I do find myself doing it now. Another simple step is cooking with the saucepan lid on – and steaming vegetables, which has the added bonus of being healthier than boiling them.'

Mike suggests that it would be a good idea to fill the holes between the floorboards in the sitting room. He says this could be inexpensive if done with newspaper scraps, beading or sealant. 'Closing your curtains at dusk helps prevent heat escaping,' he adds. 'Turning the thermostat down by just one degree can save energy – you may not even notice the difference in temperature. And as your light bulbs go, make sure you get energy-efficient replacements. Lighting accounts for 10 to 15 per cent of the average electricity bill.'

Hannah offers some tips, too: 'Draught-strip external doors and window frames; pin up curtains that hang over radiators; turn down the thermostat to 17ºC; place aluminium foil behind the radiators, and turn them off in unused rooms. But don't forget the bigger picture – that our homes are responsible for about a quarter of the UK's carbon dioxide emissions. Therefore lobby for better investment in energy-efficiency measures in our housing stock – Europe's worst insulated – and support campaigns that call for an end to our reliance on oil.'

For the past few months we haven't needed to think about our energy use at home, other than for things such as cooking. Our lighting and heating requirements have both been greatly reduced by the long and warm summer days. But with the combi-boiler now back in use each night to heat up the house, the issue seems inescapable.

So I have made the first move. I have contacted the local Energy Efficiency Advice Centre and completed its DIY Home Energy Check questionnaire. The questions were fairly straightforward: what type of residence do we live in? (mid-terrace Victorian house); how many bedrooms? (three); what type of windows? (wooden sash); how old is the house? (1870s, we think); what boiler do we have? (combi), and so on.

A few of the questions did leave us a little stumped, though, such as whether we had cavity walls or not. This is important, it transpires, as more heat is lost on average through a house's walls than anywhere else – about a third. I had always assumed it was the roof, but there you go. A general pointer to the presence of cavity walls, we learned, is the age of the house. If it was built before 1930 then it probably does not have them, but another tell-tale sign is the brick pattern on the external walls.

So Jane and I tramped outside to study our bricks. We had

been instructed to look for whether the wall was made up just from 'stretchers' (the long side of a brick), suggesting it would be a cavity wall, or whether there were any 'headers' showing (the thin end of a brick), which would indicate that it was probably a nine-inch-solid brick wall. Given the age of the house and the fact that we immediately spotted headers in the pattern, we confirmed that there were no cavities in the walls. If there had been, we could have spent about £300 having the cavities filled by injection, which would have paid for itself in fuel-bill savings within about three to five years. We had to console ourselves with the thought that terraced living means that two of our walls are 'insulated' by our next-door neighbours. Which is kind of them.

The other big question that we couldn't answer before investigating further was whether we have loft insulation or not. I must confess that I had never ventured up into our loft before other than to push a few cardboard boxes stuffed with outgrown baby paraphernalia up through the hatch. So I was pleasantly surprised to discover when I shone a torch around the loft space that we did actually have loft insulation. It was a little bit patchy in places so I straightened it out as best I could, but in general it looked good and was the depth of the joists throughout. A slight concern, though, was that it is made of glass fibre, which I learned later that day, when I realized some had gone down the back of my shirt, can be a skin irritant. A natural alternative to use in any future home we move to, I've been told, could be sheep's wool. I'm sure Esme's newborn knitted cardigans are doing a handsome job of insulating the loft, too.

In the end, the questionnaire identified two main energy-waste villains in our home – the windows and our wooden floors downstairs. We both baulk at the idea of replacing our sash windows with double glazing. It would destroy the look of the house and would cost a fortune. We've been told about secondary glazing, but that seems just as unsightly to us. People have done enough damage to the external aesthetics of the houses on our street – Sky dishes, mock-Victoriana plastic lanterns and red-brick front walls – without adding PVC double glazing to the mix, too. After some digging around we have found some firms that fit double-glazed, traditional-style sash windows, but the quotes are astronomical – £5,000 plus – so we've settled on the rather unsatisfactory option of waiting until they need replacing.

We've reached the same conclusion about investing in a renewable energy source, such as solar panels. How can we justify spending thousands of pounds until it's absolutely necessary? It's fine saying that this technology pays for itself within five to ten years, or whatever, but when you don't have thousands of pounds to hand to pay for it you're unlikely to make that kind of gesture. There's a development planned just behind our house that will accommodate over a hundred families, but judging by the plans there's absolutely no provision for the site to generate its own power using renewable energy sources. If a nationwide property developer can't see the economic value of including such technology, then why should homeowners such as us? This is an area where I really believe that the government should take the lead by making it compulsory that all new housing stock, and certain conversions or housing upgrades, should be as energy neutral as possible. It's the government that's setting all these greenhouse-gas-emission targets for us to meet, after all.

Rant over. The one area where we have decided to spend some cash is filling all the gaps in our wooden floors. The draughts are very noticeable in the winter, so we have paid for someone to come in and squeeze a mixture of wood dust and glue into the gaps. And as soon as the boards are sanded smooth, the heat retention is immediately apparent. It has actually led us to turn down the thermostat to about 19°C.

But this fussing over the efficiency of our heating has made me start to obsess about the temperature of the house. I've even started to do that thing that seems to be the copyright of all middle-aged dads: backing up to a radiator, putting both hands flat on it, and with teeth sucked saying, 'Hmmm, this could do with a bleed.' To Jane's huge annoyance I've started to turn down the hot-water thermostat, too. But my efforts keep being curtailed. Each attempt to lower the thermostat only lasts as long as it takes Jane to yell from a tepid shower, 'Have you been fiddling with the bloody water heating again?'

One major frustration still to vent: why can't you get fully dimmable energy-efficient light bulbs? Wouldn't that make perfect eco sense? We've gone to the effort of changing over all our light bulbs only to find that our new ones won't work on our dimmer switches. I have discovered that a bulb called the Osram Dulux El Vario (yes, another sign that I've been obsessing about this all too much, perhaps) is partly dimmable in that it has two brightness options, and I've even found out online that such rare beasts are available in the US, but, sadly, we're still using a handful of conventional bulbs around the house where dimming is needed.

But at least we only really have to worry about these energy-saving headaches in the winter in this country. It has taken this letter from Mickey to hammer home how much energy is required to keep people at a comfortable temperature in some other parts of the world.

I live in the Washington DC area, which was one of the cities to pioneer air-conditioning due to its large office buildings and hot, humid summers. Virtually everyone who can afford it locks themselves in their air-conditioned houses all summer long, with their windows closed, and drives to their air-conditioned offices in air-conditioned cars with their windows rolled up.

On the other hand, I live in a house built in 1912 with central air-conditioning, but in the nine years I have lived here I have only turned it on twice when I had visitors. Fortunately, the age of my house means that the doors and windows are positioned to allow breezes to blow through. I have ceiling fans in the living room and bedroom, which make still nights more tolerable. I sweat, sometimes to the point of sticking to the desk, as I work on the computer. And I have few visitors from the end of June to the beginning of September. So why do I persist in tolerating the perspiration and occasional discomfort?

1) I get to hear birds, cicadas, and crickets through the open windows. Right now I have some lovely floral scent blowing in. Whoops, it just transitioned to barbecue charcoal smell.

2) I am not contributing to pollution and global warming (during the summer).

3) I am not contributing to noise pollution from the outside condenser.

4) I am acclimatized to the outdoor temperature so it's comfortable to go outside to pick lettuce, onions, tomatoes or herbs from my organic garden.

5) I appreciate the glorious cool morning breezes through the windows when all my neighbours are locked inside their controlled environment.

6) My gas and electric bills are next to nothing in the summer.

7) My skin is softer, requiring less moisturizer, and my hair looks full and curlier, rather than dry and limp as it does in the winter. I think I look ten years younger in the summer.

8) I complain less than most people when they are outside in the summer, because I am used to the temperature.

I really worry that so many Americans have accepted that they must live within air-conditioning and that we are living in the controlled environment of science fiction, with few people motivated to ensure that the natural air and water is kept clean and healthy. Fortunately, many people in Great Britain and Europe are more

conscious of the effects on the environment and
their own pocketbooks. Good luck and thank you
so much for your efforts.

Mickey Stam, Alexandria, Virginia

Things to do before you die? The predictable answers to this
question are always things such as bungee jumping, parachut-
ing, visiting the Grand Canyon and other such visual and
adrenalin stimulants. But one of my stock answers over the
years has been that I really, really want to be a juror on a trial
at some point in my life. I've never understood why people see
it as a chore and do all they can to wriggle out of it when they
get summoned, and have always been hugely jealous of those
who are called up. Whether it's because I've watched too many
courtroom dramas over the years, or I want to experience the
power and responsibility gifted to you for that short period of
time, I don't know, but for as long as I can remember I've
always wanted that letter to fall on my doormat.

About a month ago, that dream came true. The letter said I
was being called up to attend two weeks of jury service. Barring
illness or any other extreme unforeseen event, it said I must
attend and would be recompensed for my troubles. I was
thrilled. Jane did jury service about five years ago and found
the whole experience fascinating, exciting and rewarding. I
couldn't wait. The only advice she gave me as I set off for my
first day's duty was to take a book to read – there can be a lot
of waiting around.

As I entered, the presence of the crown court building – the austere wooden panelling on the walls, the grand pillars either side of the staircase, the security screen by the entrance – spooked me considerably. Waiting in the foyer were relatives of the defendants, as well as numerous court staff, solicitors and barristers. Even the musty smell of the place gave the sense that serious business took place inside.

I was led up the stairs, under the sign 'Jurors only', to a large waiting room where about a hundred other members of the public were waiting for instruction. I sat in the corner and got my book out. It took nearly half an hour before the clerk came to put on a video to explain proceedings. But I didn't get much of my book read; instead I sat and eavesdropped on some of the conversations going on around me. People talked about what a waste of time this whole thing was and how much money or business they were losing by having to be here today. Then there were the old hands who had been here a week already and were now filling in the newbies with the workings of a trial. Some even told in considerable detail how they'd already, in the words of one woman, 'sent down some bad uns'.

The cross-section of society was extraordinary. I loved the thought that we were all here simply because our names had been pulled randomly from a computer; there was no other motivating factor. Where else does that happen in life? Living in London can leave you blasé to the presence of such diversity, but what struck me most was not the different ethnicities on show, but the extremes of class and wealth. And more significantly, how quickly like-minded people had clustered to be with their own 'sort'. I couldn't recall ever before witnessing instinctive segregation occurring right before my eyes, and wondered how this would manifest itself in the jury room once a trial was under way.

But after a few hours more of waiting around and ear-wigging, the clerk announced over the tannoy that no new trials would be starting that day and that we were dismissed. It was desperately frustrating.

Worse still, it happened for the next three days. It wasn't until the Friday of that first week that I was finally selected to be put on a trial. Fifteen of us were led by the usher into the courtroom, of whom twelve were chosen to sit in the jury box. My name was the twelfth to be called out, to my great relief.

The judge then instructed us as to our duties and about what we were going to experience. I scribbled down everything diligently on the paper we had been provided with. Then the defendant was brought in and the charges he faced were read out to the court. I could sense a collective sigh among the eleven jurors around me when it was announced that these were, in summary, conspiracy to defraud his local council out of housing benefit. How dull, we all thought. Why couldn't we have a murder or bank robbery to get our teeth into?

I felt incredibly guilty for thinking such a thing. I hadn't waited all my life to be involved in a case as dull as this, surely? But then I tried to tell myself about the responsibility we all had to this man. I didn't know exactly what the tariff for such a crime might be if he was found guilty, but I guessed it might mean a short spell behind bars. We had his fate in our hands, I kept reminding myself. A few hours of our time for a few months, or even years, of his.

It didn't take too long – three hours at the most – for the case to be presented to us. But it seemed clear to me within about ten minutes where the other jurors' sympathies lay. Their body language and the odd sigh upon certain revelations suggested they thought he was nothing more than a sponger, who had blatantly been trying to rip off the state for all he could.

How wrong I was. After just under an hour of deliberation we were back out in the courtroom to announce that we had found the man not guilty on all the related charges. What was it, I wondered, that had convinced the jurors, including me, that he should be acquitted? Was it the strict application of the 'beyond reasonable doubt' rule, as instructed by the judge? Or was it the irritating and condescending manner of the prosecution barrister, who had, in my opinion, probably lost the Crown its case due to his inability to connect with us? Or was it nothing more than just the impression on us of the bare facts placed before us?

I couldn't help but think about how important the interpretation of these facts truly was. As the discussion had continued round the table in the juror room, my faith in the justice system rose and fell depending on each juror's reasoning. It seemed corny and obvious at the time, but I couldn't help thinking of *Twelve Angry Men*, the film and play about the juror who manages to reveal, one by one, the prejudices of the other jurors and thereby acquit an innocent man who looked certain at first to be found guilty. Should I make an effort to shout down people's clear attempts to introduce their prejudices into the discussion? Or was listening to them a natural and necessary part of being on a jury? Maybe I was just being as prejudiced as them?

I was annoyed that I could be arrogant enough to assume my thoughts were superior to everyone else's around me. I didn't like the 'me and them' way my brain was working. I began to wonder whether the consensual view of all twelve of us was really the best way to find out whether the defendant was guilty or innocent of the charges. It all seemed so arbitrary – a random selection of people from the electoral register hear some evidence presented to them by people who can be either persuasive or offputting, before thrashing it out together behind closed doors with the possibility of one or two dominant personalities swinging everyone else's views.

In the end, all my angst accounted for little. The prosecution barrister was visibly distraught that he'd been 'defeated' by the young solicitor with the ill-fitting suit and spiky gelled hair who had represented the accused man. In contrast, the young solicitor was jubilantly punching the air and muttering 'Yes!' to himself and then to the defendant behind him. We were all led back to the jurors' waiting room.

The next week I again had to wait three days before being chosen for another trial. But this one was altogether more engaging than my first. It centred on a burglary in which a policeman had been assaulted trying to make an arrest as the two defendants fled the scene. We, the jury, had to decide whether the defendants were individually guilty of, first, the burglary, and, second, the assault on the policeman.

Again, if I'd been asked my opinion on hearing a summary of the evidence I would have thought a guilty verdict would have been a dead cert. A policeman's word against that of two suspected burglars who really looked the part. Mmm, tricky one. In the end, we did indeed find them guilty, but only after much heated debate and lurches of opinion – all chaired somewhat ineffectually by me, having been bumped by the other jurors into being the foreman.

Overall, the two weeks were a fascinating insight for me into how justice is dished out in this country, but they didn't leave me feeling wholly confident in the system. Far from it. I just couldn't stop dwelling on how arbitrary it all seemed, especially inside the jurors' room. People had changed their minds – and therefore the fate of the defendants – in a flash, usually under pressure from another outspoken juror. Is this the best way to obtain justice? I kept thinking. It struck me just how important it is for the blend of jurors to be right if justice is to be reached. Just one strong voice – be it a witness, barrister, judge or fellow juror – is evidently all it takes for all the jurors to swing one way or the other. It led me to think a lot about what is justice, what is right and wrong, and how important it is for people to be defended well.

But most of all, I came away from the experience wondering about what having a role in society really means; about how we – however fleetingly or dramatically – impact on other people's lives, not only through our actions, but also through our beliefs, words and prejudices. I felt a real wave of guilt about what self-centred lives we lead, feathering our nests, looking out for our own, and fearing and shunning the unknown. It left me wondering how much of my ethical living was about making my life better and how much was about improving the lives of others. And if both, does that matter?

* * *

I've always had a problem with the term 'local community'. What exactly do people mean by it? I can understand it in the context of living in the countryside, where a community's boundaries are more clearly defined, but in a city such as London it's harder to pin down. Is the local community the street or estate you live on? Or is it one of the many other links people have: the postal code, the local authority, the parish, the train station, the football club, the school catchment area, the supermarket catchment area, the parliamentary constituency, or even the city as a whole?

Even if, for argument's sake, I assume it to mean anyone living within a two-mile radius, I can't boast much of a track record in working to improve the local community, merely trotting out some lame I'm-just-too-busy-to-find-time excuses: baby to raise, full-time job, that kind of thing. The most I can offer in the way of having given time to others, in fact, is that during my sixth-form years I used to help out at the local hospital radio.

The highlight of this one spell of Doing Something for the Community wasn't so much feeling the inner warmth of touring the wards asking for record requests, but trying to outwit the radio manager's ruling on what he deemed acceptable to be transmitted to the patients. 'Nothing should be played that's stronger than "Woman" by John Lennon,' he would repeat. I would spend each weekly session asking myself whether I could get away with a current Top 40 track (as requested by patients), or whether it would be better just to stick to Perry Como's Greatest Hits as instructed. I think I saw myself more as a budding John Peel than John the Baptist.

℗ 'What do you do for your local community?' The
question hangs in the air for an uncomfortable length
of time.

'Well, I don't do volunteering for the local meals-on-
wheels or pull shopping trolleys from canals, if that's what
you mean,' I respond a little defensively. 'We haven't lived in
the area for too long, but we are getting to know more local
people. Is that what you mean?'

The auditors ask Jane and me if we vote. Always, we
respond. The questions keep coming. Do we use locally
owned and run shops? Do we know which councillor
represents the ward we live in?

No, we say.

'Does anything about the area annoy you?'

Beyond the obvious inner-city gripes, such as litter,
graffiti and fear of crime, we mention that the acquisition of
the school behind our house by property developers concerns
us – as it does many other local residents.

'By not getting involved with your local community,' says
Mike, 'you are probably missing out on opportunities to
influence what goes on in your area and help shape a
community that you want to live in.'

Mike adds that the first act to feeling more empowered is
to engage more with local democracy. 'The quality of life in
your local community is very much affected by the actions
of your local authority,' he says. 'But how can you object to,
say, plans concerning the redevelopment of the school if you
don't even know who to contact about the decision? It has to
be said that local authorities don't make it easy for people

to comment on plans, or for people to give feedback on the quality of the services they offer. But local councils are getting better at it. If people don't engage with their local councillors and let them know what they think the council is doing well or what it should be doing better, then they can't really complain when they fail to perform.'

Hannah is keen to pin down what the term 'local community' means for us. 'Is it the street you live in, your local friends with similar aspirations, or something else? A central criticism of "gentrification" is that middle-class home-buyers such as yourselves change the nature of the community precisely through their lack of desire to be part of it. Existing residents of a place like Brixton, which is known for its vibrancy, street life, pubs, busy market and multiculturalism, may well resent newcomers who spend no money in local businesses and take little interest in the area. Could you, for example, reverse your shopping habits and visit the supermarket just for items that are unavailable or unaffordable locally?'

This is a subject that sparks Renée's interest. 'For me, supporting the local community means buying local goods from local, independent stores where possible. Supporting your local economy – whether this means, say, the village, Yorkshire or even Britain – is good for jobs and the economy of your own region and country. And you're also not travelling unnecessarily.'

But it should go wider than just supporting local shops, says Mike. 'Supporting local services, such as libraries and swimming pools, also gives the clear message that these facilities are needed and wanted by local people.'

Hannah asks us if we buy a local weekly paper to keep abreast of local issues. I say that this is actually a bit of a bugbear of mine, as I have searched high and low for a local newsagent that will deliver newspapers but all of them say that, despite their best efforts, they can't find any local kids interested in doing a paper round. I say that I would certainly be interested in receiving a local paper if it was delivered, but that it doesn't really cross my mind to pick one up otherwise.

'OK, well why not join the Brixton section of the online Urban 75 forum (www.urban75.org)?' she says. 'When twenty-eight African asylum seekers were stranded locally, Urban 75 members quickly knew and could take over food and blankets and fire off press releases to alert the media.'

Hannah adds that we should ask ourselves the question, 'Who is poor and why?' 'Global social-justice issues play out in Britain's cities as much as on the coffee plantations of Colombia. Are corporate interests displacing people or threatening a way of life? With its slightly fragmented but still strong radical counterculture, Brixton is an ideal place to live if you want to grapple with concepts of power structures, ethics and resistance. You could help, say, groups fighting displacement or support positive eco-initiatives such as community gardens. You should also challenge racist or classist comments when you come across them.'

Mike says that he took the time before visiting us to research how many local groups were seeking help. 'Local community organizations and charities are often looking for volunteers and for financial support. There are sixty different charities and voluntary organizations within a mile of your home, so there are plenty of opportunities to get involved.'

Doing jury service has really left me resolved to connect more with the community and fulfil my 'civic duty', whatever that might be. But neither Jane nor I are really sure where to start. Some things sound as if they should be quite easy, such as frequenting more local shops, but the bigger themes such as 'grappling with power structures' all seem a little heady. I've never really seen myself as the grappling type. I sign the odd petition if someone in the street asks me, but that's often more out of the embarrassment of saying no than particular empathy to the cause. I've never been on a march or picketed outside the town hall. The closest I get to the white heat of democracy in action is probably watching *Question Time*.

The auditors seemed to be urging us to donate some of our time not to our own needs but to those of the wider community. We both agree that this is indeed a noble sentiment; it is just a matter of finding something, or someone, that would benefit from such a gesture. The danger, of course, is that by procrastinating we will never get around to doing anything, as is so often the case in our lives.

But I recently received an email at work that more or less shoved the solution in my face. It was asking for volunteers to help community projects near the office. I had seen this email do the rounds before, but, although I had been interested, had never acted on it, though I knew about a hundred or so people in the company took part. But the email seemed to answer one of my biggest concerns: just when was I going to find the time to volunteer when I already struggled to clear any spare time in the day? The answer was to give up my lunch hour once a week, hardly my most productive time of day, considering that it is usually spent reading the sports reports or sitting in the local park. So I put my name down for helping out with one-to-one reading for under-performing pupils during the Literacy Hour at a local primary school.

It wasn't long before I was attending a training session with Community Service Volunteers, the UK's largest volunteer organization, which oversees the scheme (not, I must add, training me how to read, but how to help six-year-olds read and how to answer their questions). Much of the training focused on what I should do if one of the pupils wanted to tell me something in confidence about problems at home or with other pupils, such as bullying or any other abuse. To my relief, I was told this was precautionary and that it only occurs on very rare occasions.

But it meant that I was even more nervous than I might otherwise have been when it came to the first reading session a week later. What if a pupil asked me something that I couldn't answer, or worse, answered incorrectly? I had major doubts as to whether I was made of the right material for this. I waited in the school reception to be collected by a teacher and taken to my class. (Waiting in reception for the teacher is still an unsettling experience, I can confirm, even a decade or more after leaving school.)

I felt like a new boy when I entered the classroom. I didn't know the ropes – where to put my coat, what the class were studying, whether I should sit down on one of the tiny chairs and wait quietly. Then thirty-odd children came running in from the playground, no doubt wondering who on earth this tall man standing awkwardly in the corner next to their hand-made 'Countries of the World' wall display was. They all looked at me quizzically before settling on the floor at the feet of Mr Burne, the archetypal stern-but-fair teacher. After the register was taken, I was introduced. Mr Burne asked who wanted to read with me. A surprising number of hands flew up, followed by a chorus of 'Me, sir! Me, sir!' Did they really want to read with me? Or did they simply see me as putty in their hands, someone who could provide them with half an hour of effort-less comedy and mischief? I suspected the latter.

Alfie, a slight boy with a mischievous smile as cheeky and wide as that of Dick Dastardly, was chosen to be my first reader. I wondered whether I was being thrown in at the deep end.

'Hello, Alfie. I'm Leo,' I said nervously. 'Do you want to go and choose a book from the reading corner to read to me?'

He skipped off to the books and came rushing back with one called *Where are you, Blue Kangaroo?* I could sense immediately that he knew it well, as he would try to second-guess the difficult words as he followed with his finger. It was so tempt-ing to do it for him, but I tried patiently to get him to spell each word out slowly and phonetically until he could guess what it was.

Despite my initial doubts, we hit it off immediately. Like any child, he was constantly trying to test my barriers of tolerance and levels of strictness, but we got on well with the book, albeit at a slow and methodical pace. The best sign that Alfie had enjoyed the one-to-one reading session with me was that he begged to finish the book when Mr Burne said our time was up. It had lasted only half an hour but I felt as though I had made a huge advance personally. More importantly, Alfie asked me if I was coming next week. 'Can I read with you?' he said, as I went to get my coat from the knee-high coat pegs by the reading corner. It was the best thing he could have said.

I have now attended several classes and I cherish and look forward to the time more and more each week. Even in such a short time, I feel as though I have already worked my way through the complete repertoire of the reading corner, which means we must be advancing. Alfie is my regular reader, but I have had the opportunity to be read to by a wonderfully engaging selection of members of 2P. It sounds a little silly now, but in the first couple of weeks I felt rather guilty that I was actually enjoying it. I think part of me believed that volunteering should be about suffering for a cause. It has only just dawned on me that it can only really work when both parties are getting something out of it.

14

THE ONE THING I DREAD most with the change in seasons is the need to buy new clothes. Shopping for clothes means one thing to me: standing outside a changing room in, say, Diesel/LK Bennett/Zara/Jigsaw/M&S/Joseph/Gap – they all blur after a while – waiting for Jane to try something on while I bemoan the lost opportunity to be at home watching *Football Focus*.

I really can't think of many things I'd less rather be doing. I'm of that uniquely male mentality, it seems, that sees clothes shopping as a mundane, functional fact of life that should be performed with near military precision and efficiency – get in there, get the job done, and then extract yourself from the theatre of war as fast as possible.

I say 'war' because if I don't manage to express exactly the right order of compliments, in the exactly the right tone – a delicate skill that I've yet to master – the shopping trip will invariably end with a full-blown domestic on the pavement outside Hobbs or wherever, with me facing a tirade of abuse: 'Why do you always have to harrumph around behind me when we're shopping? . . . How do you know a pair of trousers won't fit you if you don't try them on? . . . Clothes cost that much these days – do you want me to look cheap?' – that sort of thing.

I'm not ashamed to say that I'm entirely happy for Jane to dress me. Not literally, of course. I mean when Jane comes home from a shopping trip (from bitter experience she now tends to go alone or with friends) and hands me a bag of clothes and says, 'Here, I bought these for you.' It's an arrangement that suits us both. I'm happy to wear the same old clothes – as long as they're still presentable – from one year to the next. Needless to say, Jane has total control over what Esme wears, too. And so I have little say in how our family buys its clothes.

The auditors cast their eyes over what Jane and I are wearing, then Hannah begins by asking us a few questions about what sort of clothes we tend to wear and where we buy them. My response is much quicker than Jane's.

'From what you say,' says Hannah, 'it seems that you tend to go for quality rather than label-laden clothes. And you don't suffer from Imelda Marcos tendencies.'

I glance at Jane to see whether she has taken this woman-to-woman fashion assessment with grace. I fear this could be quite a volatile part of the ethical audit if the right advice isn't expressed in the right order, given Jane's sensitivity to the threat of being told to change the way she dresses.

'This is good,' says Hannah (dressed herself, remember, in jeans, T-shirt and velour hooded top), probably sensing the tension, 'because over-consumption of clothing, driven by fashion – that handy economic instrument predicated on gullibility and conformity – is taking a huge toll on the environment.'

Worried that this may not be the best way to persuade Jane to reassess her clothes-shopping habit, I look to the others, urging them to speak.

'Like most people, you buy your clothes on the high street,' says Mike (jeans and green cotton shirt). 'While this scores highly on the convenience front, it leaves a lot to be desired from an ethical point of view. Mass-produced fashion is a globalized industry, raising concerns about sweatshop labour, health, safety and environmental standards, as well as the environmental concerns associated with goods being transported around the world. Cheap fashions tend to be disposable in nature, with few garments designed to last more than a season.'

Using the word 'cheap' in relation to our clothes is potentially incendiary, so I hurriedly look to Renée (black trousers and cream silk twin set).

'I don't think you're wearing organic clothes, are you? You look too trendy,' she says.

I smile, but again I'm not sure flattery is going to win over Jane.

'But,' continues Renée, 'it is worth considering organic cotton, particularly for Esme, because cotton is the most highly sprayed textile in the world. It accounts for nearly 25 per cent of the total global insecticide market. If you choose fabrics made from organic cotton, you are getting clothes that not only do not carry pesticide residues – which do not wash out after several washings – but are also not bleached with chlorine dyes, nor coloured with heavy-metal dyes. And you should also try to avoid fabrics that are "easy care" or "non-iron". Many have been treated with formaldehyde – classified by the US Environmental Protection Agency as a probable human carcinogen under conditions of "unusually high or prolonged exposure".

Jane – a little dismissively, if I'm honest – asks about the range of organic clothing now on offer.

'Organic clothes are also available in hemp and wool,' says Renée. 'There are now dozens of companies producing a wide range of organic clothes, including jeans, T-shirts and yoga wear.'

Jane gives me one of her looks.

'Some of these are fashionable and well designed. And clothes from these designers don't necessarily cost more than equivalent, chemical-laden items from a high-street retailer.'

Hannah agrees that hunting down clothes made from organic textiles is an important step to take when sourcing clothes. 'As well as being heavily sprayed with pesticides, cotton – 45 per cent of which is now genetically modified – is also one of the most heavily irrigated crops, partly because water run-off is rapid where the soil structure has been destroyed. In countries with weak or non-existent pollution controls, where dyeing activities are concentrated, reactive dyes and wastes are regularly flushed straight into watercourses. Also, petrochemical-derived synthetic fabrics are often non-biodegradable as well as being heavily polluting and energy-intensive to produce. And the manufacturing of nylon emits large amounts of nitrous oxide, a greenhouse gas

310 times more effective at trapping heat in the atmosphere than carbon dioxide. Leather tanning can also be a highly toxic process.'

'What about the issue of sweatshops?' I ask.

'It almost goes without saying that the price of our clothes-buying addiction is paid by those at the bottom of the supply chain,' responds Hannah. 'But you should note that high-profile workers' rights campaigns, targeted at well-known clothing brands, are not always calls for a consumer boycott. They are often about getting companies to ensure that subcontractors provide fair wages and conditions, and persuading them not to relocate whenever abuses are exposed, thereby leaving workers without jobs. The websites www.cleanclothes.org and www.sweatshopwatch.org both explain the difference between "worker-called" boycotts, which should be supported, and campaigns which prefer customers to routinely question retailers on, for example, whether they enforce an independently monitored code of conduct, and fix prices to suppliers in function of what is needed for them to pay a living wage.'

Jane makes the point that she's never seen any clothing in the shops that promises to answer these concerns.

Mike nods. 'Buying clothes should not create an ethical dilemma,' he says. 'However, it is a sad reflection of our global economy that this is the case. But alternatives for the ethical shopper do exist, although they tend to involve extra effort or extra cash. Ethical clothing outlets can be found, especially online, with manufacturers such as Ethical Threads. Naturalcollection.com includes more environmentally friendly clothing and, although it is unlikely to satisfy logo junkies, it does the job with some style.'

As I make little contribution to the buying of our family's clothes I'm always going to be on thin ice when it comes to trying to coax Jane into reassessing her – our – wardrobe. My efforts haven't been helped by a rather ham-fisted attempt a couple of months ago to surreptitiously sign Jane up to some ethical-clothing mail-order catalogues. A few days later, when the first one was delivered, she picked it up from the doormat disdainfully between finger and thumb and asked, 'Was this you?'

'At least have a flick through it,' I said.

Several pages in, she thrust it into my hands. 'I don't do drawstring. Or tie-dye,' she sighed.

My only comfort was that at least the catalogues were placed in the recycling box.

'I know, let's go on an ethical clothes shopping trip,' I say. 'You'll get to go out to the shops as usual and I'll get to act on the auditors' advice.'

I'm taking a big gamble. I feel as though I've dodged the subject of clothes shopping for long enough and am keen to see, now that we've gone through so much since the auditors left, if Jane is more prepared to consider what they had to say. Somewhat deviously, perhaps, I'm trying to lure her with the bait of a shopping trip – a sure-fire banker for winning her over. She seems surprised, but pleasantly so, I feel.

My mistake, alas, is thinking that by living in London there are myriad options when it comes to finding ethical clothes shops. Other than the local charity shops, I'm left scratching my head when I actually start giving it some proper thought. However, after some research online, I find that two 'ethical' clothes retailers have recently opened up in central London – American Apparel in Carnaby Street and People Tree inside Selfridges on Oxford Street. Both are locations I can easily tempt Jane to. I also discover there is a Traid shop in Brixton near where we live – a place I have always assumed to be just another charity shop full of musty granddad trousers, but now learn is actually a good place to find 'vintage' clothes – fashionable, apparently – and second-hand designer wear. The irony of how our traditional roles have been reversed – me, for once, being the one keen to go shopping – isn't lost on either of us.

So we set out on our mission: to boldly shop for clothes where no self-respecting woman has ever shopped for clothes before. I decide – I'm holding the reins here, remember – that our first destination should be Selfridges, my thinking being that at least this will help Jane acclimatize, as the People Tree clothes are sure to be surrounded by labels familiar to her.

This proves to be the first mistake of the day. After much hunting around, we finally find the People Tree concession on the second floor. People Tree, I have learned on their website, use organic cotton and help 'marginalized producers to improve their lives by giving design and quality skills a fair price, regular orders, and advance payment as needed'. But Jane stands in front of the two racks, looks at the merchandise and says, 'No, to all of that,' sweeping her hand dismissively across the two rails of green and black stripy jersey organic-cotton clothes. 'Have you lost all sight of who I am?' she storms.

To be fair, it is all a little too, in her words, 'eighties retro' – not a look she is accustomed to sporting, however trendy it may be. Before I can encourage her to reconsider, she is already rifling through the Miu Miu items across the aisle. Before we leave, though, I do manage to get Jane to agree to look through People Tree's entire range online. Seeing that I've been upset by her reaction, she consoles me by saying that she did actually like the look of the organic cotton and alpaca wool winter wraps in one of the catalogues I ordered a couple of months back, but didn't want to admit it at the time.

We walk down Oxford Street to Carnaby Street to search for the new American Apparel shop, whose clothes, I've learned, are produced 'sweatshop-free' in a factory in Los Angeles where employees are paid $12.50 an hour, more than double the US federal minimum wage. We get a bit lost looking for it, and I work hard to prevent Jane from drifting into all the other shops nearby, but when we finally locate it we're pleased to discover that, unlike the rather meagre People Tree offering, it's an entire shop over two floors. As soon as we walk in it becomes immediately apparent that we're not their core market. Everyone is wearing clothes about three sizes too big for them and chewing gum, and the staff look as if they've walked straight out of a Benetton advert. I think the correct classification for this particular fashion sub-species is the skater kid.

We keep our heads high, though, and try not to look too self-conscious. And we surprise ourselves by finding some things we like. Admittedly, they're nothing more than some harmless pastel-coloured logo-less T-shirts, tops and items for Esme. It's not the high fashion Jane is craving, but we've made a start.

The trip on the way home to the local Traid shop in Brixton is successful, too. For me, at least. Jane says that she just can't get over her phobia of wearing second-hand clothes, but I manage to find a pair of jeans for £15 and a John Rocha jacket for £30. Our visit to the shop produces some comedy moments, too: Jane is left in hysterics as I keep walking out of the changing rooms in clothes either way too large or too small for me. Without size labels to guide me, the fitting session descends into farce as I can't seem to judge by sight alone whether anything is the right size. Even Esme seems amused, as Mummy points to show her how silly Daddy looks.

The one thing missing from my new head-to-toe ethical look, as Jane mockingly describes it upon our return home, is a pair of shoes. Hannah had mentioned to me that *Adbusters*, the Canadian anti-corporate magazine, sell a pair of trainers that are 'sweatshop-free', but I've learned since that a similar concept trainer, this time made by US-based No Sweat Apparel, is now available online.

So I order a pair. When they arrive they look a bit like a pair of Converse All Star sneakers I had as a child, and for £25 seem like good value, too. Furthermore, they boast on the box that they're 'union-made and vegan'. My favourite thing about them, though, is that there's a little card inside the box that lists the monthly rice allowance, health insurance, maternity pay, Ramadan allowance, pension, family burial allowance and wage – equivalent to $90 a month, based on a forty-hour week

– earned by the Indonesian worker who made them. Jane says she wouldn't be seen dead in them, but I rather like them.

I have actually found our attempt at overhauling our clothes shopping habits rather successful – well, given where we were coming from. Even though it's largely been me who has made the changes, I do feel as though Jane is now more willing to step outside her normal tight circle of clothes shops that she usually entrusts her cheque book to. I don't think, though, she's ready for the following letter quite yet. I suspect I'll have a long wait before I see Jane walking round in an outfit she's stitched together herself . . .

> Fashion is a particular bane of mine – not that I have ever been particularly interested in it, thankfully, but the way you dress has so much influence over the way others interact with you. I hate to buy into it – both personally and ideologically. However, I think I have come to a satisfactory solution, and felt I had to share it with you. I am going to make my own clothes!
>
> I have never tried this before, but I feel very optimistic that I will, with trial and error, eventually create a unique wardrobe. My first project will be a poncho. I bought the pattern (tres facile) the other day. I will get a second-hand sewing machine and experiment with materials from charity shops for mock-ups until I am confident that I have got the hang of it. Then I will buy hemp and organic materials to make my clothes.

Have you or your wife ever tried to make your own clothes? I'm sure it is a very time-consuming process, but what better way to spend those long winter evenings? Like you said in your latest posting, we live in an instant world and are used to getting what we want straight away. This, in contrast, is a bit of a step back in time.

Undoubtedly, the clothes I make will be influenced to a degree by fashion, but I hope that it will be another step towards a more individual and independent lifestyle. I also hope that the act of creation will bring an extra satisfaction to my life, like growing your own vegetables, and baking bread (other aims I have).

Liz Hofmann

'Just wait for Christmas,' someone wrote to us recently. 'That will be the true test of your ethical-living experiment.' What a Scrooge, we thought. But how right they are.

For a season of so-called goodwill and cheer, Christmas this year has, so far, been one huge ethical headache. It seems that every decision Jane and I have had to make in preparing for the big day has thrown up dilemma after dilemma. The problem is compounded by the fact that this is a big Christmas for us – it is Esme's first, and we are also hosting Christmas for the first time, with Jane's parents and siblings coming to stay with us. And now even our friends are starting to mock us in our plight.

'You are not alone. Together, we can resist Christmas.' This is the header of an email recently sent to us by a friend who 'understands' what dilemmas Christmas must be throwing up within our household. Her sympathy came in the form of a link to the website of the Christmas Resistance Movement, which is calling for the end of 'compulsory consumption' at Christmas. Here's a taster of the movement's mission statement. It doesn't make cheery reading, but I'm so frazzled by the tougher-than-normal run-up to Christmas I'm now beginning to agree with most of it:

> You know Christmas shopping is offensive and wasteful. You know Christmas 'wish lists' and 'gift exchanges' degrade the concept of giving. You know Christmas marketing is a scam, benefiting manufacturers, stores and huge corporations, while driving individuals into debt. You know this annual consumer frenzy wreaks havoc on the environment, filling landfills with useless packaging and discarded gifts. Yet, every year, you cave in and go shopping . . . Together, we boycott Christmas shopping, Christmas decorations, Christmas cards, and every variety of Christmas crap. We show our love for friends and family by giving our time and care, not by purchasing consumer goods. We maintain the integrity of giving by giving spontaneously and from our hearts, rather than during a specified season.

What bloody sensible advice. Christmas is making me feel like high-fiving Ebenezer for having the common sense – before Marley's ghost stuck his oar in, at least – to turn his back on it all and say 'sod you' to the whole festive period. I seem to be super-heightened to all of Christmas's negatives at the moment: the wanton waste, the excessive consumption, the consumer debt, the peer pressure to give, the abandoned pets, the sharp rise in calls to the Samaritans, the travel misery, the degrading race to secure this year's 'must-have' toy. I have been largely stripped of my Christmas spirit. Instead of simply dwelling on the good that comes out of this period of the year – the bringing together of families, the rise in voluntary work, the amounts raised for charities, etc. – these are now the kinds of dilemmas that seem to be gnawing away at me (and to a lesser extent Jane):

- Why is it so hard to get an advent calendar for Esme without a bloody chocolate behind each door?
- Why do people think flying to New York to do their Christmas shopping is a good thing? What about the resultant greenhouse-gas emissions such a trip would cause?
- How much electricity are all those high-street Christmas lights actually consuming?
- Why are we all being made to feel guilty about 'harming the UK economy' if we don't spend freely this Christmas?
- Why are we arguing the toss at home about whether to buy Esme a toy grocery shop for Christmas? Is it a needless introduction to the addictive allure of shopping, or a harmless role-playing toy? (A friend has suggested we just re-label it a fair-trade shop and have done with it.)
- Should we introduce the Santa myth to Esme, or shield her from what is now largely a powerful marketing tool? (I can

just imagine her in years to come saying to me, 'Why can't I have a Coke? Santa drinks Coke.') Is it even possible to shield her from him in our Santa-saturated world?

The pressure of hosting Christmas is only making it worse – as if that wasn't pressure enough. Of course, we want to be the perfect hosts, but it is hard to know if we should be imposing the tenets of our ethical-living experiment on all our guests too. It is our duty, after all, to ply everyone with alcohol, serve up a constant stream of mince pies, and give great presents. And this is all before we come to the most pressing test facing us: The Meal. Turkey with all the trimmings was, naturally, our first thought when we started to plan ahead, but after checking the prices of organic turkeys (£50-plus for a decent-sized bird) we've gone a bit cold on that idea – or should that be cold turkey? We briefly thought about a vegetarian alternative but, to be honest, don't really feel confident about imposing this on other people who may not be dreaming of an ethical Christmas. In the end we've decided to opt for an organic rib of beef – still expensive but slightly less intimidating than cooking a huge turkey in our rather meagre oven, and certainly requiring much less energy to cook.

This isn't the first time that the question of whether it's OK to impose our ethical standards on our guests has raised its head. For example, when someone asks for something for Christmas to which you have an ethical objection, should you make an issue of it and risk upsetting them, or just let it be? Is refusing to buy someone, say, the Disney film on DVD that they've asked for, because the corporation has received criticism in the past about using 'sweatshop' labour, the right thing to do?

Personally, this experiment has left me not in favour of lecturing to others, if at all possible – though Jane would no doubt argue that she's had more than her fair share of lecturing. I'm only really interested in trying to analyse and question my own actions and decisions, but it is hard to bite your tongue sometimes, even though I know how annoying it can be to listen to someone lecturing you about their beliefs.

There's also the vexing question of your guests' expectations. I'm certainly not keen to explain that certain traditions have been omitted this year on ethical grounds, but there are some aspects of Christmas that do not sit well with this experiment. It all came to a head when Jane and I debated whether it was OK to get a Christmas tree. Whatever way you look at it, cutting down a tree, transporting it hundreds of miles, draping electric lights over it, then discarding it three weeks later is a little mad. The best option would probably be not to have a tree at all and just decorate a houseplant, but somehow that doesn't seem to have the same magic. ('Mummy, Mummy, when can we decorate the cheese plant?') The tree is so much part of the festive period that it is hard to think of Christmas without one. Furthermore, we have never had a Christmas tree before – despite Jane's protestations – principally because we have never really had the room and because we have never been at home for Christmas, so we thought it would be nice to have one in our new home, given that family will be staying with us.

So off we trundled to visit the local Christmas-tree seller. We pondered briefly whether, in terms of energy and resource consumption, it was better to get a last-a-lifetime, small plastic tree instead of a real one, but came to the conclusion that, in the grand scheme of things, it must be better to get a real tree even if it does only have a two- to three-week shelf life. After all, there are worse things in the world one can do than encourage sustainable tree farms. OK, so Christmas trees are somewhat wasteful and extravagant, but as long as we make the effort to take it to the council's tree-recycling point on 6 January – even if the recycling point is miles away and we don't have a car – to get it shredded into garden mulching chips then at least it won't just be thrown on to the nearest landfill site. Next year, though, we are going to make the extra effort to find one that comes in a pot so we can keep it in the garden and re-use it each year. We asked about these this time, but the bloke just laughed. 'Why would I sell a tree with roots? You wouldn't come here again next year then, would you?'

Decorating the thing has been another concern. It just wouldn't seem the same not having fairy lights on the tree, and so we had a rather comical debate in the shop about whether flashing lights use half the power of stay-on lights. We even considered getting all Dickensian and using real candles, but then worried about burning the house down after drinking too much port one night. I did cut out some old Christmas cards and make paper chains out of recycled newspapers, though. 'What if the neighbours see them through our window?' Jane said. 'They'll think we're mad – if they don't already.'

But final confirmation that our lives have been irrevocably changed by our experiment came when Jane agreed that I could get her a goat for Christmas. I wasn't sure how she would take it, but I threw it in as a suggestion as she ran through her Christmas wish-list. It took a bit of persuading.

'What I'd really like is a pair of Prada shoes,' she said when I asked her.

I couldn't bite my tongue. The idea of spending hundreds of pounds on a pair of shoes is complete anathema to me, regardless of what the auditors would have to say. I suspected she was just winding me up.

'What a waste of money,' I said. 'You'll never wear them. Why don't you have something practical? Like a goat?'

Jane reeled, reddened and then bollocked me. 'What the hell am I going to do with a goat in the middle of Brixton?' she screamed.

'It's not strictly for you,' I said quickly. 'It's a revolving goat shared between families in war-torn communities that are slowly rebuilding themselves. You get them for fifteen pounds from the Good Gifts catalogue. It's a way of giving something meaningful rather than just blindly spending money on totally pointless presents – like Prada shoes.'

'OK,' she said calmly. 'Get me the goat . . . and the Prada shoes. That way, I can look good, you can feel good, and everyone's happy.'

Afterword

'WHAT ASPECTS OF THE EXPERIMENT are you still doing?' It's now well over a year since the auditors first entered our lives, and this is the first question people ask me. It's followed closely by another: 'Have you returned to your normal life now?'

I always struggle to answer such questions. The experiment certainly hasn't stopped. I haven't packed up the wormery, cancelled the box scheme and ceased sorting out the recycling. I can't just delete from my head what the auditors told me. I always knew that this was going to be a one-way trip; a Pandora's box that, once opened, there would be no turning back from. This has become my 'normal' life now, whatever that really means.

I'm trying to continue with all of it as best I can, but it's hard to deny that I have my pet favourites. The volunteering, our new food regime, the garden, the wormery – all of these have engaged me more than I would have first imagined. For example, I recently started mentoring at a local secondary school where English is a second language for over half the pupils – the theory being that I can in some small way guide a fourteen-year-old through GCSEs and beyond. (The reality was that, on our first encounter, it was me doing the learning: I went back to work knowing how to say 'My name is Leo' in Bengali.) Equally, I still find certain things a real chore and can't foresee myself ever actually gaining much satisfaction, let alone enjoyment, from them. These include struggling on a bus with a pushchair and using vinegar and a lemon to clean the loo.

Likewise, the thought of never being able to fly again leaves me with a sense of huge regret and there's no doubt in my mind – or Jane's – that this is one aspiration that we will inevitably fail to meet rigidly in coming years, albeit with a heavy heart and burning sense of guilt. We will forge out a compromise: while we can both see the obvious benefits to the environment of cutting out flights from our lives, we would not wish to relinquish the opportunity of travelling beyond Europe ever again. The solution to this dilemma for us is to try to find alternatives whenever possible, but to never say never.

Looking back, how did I find the whole experience? Living through an experiment that invites constant criticism of your life certainly leaves you vulnerable and raw, especially at the beginning. At times there seemed to be few highs and many lows – you always feel guilty, it is hard work and you have to battle against appearing smug and self-righteous. (I'm convinced that some people still think we must have a sign on our front door that says, 'You are now entering an ethical area. Leave any trace of your wasteful, thoughtless life here.') But I have found the trick to avoiding the feeling that your life is one drawn-out exercise in self-flagellation is to make sure you retain a sense of perspective and humour throughout. No, you can't save the world single-handedly, but you can make more of an effort than you did yesterday. Hey, you might even enjoy the experience. Likewise, if you try to do everything at once you will fail. Admittedly, it has taken me a while to realize this; a lesson that was largely learned as a result of the letters I received and Jane's reaction to much of what we tried.

In fact, the question of Jane's reaction to this whole experiment is an important one to me and a vital indication, in my opinion, of whether the experiment 'worked'. I soon learned that we each engaged with different issues at our own pace. Sometimes we have been united in our response, but often we have clashed, or struggled to empathize with or act on a problem with equal vigour. I realize now that my initial strategy of including Jane in the experiment was foolish. There was never any way that she would be railroaded into something like this. I have been frustrated not to be able to engage her further in certain matters. Equally, there have been some things that she has connected with arguably more than me, such as the organic box scheme, the cosmetics and toiletries regime (even if it was a slow start) and the TV-free week. I had assumed, incorrectly, that we would both share the same concerns to the same degree. But when I found that not to be the case, I became the household bore, parroting what the auditors had said to us back to Jane. I'm surprised that I didn't end up covered in vegetable peelings destined for the wormery, to be honest. But over time I have learned that it is best just to let Jane find her own way, rather than constantly trying to coax her to join me. It took me a surprisingly long time to learn not to sound like another auditor lecturing her on how to live her life.

Far from having now finished the experiment, I feel in some ways that it has only just begun. It's as though I have only recently had the stabilizers taken off my bike and am now confident enough to pedal on alone, without the reassuring, if overbearing, influence of the auditors behind my every move. In fact, the biggest test is just around the corner. At the time of writing, Jane and I are a matter of days away from the birth of our second child. Esme was three months old when the auditors called by with their clipboards, but our new baby will be entering a world where Mummy and Daddy fret about washable nappies, worry themselves silly about lurking toxic chemicals, and struggle on public transport with what will now have to be a double buggy. (How on earth do people actually do that?) Poor little thing. I suppose that at least they will have Esme, a sibling in waiting who is now battle-hardened to the realities of ethical living, to guide them through the experience. But I fear the prospect of revolt is one that will be constant as they both grow older. ('Oh no, Daddy, not homemade organic carrot and lentil soup in a flask again. Can't we go and get a Happy Meal from the Drive-Thru like the rest of our friends?')

If I had to name our proudest achievement I would have to say that it's been to remain car-free. In the words of the Union of Concerned Scientists, an alliance of scientists in the US concerned about the environmental and social legacy of our current use of scientific research and technological advance: 'The choice of vehicle you drive has a greater effect on the environment than any other choice you make as a consumer.' But with the reality of life with two children just around the corner, we now worry – much more than when we first had Esme – about how we are going to continue coping without a car in such a car-oriented world. It's the 'alleviating short-term pain versus achieving long-term gain' argument in extremis. I suppose we will soon find out just what it takes to stay car-free, but all I can say is that I have huge admiration for people who, be it through design or circumstance, do so with two or more children.

The conclusion of a book seems to be the time to trot out some sage words that transcend time and sum up succinctly the core findings of the pages within. I could turn to the likes of Gandhi ('We must be the change we wish to see'), Aristotle ('For the things we have to learn before we can do them, we learn by doing them') or Proust ('The real voyage of discovery consists not in seeking new landscapes but in having new eyes'), but for me the profound, ageless words of pretzel-loving George W. Bush speak loudest about the need to consider in advance the true impact of our actions:

'Chew before you swallow.'

Six Months Later

Six months on from the last update, the big news for Jane and me is, of course, the birth of our second child. Jessie Lily Jane Hickman was born after a forty-five-minute labour at King's College Hospital, London, weighing 6lbs 9oz. Her parents and big sister were delighted by her safe arrival and entry into the family.

That's the official birth notice out of the way. But tending to a newborn inevitably means that fretting about ethical nuances such as reducing your energy consumption or buying fair-trade apples rapidly fall off the to-do list, to be replaced by the constant struggle to get enough sleep, mundane parental anxieties such as worrying whether the baby is the right temperature, and tackling the pyroclastic flow of unwashed clothes that spill from the laundry basket. The hour-by-hour responsibility for a newborn – and their toddler sibling – sadly means that loftier concerns, temporarily at least, go the way of the baby's bath water. (Jane believes that her waters breaking slap bang in the middle of her beloved *Desperate Housewives* was Jessie's way of letting us know that we should abandon all thoughts of having any 'me time' for at least the next few months.)

Esme was already three months old when our experiment first started so Jessie's arrival has presented brand-new challenges for us. Having now had some time to look back and reflect a little on our choices when Jessie was first born, it is easy to see how quickly the tenets of ethical living became distant to us – if just for the first few anarchic weeks until we refound our feet and started to establish more of a steady routine. The fact that she was (and still is) being breastfed certainly made life a lot easier in many respects – no bottles to heat and sterilize, no worrying about supporting infant formula companies – but our gains there were counteracted somewhat by our rapid, if temporary, abandonment of washable nappies. Without going into explicit detail, there was a major leakage issue. In fact, it wasn't until we began to wean Jessie – meaning, for any non-parents, that her poo became less fluid – that washable nappies became a truly viable and lasting proposition again. We did use the so-called 'eco-disposables' in an attempt to reduce our guilt, but we haven't really doused ourselves in pride with regard to nappies, even though we're back on track now. But thankfully, at least Esme is now (despite the odd accident) potty trained, which has made life somewhat easier.

Away from the domestic travails of trying to live ethically with a babe in arms, we are continuing well. I'm pleased to report that we are still resisting the temptation to get a car. In fact, the urge has retreated somewhat, even though we are now 'double buggered' in terms of travelling by public transport. Life as the proud owners of a double buggy is going OK, although we have had to learn to tolerate audible harrumphs from some members of the public whilst out and about. Take travelling on the Tube: lifting a loaded double buggy down an escalator requires deep concentration, if not a controlled rush of bravery, but the tension rises further the moment you realize that dozens of people are backing up behind you because they can't get past you and your hog of a pavement 4×4. On a more positive travel-related note, we're still resisting those flights where possible – just one in the last three years – though the allure is still very much present. Elsewhere, we're still in love with our vegetable box, we're still trying to reduce our meat intake and the supermarket breakaway continues.

The gardening is going from strength to strength, too. In fact, this summer we finally got round to heeding Renée's advice and built some raised beds in the back garden. Better still, we got rid of the dreaded decking by recycling the wood to build our beds. Arguments developed over what we should plant in them, so we decided it best to each have our own beds. I now have full responsibility for the largest bed, which is used exclusively to grow vegetables, and Jane has two smaller beds in which she grows flowers. It's the clichéd gender divide, I'm afraid, of the utilitarian versus the aesthetic. But it keeps us from bickering.

One of the most warming aspects of my vegetable gardening this year has been the fact that the compost I used to enrich the soil was taken from the wormery. Therefore last year's kitchen waste has now been used to help grow this year's bounty, which included courgettes, tomatoes, potatoes, sweetcorn, Swiss chard, spinach and herbs such as lovage, parsley, basil, tarragon, mint, bay and borage.

A most welcome side effect of all the new foliage and flowers in the garden has been the noticeable increase in visiting wildlife. We've had lots more butterflies this summer (mainly homing in on the flowers on our potato plants), as well as many more bees drawn to the lavender in Jane's beds. Esme has now become quite the wildlife boffin – she spent two weeks in early summer anxiously peering out of the French doors that lead to the garden, monitoring the progress of a baby sparrow as it struggled to gain its wings before the local tabby could find it. Thankfully, the saga of the fledgling had a happy ending, but the drama unfolding before her gave Esme a memorable lesson about the fine line in nature between success and failure. Jane and I, meanwhile, identified with the bird's struggle to get off the ground and keep aloft.

Leo's DIY Ethical Audit

☆ **Calculate your carbon footprint**
Go to www.myfootprint.org and answer a short list of questions about your lifestyle. It will calculate how many 'biologically productive hectares' of land are required to support your lifestyle – and show you ways to reduce your 'footprint'. The UK average is 5.3 hectares, whereas the planet can only sustainably support 1.8 hectares per person. In other words, we would need nearly three Earths if everyone on the planet lived like we currently do in the UK.

☆ **Look long and hard into your supermarket trolley**
Beware items with excessive food miles. Try to source local, seasonal food. Also support organic and fair-trade foods wherever possible. Cut back on heavily processed foods.

Given its environmental impact, try to reduce your intake of meat. If you do eat it, always source organic meat, or meat of which you know the precise provenance. Likewise with fish and dairy products. Buy items with minimal packaging and remember to re-use old carrier bags when carrying your shopping home. Alternatively, reduce your reliance on supermarkets by signing up with a local organic box delivery scheme.

☆ Check your cupboards

Look for excessive amounts of synthetic chemicals in items such as toiletries, cosmetics and cleaning products. Isolate items that use lots of needless packaging. Check brand names, then research the background of each company for any practices such as animal testing and political lobbying.

☆ Work out the shortest distance you last travelled by car

If it was less than two miles then you're probably guilty of using your car for needless journeys when you could have just bussed, biked or walked instead. Opting for alternatives to the car wherever possible is an important part of ethical living. Perhaps consider getting a bicycle.

☆ Check your home's thermostat

It is easy to overheat the home needlessly by not regularly monitoring the thermostat or the timer on your heating system. Try incrementally lowering the thermostat by one degree to help acclimatize yourself to a lower household temperature. Also, check your home for places where heat may be being wasted such as rattling windows, poorly insulated lofts or gappy floorboards. Better still, get an Energy Savings Adviser (www.est.org.uk/myhome, tel: 0845 727 7200) to complete an energy audit of your home. Also consider switching to an energy supplier that offers a green tariff or green fund which supports renewable energy technologies.

☆ List your last five holidays

If you travelled by plane each time then your habit is responsible for emitting above-average lifestyle-related greenhouse gas emissions, especially if you favour long-haul trips. The only real answer is to fly less by holidaying more in the UK or western Europe, and travel by, say, train.

☆ Work out how much water you use

Do you bath or shower? Do you leave the tap running when brushing your teeth or rinsing off dishes? Do you use a hose or sprinkler to water your garden? There are many ways to save water around the home. The best way to monitor your habit – and to save money – is to get a water meter installed.

☆ Look into your wheelie bin

Do you fill it to the top each week? If so, you are sending far too much of your waste to landfill. Much of our waste can be recycled or composted. But it is also important to think hard before we buy items which lead to waste, such as over-packaged foods. For more information about reducing your waste output, visit www.recyclenow.com.

☆ Hold your money to account

Who do you bank with? Do you know where your money is being invested? Whether it's your current account, mortgage or insurance, it's worth interrogating all of the financial services that you give your business to about their investment policies. For example, do they invest in firms that sell military hardware? Or are involved in the felling of virgin rainforests? Or use animal testing on domestic cleaning products? For more information about the range of ethical investments and financial services available, visit www.eiris.org. Also, how much of your income do you spend on charitable donations? Look into the most tax efficient ways of giving by visiting www.allaboutgiving.org.

☆ List what activities you do in your spare time

We've all got busy lives, but how much time do you spend on yourself and how much on others? There are dozens of ways to volunteer any spare time for good causes, such as local environmental projects or helping those living less fortunate lives than yourself. A national database of volunteering opportunities can be found at www.do-it.org.uk.

If you have enjoyed A Life Stripped Bare *and would like further information about ethical living, we recommend:*

A Good Life
The guide to ethical living
Leo Hickman

ISBN: 1-903-91959-2   £15.00 paperback

Addressing every area of our lives, from the food we eat to each room in the house, from our leisure time and healthcare to our travel and financial arrangements, *A Good Life* examines all the dilemmas we face, provides a guide through the choices and their consequences, and gives a detailed directory of goods, suppliers, companies and organizations.

Whether you just want to dip a toe in the water or try the whole ethical life 24/7, *A Good Life* is the essential reference.

Turn over for a short extract.

For further information about other Eden Project Books, visit *www.booksattransworld.co.uk/eden.*

Fruit and Veg

The advice from health professionals is consistent and straightforward: eat five portions of fruit and vegetables a day – equal to 400g – to help yourself stay healthy. The truth is that, on average, we eat nearer three. This figure is even more depressing when we learn that we should actually be eating nine portions a day, according to nutrition researchers at Cambridge University. The reason we're not told this, it seems, is because there's a fear that we would ignore this advice if confronted by such a high total.

But as important as our low fruit and vegetable intake is the way in which we consume it. According to government figures released each year about typical food consumption in the UK, we are now eating fewer green vegetables and more fruit 'products', i.e., processed foods containing fruit. In 1975, for example, we ate over 341g of fresh green vegetables a week, whereas in 2002/03 the figure stood at just 231g. In comparison, in 1975 we ate just 228g of fruit 'products' in a week. In 2002/03 that weekly figure had risen to 413g.

Thankfully, it's not an issue that is being ignored – fresh fruit and vegetables are now distributed free at most primary schools and 'Healthy Start' vouchers worth at least £2.80 a week were introduced from

2005 to encourage low-income families to buy more fresh fruit and vegetables. (In 2002/03, the average household spend on fresh fruit and vegetables each week was £5.40. In contrast, £5.50 was spent on buns, cakes, biscuits, chocolate and soft drinks.)

But while encouragement and assistance from the state is welcome, much of the responsibility remains with us. So rule number one when it comes to eating fruit and vegetables is quite simple – just eat more of the stuff. You will be more healthy for it, you should require less medical help later in life (many studies now show consuming fresh fruit and vegetables reduces the risk of heart disease and certain cancers) and you will be giving less money to the processed food industry.

To eat ethically, it's not just a case of consuming more fruit and vegetables, but also asking other questions of the produce we eat: Who grew my apple, for example? Who picked it? Where and how was it transported? Was it sprayed with pesticides? Is it currently the right season for such produce?

Four key things – all of them interconnected and all driven overwhelmingly by market desire to 'satisfy' you, the consumer – should be in the forefront of your mind when buying fruit and vegetables:

- Pesticide residues
- Food miles
- Grower and picker rights
- Seasonality

DILEMMA:

Should I eat the New Zealand organic apple, the Kent non-organic apple, or the fair-trade apple from South Africa?

The simple answer is all of them, but it depends where your priorities lie.

Friends of the Earth now annually highlight the plight of UK apple farmers, saying that retailers need to start supporting homegrown apples more. If not, the accelerating loss of orchards will affect biodiversity on our farmed land, rural economies will suffer yet further and even more food miles will be burned. In its 2003 survey of the apple market, it found that just 38 per cent of apples sold in supermarkets were grown in the UK. It also found a poor range of varieties on offer with just 14 British varieties on sale in supermarkets. In contrast 28 varieties were found on market stalls.

The survey also revealed that homegrown apples from market stalls (including farmers' markets) were actually cheaper than at supermarkets, despite the ever-present price wars. The average price of a kilo of Cox apples in the supermarkets was £1.18 whereas at the local market it was just £1.02.

Therefore, when in season, buy your apples from local market stalls, or direct from the farmers where possible. Outside the British apple season (which runs from the end of July through, if cold stores are used, to the following April), if you must have an imported apple, your choice should be limited to either organic or fair-trade. Both have the major disadvantage of needing to be transported from afar. However, both are a better choice than imported non-organic apples that may have been sprayed up to 35 times with pesticides.

If only because of the lesser distance they need to travel, you should probably favour fair-trade apples from South Africa, if you can find them, over the more available organic ones from New Zealand. Fair-trade apples have been available to buy in the UK since 2003. They are grown by South African farmers who are part of the Thandi Initiative. This was launched in 2002 by the Capespan Foundation as part of the South African government's land transformation programme. It encourages joint ownership and empowerment through 'capacity building' (improving local social capital) in the country's fruit industry. The Thandi Initiative also supplies fair-trade seedless grapes, oranges and lemons. (NB. Fair-trade farmers around the world are encouraged to farm sensitively with regard to pesticides and the environment. Some are even certified organic.)

Dancing at the Dead Sea
Journey to the heart of environmental crisis
Alanna Mitchell

ISBN 1903 919630   £8.99 Paperback

Does the human race have a death wish? One hundred and fifty years after the publication of *On the Origin of Species*, award-winning writer Alanna Mitchell sets out on a journey to the world's hotspots – where the environment has been all but destroyed – to pick up where Darwin left off and examine not the origin but the ultimate fate of the human species and the world we inhabit. Grappling with Richard Leakey's contention that a massive extinction of the planet's species is well under way, she travels from Madagascar, the 'last living Eden', to the Galapagos, Darwin's natural laboratory, from the Azraq Oasis in Jordan to the Arctic desert of Banks Island.

Intertwining scientific theory with travel adventure and history, here is a dramatic, and refreshingly optimistic, narrative voice.

'*Dancing at the Dead Sea* is a powerful narrative on a critically important topic. This is not a pessimistic tirade, but instead a factual commentary that will convince many, written by a gifted writer with an independent mind. I recommend this book without reservation.'
RICHARD LEAKEY

'An important and uplifting read. Alanna marches energetically around the world to find out what every single one of us needs to know: what's really the state of health of our long-suffering little planet? '
BENEDICT ALLEN

Rubbish!
Dirt on our hands and crisis ahead
Richard Girling

ISBN 1903 919444   £7.99 Paperback

We can no longer cope with our waste. Every hour in the UK we throw away enough rubbish to fill the Albert Hall. Yet our systems for disposal remain as crude as ever. Plan A: chuck it in a hole. Plan B: dump it on someone else's doorstep.

The story of our rubbish - a mucky saga of carelessness, greed and opportunism, wasted opportunity and official bungling – is at the heart of Richard Girling's book. But it is also a plea for us to reconsider other kinds of waste: our trashing of the landscape; our defilement of towns and cities with tawdry architecture and thoughtless planning; our obliteration of wildlife; the unstoppable floods of junk that clog our mailboxes, litter the skies and foul the airwaves.

Hard-hitting, passionate, provocative, Girling is also persuasive, often funny and always entertaining.

'Be scared. Be very scared. But be sure to read this book.'
BEN ELTON

'With a subject that ranges from the noxious to the infernal, it is a wonder that Girling's book manages to b e compulsively readable and often hilarious, as well as important.'
JOHN CAREY, *Sunday Times*

When the Rivers Run Dry
What happens when our water runs out?

Fred Pearce

ISBN 1903 919576 / 9781903 919576   £18.99 Hardback

Few of us take the trouble to consider how much water
we use. We drink no more than 5 litres each in a day
and even after washing and flushing toilets we consume
only 150 litres; but it can take as much as 5,000 litres to
grow just one kilo of rice; 11,000 litres to feed enough
cow for a quarter-pound burger; and you could fill 25
baths with the water it takes to grow the cotton for a
T-shirt. In such ways we consume a hundred times our
own weight in water every day.

But the world is running out of water. Some of our
largest rivers now trickle into sand miles from the ocean,
exhausted by human need. By 2025 three billion people
will face chronic water shortages and the spectre of
water wars looms. Water is 'the new oil' – except we can
live without oil; there are no alternatives to fresh water.

Fred Pearce has travelled all over the world preparing the
most complete portrait yet of the growing world water
crisis. His vivid reportage reveals the personal stories
behind failing rivers, barren fields, desertification,
floods, water wars, and even the death of cultures.
Terrifying about the consequences if governments fail
to act, Pearce is also truly empowering in his advocacy
of the ways we all need to change.

'If ever a book has been written that demands to be read
it is this one.'
TIM SMIT

Seasonal Food
A Guide to What's in Season When and Why
Paul Waddington

ISBN 1903 919525   £10.99   Paperback

A month-by-month guide to British food at its freshest.
Writing with the relish his subject deserves, Paul
Waddington explains why lamb is perfect one month,
but not lobster, when you should choose strawberries
and not blackberries, when you should look for
elderflowers and what to do with them, and why you
should choose this potato over that. His book includes
culinary history, notes for preserving and storing,
supplier advice and suggestions for what will work
with what. This is the essential companion for all food
enthusiasts; it is also an absorbing and entertaining
reference for anyone wanting to buy locally, eat well,
and contribute to sustainable, local agriculture.

'The perfect reference book for all keen cooks.'
ANTONY WORRALL THOMPSON

'A must for the discriminatingly greedy.'
ANDREW MARR, *Daily Telegraph*

For information about other Eden Project Books,
please vist our website at
www.booksattransworld.co.uk/eden